Eusebius of Caesarea

History of the martyrs in Palestine

discovered in a very ancient Syriac manuscript

Eusebius of Caesarea

History of the martyrs in Palestine
discovered in a very ancient Syriac manuscript

ISBN/EAN: 9783742860194

Manufactured in Europe, USA, Canada, Australia, Japa

Cover: Foto ©ninafisch / pixelio.de

Manufactured and distributed by brebook publishing software
(www.brebook.com)

Eusebius of Caesarea

History of the martyrs in Palestine

HISTORY

OF THE

MARTYRS IN PALESTINE,

BY

EUSEBIUS, BISHOP OF CÆSAREA,

DISCOVERED IN A VERY ANTIENT SYRIAC MANUSCRIPT.

EDITED AND TRANSLATED INTO ENGLISH

BY

WILLIAM CURETON, D.D.,

MEMBER OF THE IMPERIAL INSTITUTE OF FRANCE.

WILLIAMS AND NORGATE:

14, HENRIETTA STREET, COVENT GARDEN, LONDON;

AND

20, SOUTH FREDERICK STREET, EDINBURGH.

PARIS: C. BORRANI.

MDCCCLXI.

THIS ACCOUNT OF

MARTYRS FOR THE TRUTH OF THE HOLY RELIGION OF OUR LORD JESUS CHRIST

IS

Dedicated to the Memory

OF

FRANCIS EGERTON EARL OF ELLESMERE

K. G.

IN PIOUS RECOGNITION OF MUCH AND LONG-CONTINUED KINDNESS AND

IN GRATEFUL REMEMBRANCE OF THE PRIVILEGE OF ENJOYING THE

FRIENDSHIP OF ONE WHO SO EMINENTLY ADORNED THE HIGH

STATION TO WHICH HE WAS BORN BY HIS OWN PERSONAL

VIRTUES AND ADDED REAL DIGNITY TO THE RANK

WHICH HE INHERITED BY THE ACQUIREMENTS

OF A SCHOLAR THE ACCOMPLISHMENTS

OF A GENTLEMAN AND THE

GRACES OF A CHRISTIAN.

PREFACE.

THE manuscript from which this work of Eusebius has been at length recovered, after the lapse of several centuries, is that wonderful volume of the Nitrian Collection[a] now in the British Museum, whose most curious and remarkable history I have already made known in the Preface to my edition of the Festal Letters of St. Athanasius.[b] It is not necessary, therefore, for me in this place to give any further account of it than to state that it was transcribed fourteen hundred and fifty years ago,—as early as the year of our Lord four hundred and eleven.

The several works contained in it are now all printed, and thereby rescued from the chance of being lost for all future time. The first—a Syriac translation of the Recognitions of St. Clement, which I once intended to publish, and had transcribed the greater part of it for that purpose—has been edited by Dr. P. de Lagarde,[c] to whom I

(a) British Museum, Additional MS. No. 12,150.

(b) P. xv. The Festal Letters of Athanasius, discovered in an antient Syriac version. 8vo. London, 1848.

(c) Clementis Romani Recognitiones Syriace. Paulus Antonius de Lagarde edidit. 8vo, Lipsiæ, 1861.

gave my copy. The transcript was completed by him, and compared with another manuscript of the same work, and afterward printed with that great care and accuracy which gives so much value to all the Syriac texts which he has edited. The second treatise in this manuscript is the book of Titus, Bishop of Bostra, or Bozra, in Arabia, against the Manicheans. We are also indebted for the publication of this important work to Dr. de Lagarde.[a] The third is the book of Eusebius on the Theophania, or Divine Manifestation of our Lord. The text of this was edited by the late Dr. Lee,[b] who also published an English translation of it,[c] with valuable notes and a preliminary dissertation. The last is this history of the Martyrs of Palestine, also written by the same Author.

In the eighth book of the Ecclesiastical History, upon the occasion of his giving a short account of certain Bishops and others, who sealed their testimony for their faith with their blood, Eusebius stated his intention of writing, in a distinct treatise, a narrative of the confession

(a) Titi Bostreni contra Manchæos libri quatuor Syriace. Paulus Antonius de Lagarde edidit. 8vo. Berolini, 1859.

(b) Eusebius, Bishop of Cæsarea, on the Theophania, or Divine Manifestation of our Lord and Saviour Jesus Christ. A Syriac Version, edited from an ancient Manuscript recently discovered. By Samuel Lee, D.D. 8vo. London, 1842.

(c) Eusebius, Bishop of Cæsarea, on the Theophania, or Divine Manifestation of our Lord and Saviour Jesus Christ. Translated into English with Notes, from an ancient Syriac Version of the Greek Original now lost. To which is prefixed a Vindication of the Orthodoxy and Prophetical Views of that distinguished writer By Samuel Lee, D.D. 8vo. Cambridge, 1843.

of those Martyrs with whom he had himself been acquainted.[a] Up to the time of the discovery of this Syriac copy, no such work was known to exist in a separate form, either in Latin or Greek. There is indeed a brief history of those contemporaries of Eusebius who suffered in the persecution of the Christians in Palestine, found in several antient Greek manuscripts, inserted as a part of it, and combined with the Ecclesiastical History: but it does not occupy the same place in all the copies of that work. In one it is placed after the middle of the thirteenth chapter of the eighth book;[b] in two[c] at the end of the tenth book; and in several,[d] at the end of the eighth; while from two

(a) Οις γε μην αυτος παρεγενομην, τουτους και τοις μεθ' ημας γνωριμους δι' ετερας ποιησομαι γραφης. "Moreover, there were many other eminent martyrs who have an honourable mention among the Churches, which are in those places and countries. But our design is not to commit to writing the conflicts of all those who suffered for the worship of God over the whole world, nor yet to give an accurate relation of every accident that befel them; but this rather belongs to those who, with their own eyes, beheld what was done. *Moreover, those ourselves were present at, we will commit to the knowledge of posterity in another work.*" See Ecc. Hist., B. viii. ch. 13, *Eng. Trans.* p. 148.

(b) Codex olim Regiæ Societatis, nunc vero Musei Britannici. This is G. of Dr. Burton's edition: Oxford, 1838. See the same, pp. 572 and 591.

(c) Duo Codices Florentini Bibliothecæ Mediceo-Laurentianæ. Plut. lxx. n. 7 et 20. I. and K. of Burton. See *Ibid.* p. 591.

(d) 1. Codex Regius Bibliothecæ Parisiensis n. 1436; 2. Codex Mediceus, *ibid.* n. 1434; 3. Codex Mazarinæus, *ibid.* n. 1430; 4. Codex Fuketianus, *ibid.* n. 1435; 5. Codex Savilianus, in Bibliotheca Bodleiana, n. 2278; being A. B. C. D. and F. respectively of Burton. *Ibid.*

others,[d] as well as from the Latin version made by Ruffinus, it is omitted altogether. There is no distinct title prefixed to it in any copy but one, the Codex Castellani,[a] where it bears the inscription:—*Ευσεβιου συγγραμμα περι των κατ' αυτον μαρτυρησαντων εν τῳ οκταετει Διοκλητιανου και εφεξης Γαλεριου του Μαξιμινου διωγμου*; but two copies, the Mazarine and Medicean, have at the end—*Ευσεβιου του Παμφιλου περι των εν Παλαιστινῃ μαρτυρησαντων τελος.*[b]

That this was the history of the martyrs who were known to Eusebius which he had promised, has never been doubted by any one; while, on the other hand, almost every one who has undertaken to write on the subject has judged it to be but an abridgment of the original work which formerly existed in a more extended form.[c] The

(d) Codex Bibliothecæ Regiæ Parisiensis n. 1431, and Codex Venetus n. 838; being E. and H. of Burton. *Ibid.*

(a) See N. of Burton. *Ibid.*

(b) See Valesius, note (a), p. 154, *Eng. Trans.*

(c) See Valesius and Ruinart, cited in the notes to this, pp. 50, 51, 55, 59, 60, 64, 69, 84. Also S. E. Assemani remarks:—"Græcam S. Procopii, Martyrum Palæstinorum in Diocletiani persecutione antesignani, historiam, quæ in laudato de martyribus Palæstinæ libro habetur; ab alia fusiori, atque explicatiori fuisse contractam atque truncatam, certum et exploratum est, nam quæ ad patriam atque institum pertinent omittere nunquam consuevit Eusebius."—*Acta SS. Mart.*

"Horum sanctorum martyrum historiam concisam pariter jejunamque exhibet nobis Græcus Eusebii Cæsariensis textus in libro de martyribus Palæstinæ; eandemque prorsus fortunam experta est, quam prior Procopii, ex latiori scilicet narratione in brevem summam. Atque priorem illam Latina, quæ superfuit, versio supplerit, hæc autem suppleri aliter non potuissent, nisi, favente Deo, Chaldaicus

antient Latin copy of the Acts of Procopius,[a] the Acts of Pamphilus and his companions, as exhibited by Simeon Metaphrastes,[b] in much fuller detail than they are now found in the Greek text of Eusebius, and the additional facts respecting other martyrs who suffered in Palestine, supplied by the Greek Menæa and Menologia, were adduced as evidence of the existence at one time of a more copious work, and as a proof that the narrative inserted in the Ecclesiastical History was only an abridgment.

The correctness of this critical induction has been completely established by the discovery of this copy of the work of Eusebius of Cæsarea on the Martyrs of Palestine, in the vernacular language of the country where the events took place, and actually transcribed within about seventy years after the death of the author.[c]

S. E. Assemani goes so far as to express his conviction that this history of the sufferings of the martyrs in Palestine was originally composed in Syriac, a language with which Eusebius, Bishop of Cæsarea, was necessarily well acquainted,

Codex noster e tenebris Ægypti vindicatus emersisset in lucem."—*Ibid.* p. 173.

Baillet:—"Eusebe de Cesarée avait recueilli à part les Martyrs de Palestine: et quoique les Actes qu'il en avoit ramassez avec beaucoup de soin et de travail ne paroissent plus, il nous en reste un bon abbregé dans le livre qui se trouve joint à son histoire generale de l'Eglise." See *Les Vies des Saints*, vol. i. p. 55.

(a) See these printed p. 50 below and Valesius' note thereon.

(b) The Latin, by Surius, of this, will be found in the Notes, at p. 69.

(c) Eusebius died A.D. 339 or 340 (Fabricius, *Bibliotheca Græc.* lib. v. c. 4. p. 31), and this copy was transcribed A. D. 411.

as being the vernacular speech of his own country and diocese.[a] It is not at all improbable that Eusebius might made have use of the Syriac for ordinary purposes, or, indeed, as a safer deposit for any memoranda which he might wish to commit to writing than the Greek, during the time that the persecution continued. Could this inference of S. E. Assemani be established, it would give still additional interest and value to the work which I now publish. I must, however, own that I cannot admit the supposition that this work was originally written in the Syriac language. Indeed, it seems to me to be sufficiently disproved by the fact, that the Syriac copy of such of the Acts of Martyrs in Palestine as have been published by S. E. Assemani, while it agrees completely in substance with this, is evidently a translation by another hand; and that the variation and errors which occur in some of the proper names are of such a kind as could only have arisen from confounding two similar Greek letters of the writing at that period;[b] and further, there are some obscure passages in this Syriac, which obviously seem to be the result of a translator not fully apprehending the meaning of the Greek passage before him.[c]

How long the entire Greek text of the original work continued to be read, we have now no means of learning with any degree of certainty. It must have been in existence in the time of Simeon Metaphrastes, in the tenth century, for he has supplied many facts[c] from it

(a) See Note, p. 51, below.

(b) See Notes, pp. 57, 60 below.

(c) See p. 66, below.

which the abridged form of the Greek does not contain, and has also given entire the long passage relating to Pamphilus and his companions.[a] Neither can there be any doubt of its having been in use at the period when the Greek Menæa and Menologia were compiled.[b] The fact that many of the circumstances and events which it described had been inserted in the abovementioned books, and that an abridgment, which, I cannot doubt, was made by Eusebius himself, had also been incorporated into the Ecclesiastical History, seems to have led to the discontinuance of the transcription of the larger work, and to have been mainly the cause of its being no longer found in the Greek in a separate form. The preservation of this work in its complete state up to the present time, in the Syriac, is chiefly due to the circumstance of its having been transported, at a very early period, to the Syrian Monastery in the solitude of the Nitrian Desert, where the dryness of the climate kept the vellum from decay, and the idleness and ignorance of the monks saved the volume from being worn out and destroyed by frequent use.

Independently of the great interest of the subject of which it treats, this work of Eusebius has especial claims to consideration, on the ground of the author having been himself an eyewitness of most of the events which he de-

(a) A Latin version of this, as it is found in Simeon Metaphrastes, translated by Lipomannus, I have printed in the Notes, p. 69, below, for the sake of comparison with this text. It also still exists in Greek, and was first published by D. Papebrochius from a Medicean MS. in the *Acta Sanctorum*, June, vol. i. p. 64; and afterwards reprinted by J. Alb. Fabricius in *S. Hippoliti Opera*, 2 vols. fol. Hamb. 1716—19, vol. ii. p. 217.

(b) See notes pp. 53, 56, 59, 60, 64, 68.

scribes. There are some, indeed, at which he could not have have been present; for instance, the Confession of Romanus, who suffered at Antioch on the same day as Alphæus and Zacchæus did at Cæsarea, where he was then residing. He has, given a narrative of the sufferings of Romanus, in his history of the Martyrs of Palestine, because he was a native of Palestine, and had also been a deacon and exorcist in one of the villages of Cæsarea; and Eusebius was anxious to claim for his own country and diocese the honour of this man's confession. This may perhaps be the reason why there are found two distinct accounts of the Acts of Romanus in Syriac, as well as in Greek and Latin.

It is not my intention to enter into any discussion respecting the time of the composition of this treatise, or that of the great Church History by Eusebius: nor will I consider at any length the question of the abridgment of the account of the Martyrs of Palestine inserted in most of the copies of the Ecclesiastical History, or that of the different recensions of this latter work by the author himself.[a] These are certainly very interesting subjects of literary and historical inquiry; and doubtless this book will supply the critic with new data, to enable him to elucidate and determine them in a more complete and satisfactory manner than it has been hitherto possible for any one to do. These matters I would rather leave to other scholars. All now have the same materials as I have, and some may be possessed of other greater facilities and appliances, as well as better capacities for the task. I

(a) See Heinichen, *Notitia Codicum, Editionum et Translationum Historiæ Ecclesiasticæ Eusebianæ*, § vi.

believe it to be my duty to employ my own time and exertions in another way.

I will therefore content myself with briefly observing that this work of Eusebius on the Martyrs of Palestine bears evidently upon it the stamp of being a record of facts which were noted down at the time as they severally occurred, and were afterwards revised and arranged in due order at a subsequent period, when some events, which, in the earlier years of the Persecution, the author thought it probable might happen, had actually taken place; and when other occurrences of earlier date were no longer so fresh and vivid in the minds of men as they had been when all were still living who had witnessed them.

I would observe, also, that it seems to be evident that this work, in which Eusebius recounts the martyrdom of Pamphilus and his companions, was composed before he wrote the fuller history of that noble Martyr, to which he refers in the Abridgment; for no reference whatever is made to the existence of any such history in this original and more copious narrative of the Martyrs of Palestine. It must, therefore, have been composed before he wrote the Ecclesiastical History, in which he several times adverts to the life of Pamphilus as having been already completed.

The first edition of the Ecclesiastical History does not appear to have contained the history of the Martyrs of Palestine. This seems to be the copy used by Ruffinus, who neither gives any such history, nor has the passage in the thirteenth chapter of the eighth book which refers to it.

Indeed, it is evident from his own words that the abridgment must have been made by Eusebius himself.[a] When,

([a]) See Note below, p. 79.

therefore, he condensed the narrative for the purpose of incorporating it into the subsequent editions of the Ecclesiastical History, he also took that opportunity of supplying several facts which, either from considerations of prudence, or from not having had knowledge of them at the time when the work was originally composed, he had previously omitted; and also ventured to speak more plainly of persons, because the altered condition of circumstances after the accession of Constantine enabled him to do this without any apprehension of danger. This, I think, will be obvious to those who will be at the pains to compare the general narrative of the events as they are recorded year by year, with the notes which I have added, even without having recourse to fuller and more minute researches.

The translation I have endeavoured to make as faithful as I could without following the Syriac idiom so closely as to render the English obscure. There are a very few passages in which I cannot feel quite sure that I have obtained the precise meaning of the Syriac; but the obscurity of these passages is certainly due to the Translator, who does not seem to have fully understood the Greek text which he had before him. My English translation of the long account of Pamphilus and his companions was printed before I read either the Greek text printed by Papebrochius, or the Latin translation made by Lipomannus from the same Greek, as it was preserved by Simeon Metaphrastes. The comparison of all of these together will be a good means of testing both the integrity of the transmission of the original Greek to the present day, and the fidelity of the Syriac translation.

In the notes, my chief object has been to collect such observations as may tend especially to throw light upon the time of the composition 'of this work and of the Ecclesiastical History by Eusebius, and serve to elucidate the text; but in order to keep them from extending to too great a length, I have omitted all those matters which it appeared to me an ordinarily well-informed scholar might be presumed to be acquainted with.

ON THE MARTYRS IN PALESTINE,

BY EUSEBIUS OF CÆSAREA.

Those Holy Martyrs of God, who loved our Saviour and Lord Jesus Christ, and God supreme and sovereign of all, more than themselves and their own lives, who were dragged forward to the conflict for the sake of religion, and rendered glorious by the martyrdom of confession, who preferred a horrible death to a temporary life, and were crowned with all the victories of virtue, and offered to the Most High and supreme God the glory of their wonderful victory, because they had their conversation in heaven, and walked with him who gave victory to their testimony, also offered up glory, and honour, and majesty to the Father, and to the Son, and to the Holy Ghost. Moreover, the souls of the martyrs being worthy of the kingdom of heaven are in honour together with the company of the prophets and apostles.

Let us therefore, likewise, who stand in need of the aid of their prayers, and have been also charged in the book of the Apostles, that we should be partakers in the remembrance of the Saints,—let us also be partakers with them, and begin to describe those conflicts of theirs against sin, which are at all times published abroad by the mouth of those believers who were acquainted with them Nor, indeed, have their praises been noted by monuments of stone, nor by statues variegated with painting and colours and resemblances of earthly things without life, but by the word of truth spoken before God: the deed also which is seen by our eyes bearing witness.

[P. 2.] Let us therefore, relate the manifest signs and glorious proofs of the divine doctrine, and commit to writing a commemoration not to be forgotten, setting also their marvellous virtues as a constant vision before our eyes. For I am struck with wonder at their all-enduring courage, at their confession under many forms, and at the wholesome alacrity of their souls, the elevation of their minds, the open profession of their faith, the clearness of their reason, the patience of their condition, and the truth of their religion: how they were not cast down in their minds, but their eyes looked upwards, and they neither trembled nor feared. The love of God also, and of His Christ, supplied them with an all-effective power, by which they overcame their enemies. For they loved God, the supreme sovereign of all, and they loved Him with all their might. He, too, requited their love to Him by the aid which He afforded them: and they also were loved by Him, and strengthened against their enemies, applying the words of that confessor who had already borne his testimony before them and exclaiming "Who shall separate us from Christ? shall tribulation, or affliction, or persecution, or hunger, or death, or the sword? as it is written, For thy sake we die daily: we are reckoned as lambs for the slaughter." And again, when this same martyr magnifies that patience which cannot be overcome by evil, he says—" that in all these things we conquer for Him who loved us." And he foretold that all evils are overcome by the love of God, and that all terrors and afflictions are trodden down, while he exclaimed and said: "Because I am persuaded that neither death, nor life, nor things present, nor things to come, nor powers, nor height, nor depth, nor any other creature, shall be able to separate us from the love of God which is in our Lord Jesus Christ."

At that time then, Paul, who exulted in the power of his Lord, was himself crowned with the victory of martyrdom in the midst of Rome, the Imperial City [p. 3.], because he had entered the contest there, as in a superior conflict. In that victory also which Christ granted to his triumphant martyrs, Simon, the chief and first of the disciples, likewise received the crown; and he suffered in a manner similar to our Lord's sufferings. Others of the Apostles too, in other places, closed their lives in martyrdom. Nor was this grace given only to those of former times, but it has also been bestowed abundantly upon this our own generation.

As for those conflicts, which were gloriously achieved in various other countries, it is meet that they who were then living should describe what took place in their own country; but for myself I pray that I may be enabled to write an account of those with whom I had the honour of being cotemporary, and that they may rank me also among them—I mean those of whom the whole people of Palestine is proud, for in the midst of this our land also the Saviour of all mankind himself arose like a thirst-refreshing fountain. The conflicts, therefore, of these victorious combatants I will proceed to relate, for the common instruction and benefit of all.

THE CONFESSION OF PROCOPIUS,

IN THE FIRST YEAR OF THE PERSECUTION IN OUR DAYS.

THE first of all the martyrs who appeared in Palestine was named Procopius. In truth he was a godly man, for even before his confession he had given up his life to great endurance: and from the time that he was a little boy had been of pure habits, and of strict morals: and by the vigour of his mind he had so brought his body into subjection, that, even before his death, his soul seemed to dwell in a body completely mortified, and he had so strengthened his soul by the word of God that his body also was sustained by the power of God. His food was bread only, and his drink water; and he took nothing else besides these two. [P. 4.] Occasionally he took food every second day only, and sometimes every third day; oftentimes too he passed a whole week without food. But he never ceased day nor night from the study of the word of God: and at the same time he was careful as to his manners and modesty of conduct, so that he edified by his meekness and piety all those of his own standing. And while his chief application was devoted to divine subjects, he was acquainted also in no slight degree with natural science. His family was from Baishan; and he ministered in the orders of the Church in three things:—First, he had been a Reader; and in the second order he translated from Greek into Aramaic; and in the last, which is even more excellent than the preceding, he opposed the powers of the evil one, and the devils trembled before him. Now it happened that he was sent from Baishan to our city Cæsarea, together with his brother confessors. And at the very moment that he passed the gates of the city they brought him before the Governor: and immediately upon his first entrance the judge, whose name was Flavianus, said to him: It is necessary that thou shouldest sacrifice to the gods: but he replied with a loud voice, There is no God but one only, the Maker and Creator of all things. And when the judge felt himself smitten by the blow of the martyr's words, he furnished himself with arms of another kind against the doctrine of truth, and, abandoning his former order, commanded him to sacrifice to the emperors, who were four in number; but the holy martyr of God laughed still more at this saying, and repeated the words of the greatest of poets of the Greeks, which he said that "the rule of many is not good: let there be one ruler and one sovereign." And on account of his answer, which was insulting to the emperors, he, though alive in his conduct, was delivered over to death, and forthwith the head of this blessed man was struck off, and an easy transit afforded him along the way to heaven. [P. 5.] And this took place on the seventh day of the month Heziran, in the first year of the persecution in our days. This confessor was the first who was consummated in our city Cæsarea.

THE CONFESSION OF ALPHÆUS, AND ZACCHÆUS, AND ROMANUS,

IN THE FIRST YEAR OF THE PERSECUTION IN OUR DAYS.

It happened, at the same time, that the festival, which is celebrated on the twentieth year of the emperor's reign, was at hand, and a pardon was announced at that festival for the offences of those who were in prison. The governor, therefore, of the country came before the festival, and instituted an inquiry respecting the prisoners which were in confinement, and some of them were set at liberty through the clemency of the emperors; but the martyrs of God he insulted with tortures, as though they were worse malefactors than thieves and murderers.

Zacchæus, therefore, who had been a deacon of the Church in the city of Gadara, was led like an innocent lamb from the flock—for such indeed he was by nature, and those of his acquaintance had given him the appellation of Zacchæus as a mark of honour, calling him by the name of that first Zacchæus—for one reason, because of the smallness of his stature, and for another, on account of the strict life which he led; and he was even more desirous of seeing our Lord than the first Zacchæus. And when he was brought in before the judge, he rejoiced in his confession for the sake of Christ: and when he had spoken the words of God before the judge, he was delivered over to all the tortures of punishment, and after having been first scourged, he was made to endure dreadful lacerations, and then after this he was thrown into prison again, and there for a whole day and a whole night his feet were strained to four holes of the rack.

Alphæus, also, a most amiable man, endured afflictions and sufferings similar to these. His family was of the most illustrious of the city Eleutheropolis, and in the church of Cæsarea he had been honoured with the dignity of Reader and Exorcist. But before he became a confessor he had been a preacher and teacher of [p. 6.] the word of God; and had great confidence towards all men, and this of itself was a good reason for his being brought to his confession of the truth. And because he saw that there was fallen upon all men at that time laxity and great fear, and many were swept along as it were before the force of many waters, and carried away to the foul worship of idols, he deliberated how he might withstand the violence of the evil by his own valour, and by his own courageous words repress the terrible storm. Of his own accord, therefore, he threw himself into the midst of the crowd of the oppressors, and with words of denunciation reproached those, who through their timidity had been dragged into error; and held them back from the worship of idols, by reminding them of the words which had been spoken by our Saviour, respecting confession. And when Alphæus, full of courage and bravery, had done these things openly with boldness, the officers seized him, and took him at once before the judge. But this is not the time for us to relate what words he uttered with all freedom of speech, nor what answers he gave in words of godly religion, like a man filled with the Spirit of God. In consequence of these things he was sent to prison. And after some days he was brought again before the judge, and his body was torn all over by severe scourgings without mercy, but the fortitude of his mind still continued erect before the judge, and by his words he withstood all error. Then he was tortured on his sides with the cruel combs, and, at last, having wearied out the judge himself, and those who were ministering to the judge's will, he was again committed to prison, together with another fellow-combatant, and stretched out a whole day and night upon the wooden rack. After three days they were both of them brought together before the judge, and he commanded them to offer sacrifice to the emperors: but they confessed, and said, We acknowledge one God only, the supreme sovereign of all; and when they had uttered these words in the presence of all the people (p. 7.) they were numbered among the company of Holy Martyrs, and were crowned as glorious and illustrious combatants in the conflict of God, for whose sake also their heads were cut off.* And better than all the course of their lives did they love their departure, to be with Him in whom they made their confession. But the day that they suffered martyrdom was the seventh of Teshri the latter, on which day the confession of those of whom we have been speaking was consummated.

And on this selfsame day also Romanus suffered martyrdom in the city of Antioch. But this Romanus belonged to Palestine, and he was a Deacon, and an Exorcist likewise, in one of the villages of Cæsarea. And he, too, was stretched out upon the rack, and like as the martyr Alphæus had done in Cæsarea, so did the blessed Romanus by his words of denunciation restrain from sacrificing those who, from their timidity, were relapsed into the sin of the error of devils, recalling to the minds of them all the terrors of God. He had also the courage to go in together with the multitude who were dragged by force into error and to present himself there in Antioch before the judge: and when he heard the judge commanding them to sacrifice, and they, in trepidation from their fears, were driven with trembling to offer sacrifice, this zealous man was no longer able to endure this sad spectacle, but was moved with pity towards them as towards those who were feeling about in thick darkness, and on the point of falling over a precipice, and so he made the doctrine of the religion of God to rise up before them like the sun, crying aloud and saying: Whither are ye being carried, oh men? Are ye all stooping down to cast yourselves into the abyss? Lift up the eyes of your understanding on high, and above all the worlds ye shall recognise God and the Saviour of all the ends of the world; and do not abandon for error the commandment which has been committed to you: then shall the godless error of the worship of devils be apparent to you. Remember also the righteous judgment of God supreme. [p. 8.] And when he had spoken these things to them with a loud voice, and stood there without fear and without dread, at the command of him who was constituted judge there, the officers seized him, and he condemned him to be destroyed by fire, for the crafty judge perceived that many were confirmed by the words which the martyr spake, and that he turned many back from error. And because the servant of Jesus had done these things in the place where the emperors were, they at once brought out this blessed man into the midst of the city of Antioch. And he was arrived at the spot where he was to undergo his punishment, and the things which were required for the fire were got ready, and they were busying themselves to fulfil the command with haste, when the emperor Diocletian, having heard of what was done, gave orders that they should withdraw the martyr from the death by fire, because, said he, his insolence and folly were not suitable for punishment by fire; and so, like a merciful emperor, he gave order for a new kind of punishment for the martyr, that his tongue should be cut out. Nevertheless, when that member by which he spoke was taken away, still was his true love not severed from his God; neither was his intellectual tongue restrained from preaching, and immediately he received from God, the sovereign of all, a recompense for his struggle in the conflict, and was filled with power much greater than he had before. Then did great wonder seize upon all men; for he, whose tongue had been cut out, forthwith, by the gift of God spake out valiantly, and heartily exulted in the faith, as though he were standing by the side of Him in whom he made his confession; and with a countenance bright and cheerful he saluted his acquaintance, and scattered the seed of the word of God into the ears of all men, exhorting them all to worship God alone, and lifting up his prayers and thanksgiving to God, who worketh marvels [p. 9.]: and when he had done these things he mightily gave testimony to the word of Christ before all men, and in deed shewed forth the power of Him in whom he made his confession. And when he had done so for a long time he was again stretched upon the rack; and by the command of the governor and the judge they threw upon him the strangling instrument, and he was strangled. And on the same day as those blessed martyrs who appertained to Zacchæus he was consummated in his confession. And although this man actually passed through the conflict, and suffered martyrdom in Antioch, nevertheless, because his family was of Palestine, he is properly described among the company of martyrs in this our country.

THE CONFESSION OF TIMOTHEUS, IN THE CITY OF GAZA,

IN THE SECOND YEAR OF THE PERSECUTION IN OUR DAYS.

It was the second year of the persecution, and the hostility against us was more violent than the first; and Urbanus, who at that same time had superseded the governor Flavianus in his office, was governor over the people of Palestine. There came then again the second time edicts from the emperor, in addition to the former, threatening persecution to all persons. For, in the former, he had given orders respecting the rulers of the Church of God only, to compel them to sacrifice; but, in the second edicts there was a strict ordinance, which compelled all persons equally, that the entire population in every city, both men and women, should sacrifice to dead idols, and a law was imposed upon them to offer libations to devils; for such were the commands of the tyrants who, in their folly, desired to wage war against God, the king supreme. And when these commands of the emperor were put into effect, the blessed Timotheus, in the city of Gaza, was delivered up to Urbanus while he was there, and was unjustly bound in fetters, like a murderer [p. 10.], for indeed he was not bound in fetters on account of any thing deserving of blame, because he had been blameless in all his conduct, and during the whole of his life. When, therefore, he did not comply with the law as to the worship of idols, nor bow down to dead images without life, for he was a man perfect in every thing, and was in his soul acquainted with his God, and because of his piety and his conduct and his virtues, even before he was delivered up to the governor, he had already endured severe sufferings from the inhabitants of his own city, having lived there under insults and frequent blows and contumely, for the people of the city of Gaza were accursed in the heathenism; and when they were present in the judgment hall of the governor, this champion of righteousness came off victorious in all the excellence of his patience. And the judge cruelly employed against him severe tortures, and showered upon his body terrible scourgings without number, inflicting on his sides horrible lacerations, such as it is impossible to describe; but, under all these things this brave martyr of God sustained the conflict like a hero, and at last obtained the victory in the struggle, by enduring death by means of a slow fire: for it was a weak and slow fire by which he was burned, so that his soul could not easily make her escape from the body, and be at rest.

And there was he tried like pure gold in the furnace of a slow fire, manifesting the perfection and the sincerity of his religion towards his God, and obtaining the crown of victory which belongs to the glorious conquerors of righteousness. And because he loved God, he received, as the meet recompense of his will, that perfect life which he longed for in the presence of God the sovereign of all. And together with this brave confessor, at the same time of the trial of his confession, and in the same city, the martyr Agapius, and the admirable Theckla (she of our days) were condemned by the governor to suffer punishment and to be devoured by wild beasts. [p. 11.]

THE CONFESSION OF AGAPIUS, AND OF THE TWO ALEXANDERS, AND OF THE TWO DIONYSIUSES, AND OF TIMOTHEUS, AND OF ROMULUS, AND OF PAESIS,

IN THE SECOND YEAR OF THE PERSECUTION IN OUR DAYS, IN THE CITY OF CÆSAREA.

It was the festival at which all the people assembled themselves together in their cities. The same festival also was held in Cæsarea. And in the circus there was an exhibition of horse races, and a representation was performed in the theatre, and it was customary for impious and barbarous spectacles to take place in the Stadium: and there was a rumour and a report generally current, that Agapius, whose name we have mentioned above, and Theckla with him, together with the rest of the Phrygians, were to be sent into the theatre in the form of martyrs, in order that they might be devoured by the wild beasts; for the governor Urbanus would present this gift to the spectators. When the fame of these things was heard abroad, it happened further that other young men, perfect in stature, and brave in person (they were in number six) arrived. And as the governor was proceeding to the theatre, and passing through the city, these six men stood up courageously before him: and having bound their hands behind them, they drew near before the judge Urbanus, and, in fact, by binding themselves, shewed what was about to be done to them by others, and exhibited their excellent patience, and the readiness of their mind for martyrdom, for they confessed, crying aloud and saying, We are Christians; and beseeching the governor Urbanus that they also might be thrown to the wild beasts in the theatre in company with their brethren who appertained to Agapius. For all this confidence of Jesus our Saviour, in his own champions did He manifest to all men; extinguishing the menaces of the tyrants by his champion's valour, and manifestly and clearly shewing, that neither fire, nor steel, nor even fierce wild beasts, were able to subdue his victorious servants [p. 12.], for He had girded them with the armour of righteousness, and strengthening them with victorious and invincible armour, he made them despise death. And they struck at once the governor and the whole band with him with astonishment at this their courage: and the governor gave command that they should be delivered up to prison; and there they were detained many days. And while they were in prison, Agapius, a meek and good man, the brother of one of the prisoners, arrived from the city of Gaza, and went frequently to the prison to visit his brother, and having already striven in many contests of confession before, he went with confidence to the place of imprisonment: and so he was denounced to the governor as a man prepared for martyrdom, and consequently was delivered over to bonds, in order that he might endure the trial of a second conflict. And things similar to these did Dionysius also suffer. And this good recompense was given to him from the martyrs of God as the reward of his service to them. And when the governor was made aware of this recompense of the compassion of Dionysius towards the martyrs, he gave the sentence of death against him. And thus he became associated with those who preceded him. And all together they were eight in number; namely, Timotheus, whose origin was from Pontus; and Dionysius, who came from the city of Tripolis; and Romulus, a sub-deacon of the church of the city of Diospolis; and two were Ægyptians, Paesis and Alexander; and again another Alexander, and those two respecting whom we have said that they were at last cast into prison.

All these were delivered up together at one time, to be beheaded. And this matter took place on the twenty-fourth of Adar. But there was, at the same time, a sudden change of the emperors, both of him who was the chief and emperor, and of him who was honoured in the next place after him: and those [p. 13.] who had divested themselves of the power of empire and put on the ordinary dress, having given up the empire to their associates, were rent asunder from their love towards each other, and they raised against one another an implacable war; nor was any remedy given to this malady of their hostility, until the peace in our time, which was spread throughout the whole empire of the Romans; for it arose like light out of clouds of darkness, and forthwith the Church of the supreme God and the divine doctrine was extended throughout the whole world.

THE CONFESSION OF EPIPHANIUS (Gr. *Apphianus*),

IN THE THIRD YEAR OF THE PERSECUTION WHICH TOOK PLACE IN OUR DAYS IN THE CITY OF CÆSAREA.

THAT bitter viper, and wicked and cruel tyrant, which in our time held the dominion of the Romans, went forth, even from his very commencement, to fight as it were against God, and was filled with persecution and rage against us in a far greater degree than any of those who had preceded him—I mean Maximinus: and no little consternation fell upon all the inhabitants of the cities, and many were scattered abroad into every country, and dispersed themselves, in order that they might escape the danger which surrounded them.

What words then are adequate to describe, as it deserves, the divine love of the martyr Epiphanius, who had not yet attained the age of twenty years? He was sprung from one of the most illustrious families in Lycia, famous also for their extensive worldly wealth, and, by the care of his parents, he had been sent to be educated in the city of Beyrout, where he had also acquired a great stock of learning. But this incident is not in any way connected with the narrative which we are writing: if, however, it be befitting that we make any mention of the virtuous conduct of this all-holy soul, it is very right to admire, how in a city such as this he used to withdraw himself from the society and company [p. 14.] of young men, and practised the virtues and the habits of old men, adorning himself with pure conduct and becoming manners, nor suffered himself to be overcome by the vigour of his body, nor to be led away by the society of youth. But he laid the foundation of all virtues for himself in patience, cherishing perfect holiness and temperance, and applying himself with purity, as it is right, to the worship of God. And when he had finished his education and quitted Beyrout, and was returned to the house of his parents, he was no longer able to live with those who were of his own family, because their manners were dissimilar to his own. He therefore left them, without taking care to carry with him the means of providing sustenance even for a single day. He conducted himself, however, in his travels, with purity, and by the power of God which accompanied him, he came to this our city, in which the crown of martyrdom was prepared for him, and resided in the same house with us, confirming himself in godly doctrine, and being instructed in the Holy Scriptures by that perfect martyr, Pamphilus, and acquiring from him the excellence of virtuous habits and conduct.

And for this reason I have applied myself to the narrative of the martyrdom of Epiphanius, in order that I may declare, if I be able, what a consummation he also had. All the multitudes that beheld him were struck with admiration of him. And who is there, even now-a-days, that can hear of his fame without being filled with astonishment at his courage, and at his boldness of speech, and at his daring, and at his patience, at his words addressed to the governor, and his answers to the judge? And more than all to be wondered at is the resolution with which he dedicated as it were with incense the offering of his zeal for God. For when the persecution had been raised against us the second time, in the third year of this same persecution, the former edicts of Maximinus arrived—those by which he gave command that the governors of the cities should use great pains and diligence in order to compel all men to offer sacrifices [p. 15.] and libations to devils. The heralds, therefore, through all the cities made a diligent proclamation, that the men, together with their wives and children, should assemble in the temples of the idols, and before the Chiliarchs and Centurions, as they went round about to the houses and the streets making a list of the inhabitants of the city. Then they summoned them by name, and compelled them to offer sacrifice as they had been commanded. And while this boundless tempest was threatening all men from all sides, Epiphanius, a perfectly holy man, and a witness of the truth, performed an act which surpasses all words. While no one was aware of his purpose; he even concealed it from us who were in the same house with him, he went and drew near to the governor of the place, and stood boldly before him; having also escaped the observation of the whole band that was standing near the governor, for they had not given heed when he approached the governor: and while Urbanus was offering libations, he came up to him and laid hold of his right hand, and held him back from offering the foul libation to idols, endeavouring with an excellent and gentle address and godlike suavity to persuade him to turn from his error, saying to him: That it was not right for us to turn away from the one only God of truth, and offer sacrifice to lifeless idols and wicked devils. Thus did He, who is more mighty than all, reprove the wicked through the youth Epiphanius, whom, for the sake of his reproof, the power of Jesus had taken from the house of his fathers, in order that he might be a reprover of the works of pollution. He therefore despised threatenings and all deaths, and turned not aside from good to evil, but spake gladly with pure knowledge and a glorifying tongue, because he was desirous to carry speedily, if it were possible, persuasion even to his persecutors, and to teach them to turn away from their error, and become acquainted with our common deliverer, the Saviour and God of all. When then this holy martyr of God had done these things, the servants [p. 16.] of devils, together with the officers of the governor, were smitten in their hearts as if by a hot iron; and they struck him on the face, and when he had been thrown down on the ground they kicked him with their feet, and tore his mouth and lips with a bridle. And when he had endured all these things bravely, he was afterwards delivered up to be taken to a dark prison, where his legs were then stretched for a day and a night in the stocks. And after the next day they brought Epiphanius, who, although a youth in age, was a mighty man in valour, into the judgment hall, and there the governor Urbanus displayed a proof of his own wickedness and hatred against this lovely youth by punishment and every kind of torture inflicted upon this martyr of God. And he ordered them to lacerate his sides until his bones and entrails became visible: he was also smitten upon his face and his neck to such a degree, that his countenance was so disfigured by the severe blows which he had received, that not even his friends could recognise him. This martyr of Christ, however, was strengthened both in body and soul like adamant, and stood up even more firmly in his confidence upon his God. And when the governor asked him many questions, he gave him no further answer than this—that he was a Christian: and he questioned him again as to whose son he was, and whence he came and where he dwelt; but he made no other reply than that he was the servant of Christ. For this cause therefore the fury of the governor became more fierce, and he thundered forth the more in his rage, on account of the indomitable speech of the martyr, giving command that his feet should be wrapped up in cotton that had been dipped in oil, and then be set on fire. So the officers of the judge did what he commanded them. And the martyr was hung up at a great height, in order that, by this dreadful spectacle, he might strike terror into all those who were looking on, while at the same time they tore his sides and ribs with combs, till he became one mass of swelling all over, and the appearance of his countenance was completely changed. [p. 17.] And for a long time his feet were burning in a sharp fire, so that the flesh of his feet, as it was consumed, dropped like melted wax, and the fire burnt into his very bones like dry reeds. But at the same time, although he was in great suffering from what befel him, he became, by his patience, like one who had no pain, for he had within, for a helper, that God who dwelt within him; and he appeared evidently to all like the sun: and in consequence of the great courage of this martyr of Christ many Christians also were assembled together to behold him, and stood up with much open confidence; and he, with a loud voice and distinct words, made his confession for the testimony of God, publishing by this his valour the hidden power of Jesus, that He is ever near to those who themselves draw near to Him.

And all this wonderful spectacle did the glorious Epiphanius exhibit, as it were in a theatre: for they who were the martyr's oppressors became like corrupt demons, and suffered within themselves great pain; being also themselves tortured in their own persons, as he was, on account of his endurance in the doctrine of his Lord. And while they stood in bitter pains, they gnashed upon him with their teeth, burning in their minds against him, and trying to force him to tell them whence he came, and who he was, and questioning him as to whose son he was, and where he lived, and commanding him to offer sacrifice and comply with the edict. But he looked upon them all as evil demons, and regarded them as corrupt devils: not returning an answer to any of them, but using only this word in confessing Christ, that He is God and the Son of God: [p. 18.] testifying also that he knew God his Father only. When therefore those who were contending against him were grown weary and overcome, and failed, they took him back to the prison, and on the next day they brought him forth again before that bitter and merciless judge, but he still continued in the same confession as before. And when the governor and his officers, and the whole band that ministered to his will, were foiled, he gave orders at last that he should be cast into the depths of the sea.

But that wonderful thing which happened after this act I know will not be believed by those who did not witness the wonder with their own eyes, as I myself did: for men are not wont to give the same credence to the hearing of the ear as to the seeing of eye. It is not, however, right for us also, like those who are in error and deficient in faith, to conceal that prodigy which took place at the death of this martyr of God; and we also call as witnesses to you of these things, which we have written, the whole of the inhabitants of the city of Cæsarea, for there was not even one of the inhabitants of this city absent from this terrific sight. For after this man of God had been cast into the depths of the terrible sea, with stones tied to his feet, forthwith a great storm and frequent commotions and mighty waves troubled the vast sea, and a severe earthquake made even the city itself tremble, and every one's hands were raised towards heaven in fear and trembling, for they supposed that the whole place, together with its inhabitants, was about to be destroyed on that day. And at the same time, the sea, even as if it were unable to endure it, vomited back the holy body of the martyr of God, and carried it with the waves and laid it before the gate of the city. And there was at that time vast affliction and commotion, for it seemed like a messenger sent from God to threaten all men with great anger [p. 19]. And this which took place was proclaimed to all the inhabitants of the city, and they all ran at once and pushed against each other in order that they might obtain a sight, both boys and men and old men together, and all grades of women, so that even the modest virgins, who kept to their own apartments, went out to see this sight. And the whole city together, even the very children as well, gave glory to the God of the Christians alone, confessing with a loud voice the name of Christ, who had given strength to the martyr in his lifetime to endure such afflictions, and at his death had shewed prodigies to all who beheld.

Such was the termination of the history of Epiphanius, on the second of the month Nisan, and his memory is observed on this day.

THE CONFESSION OF ALOSIS (Gr. *Ædesius*).

LIKE what had befallen the martyr Epiphanius, so after a short time the brother of Epiphanius, both on the father's and the mother's side, became a confessor, whose name was Alosis. He too, as he contended against them with the words of God, made use of his faith in the truth as armour; they also fought against him with smiting and scourging, and they stood up against each other as it were in battle array, and strove which side should get the victory. But even before his brother had given himself up to God, this admirable Alosis had applied his mind to philosophy, and meditated upon all the learned investigations of the greatest minds. Nor was he a proficient in the learning of the Greeks only, but he was also well acquainted with the philosophy of the Romans, and he had passed a long time in the society of the martyr Pamphilus, and by him had been embued with the godly doctrine as with purple suited for royalty. This same Alosis, after his admirable confession, which was accomplished before our eyes, and his sufferings of the evils (p. 20) of imprisonment for a long period, was first of all delivered over to the copper mines which are in our country, Palestine; and after that he had passed through many afflictions there, and then been released, he went thence to the city Alexandria, and fell in with Hierocles, who held the government of the province in all the land of Egypt. Him also he beheld judging the Christians severely, and contrary to just laws, making mock of the confessors of God, and delivering up the holy virgins of God to fornication, and to lust, and to bodily shame. When therefore these things were perpetrated before the eyes of this brave combatant, he devoted himself to an act akin to that of his brother; and the zeal of God was kindled within him like fire, and its heat burned within his members as in dry stubble, and he drew near to Hierocles, the wicked governor, with indignation, and put him to shame by his words of wisdom and his deeds of righteousness, and, having struck him on the face with both his hands, he threw him on his back upon the ground; and as his attendants laid hold upon him to help him, he gave him some severe blows, saying to him, Beware how thou darest to commit acts of pollution contrary to nature against the servants of God. And, being well instructed, he convicted him from the laws themselves of acting contrary to the laws.

And after Alosis had so courageously done all these things, he endured with great patience the torments which were inflicted upon his body; and as he resembled his brother in his appearance, and conduct, and in his zeal and confession, so also did they resemble each other in their punishment, and at the last, after their death the terrible sea received them from the hand of the judge.

Now this servant of Jesus exhibited his contest for the truth in [p. 21] the city of Alexandria, and was there adorned with the crown of victory; but the next confessor after Epiphanius who was called to the conflict of martyrdom in Palestine was Agapius.

THE CONFESSION OF AGAPIUS,

IN THE FOURTH YEAR OF THE PERSECUTION IN OUR DAYS.

It was in the fourth year of the persecution in our days, and on Friday the twentieth of the latter Teshri: it was on this same day that the chief of tyrants, Maximinus, came to the city of Cæsarea. And he made a boast that he would exhibit some novel sight to all the spectators that were assembled together on his account; for that was the same day on which he celebrated the anniversary of his birthday. And it was requisite upon the arrival of the tyrant that he should exhibit something more than what had ordinarily been done. What then was this new spectacle, but that a martyr of God should be cast to wild beasts to be devoured by them? while of old it had been the practice upon the arrival of the emperor that he should set before the spectators competitive exhibitions of various forms and different kinds, such as recitation of speeches, and listening to new and strange songs and music, and also spectacles of all sorts of wild beasts, and likewise that the spectators might have much delight and amusement in a show of gladiators.

It was therefore requisite that the emperor at this festival of his birthday should also do something great and extraordinary, for at all the previous exhibitions which he had furnished for them he had not done any thing new. So that—what was at once a thing desired by himself, and acceptable to the wicked tyrant—a martyr of God was brought forth into the midst, adorned with all righteousness, and remarkable for the meekness of his life; and he was cast into the theatre in order that he might be devoured by the wild beasts. His name was Agapius, respecting whom, together with Theckla, an order had been given that they should be devoured by wild beasts. The fair name of Theckla has been already mentioned in another chapter [p. 22]. They therefore dragged the blessed Agapius forward, and took him round about in mockery in the midst of the Stadium. And a tablet, with an inscription upon it, was carried about before him, on which no other accusation was exhibited against him, but this only—That he was a Christian. And the same time also a slave, a murderer, that had killed his master, was brought forward, together with the martyr of God, and they both received equally one and the same sentence. And very closely did this passion resemble that of our Saviour; for while the one was to suffer martyrdom for the sake of the God of all, the other also was to be put to death for the murder of his master; and one and the same sentence of evil went forth against both of them without any distinction. And the judge in this case was the governor Urbanus, for he was still governor in Palestine: but when Maximinus came to be present at this spectacle which has been described above, as if on account of the promptitude of Urbanus, he increased his power of evil, and liberated from death that murderer which had slain his master, and put him beyond all torture; but as for the martyr of God, he took delight in looking on with his own eyes while he was being devoured by the savage beasts. When therefore they had led the martyr Agapius round about in the Stadium, they asked him in the first place if he would deny his God, but he cried out with a loud voice and said to all those who were assembled together—Oh ye that are looking on at this trial in which I am now placed, know that it is not for any evil crime which I have committed that I am brought to this trial, for I am a witness of the true doctrine of God, and I bear testimony to you all, in order that ye may have knowledge of the one only God, and of that Light which he has caused to arise, that ye may know and adore Him who is the creator of the heavens and of the earth. And all this which is come upon me for his name's sake, I receive with joy in my mind; for they have not brought me to this place against my will, but I desire this of my own free choice, by which I stand even unto death. Moreover, I am contending for the sake of my faith, that I may afford encouragment to those who are younger than myself, that they too may despise death while [p. 23] they follow after their true life, and may disregard the grave in order to obtain a kingdom; that they should make light of that which is mortal, and keep in their recollection the life of the Giver of life, nor have any dread of punishment which is momentary, but be in fear of those flames of fire which are never quenched.

When therefore this martyr of God had cried with a loud voice and said these things, and stood erect in the midst of the Stadium, like one who felt confident that there was no danger, the wicked tyrant was filled with rage and fury, and gave orders for the wild beasts to be let loose upon him: but he, being full of courage and despising death, turned not aside to the right hand or to the left, but with lightness of feet and courage of heart advanced to meet the savage beasts. And a fierce bear rushed upon him and tore him with her teeth: he was then remanded to prison, while life was still left in him, and there he lived one day. After this, stones were tied about him, and his body was thrown into the sea; but the soul of the blessed Agapius winged her flight through the air to the kingdom of heaven, whither she was previously hastening, and was received together with the angels and the holy company of martyrs. So far then was the contest and the valour of Agapius victorious.

THE CONFESSION OF THEODOSIA, A VIRGIN OF GOD,

IN THE FIFTH YEAR OF THE PERSECUTION WHICH TOOK PLACE IN OUR DAYS.

THE persecution in our days had been prolonged to the fifth year. And it was the month Nisan, and the second day of the same month, when a godly virgin, and holy in all things, one of the virgins of the Son of God in the city of Tyre, who was not yet eighteen years old, out of pure love for those, who on account of their confession of God were set before the tribunal of the governor, [p. 24] drew near and saluted them, and entreated them to remember her in their prayers: and because of these words which she had spoken to them, the wicked men were filled with anger, as if she had been doing something unjust and improper; and the officers seized her forthwith, and took her before the governor Urbanus, for he still held the power in Palestine. And I know not what happened to him, but immediately, like one much excited by this young woman, he was filled with rage and fury against her, and commanded the girl to offer sacrifice: and because he found, that although she was but a girl, she withstood the imperial orders like a heroine, then did this savage governor the more inflict tortures on her sides and on her breast with the cruel combs; and she was torn on the ribs until her bowels were seen. And because this girl had endured this severe punishment and the combs without a word, and still survived, he again commanded her to offer sacrifice. She then raised her lips and opened her eyes, and looking around with a joyful countenance in that time of her suffering, (for she was charming in beauty and in the appearance of her figure), with a loud voice she addressed the governor: Why, oh man, dost thou deceive thyself, and not perceive that I have found the thing which I prayed to obtain at thy hands? for I rejoice greatly in having been deemed worthy to be admitted to the participation of the sufferings of God's martyrs: for indeed, for this very cause, I stood up and spake with them, in order that by some means or other they might make me a sharer in their sufferings, so that I also might obtain a portion in the kingdom of heaven together with them, because so long as I had no share in their sufferings, I could not be a partaker with them in their salvation. Behold therefore now, how, on account of the future recompense, I stand at present before thee with great exultation, because I have obtained the means of drawing near to my God, even before those just men, whom but a little while ago I entreated to intercede for me. Then that wicked judge [p. 25], seeing that he became a laughing-stock, and that his haughty threats were manifestly humbled before all those who were standing in his presence, did not venture to assail the girl again with great tortures like the former, but condemned her by the sentence which he passed to be thrown into the depths of the sea.

And when he passed on from the condemnation of this pure girl, he proceeded to the rest of those confessors, on whose account this blessed maiden had been called to this grace, and they were all delivered over to the copper mines in Palestine, without his saying a word to them, or inflicting upon them any sufferings or torture; for this holy girl prevented all those confessors by her courageous conduct against error, and received in her own body, as it were on a shield, all the inflictions and tortures which were intended for them, having rebuked in her own person the enemy that opposed them; and subdued by her valour and patience the furious and cruel judge, and rendered that fierce governor like a coward with respect to the other confessors. It was on the first day of the week that these confessors were condemned in Cæsarea; and in the month above written and in the year noted by us was this act accomplished.

THE CONFESSION OF DOMNINUS,

IN THE FIFTH YEAR OF THE PERSECUTION IN OUR DAYS, IN THE CITY OF CÆSAREA.

URBANUS was governor in Palestine; and it was the first day of the latter Teshri; and so, from day to day, he renewed himself in his wickedness, and every year prepared some devices against us. I will therefore relate how many evils he inflicted on this one day which I have mentioned. On the day then which we have spoken of, a certain man, admirable in all his conduct, and excellently skilled in the science of medicine, [p. 26] and he was a young man of tall stature and handsome, and celebrated for the holiness of his life, and the purity of his soul, and his modesty, and his name was Domninus; he was also well known to all those in our time who had been confessors. Moreover, this same man, previously to his receiving consummation by martyrdom, had endured torture in the copper mines; and on account of his patience under his confession he was condemned to the punishment by fire.

When that same judge, cunning in his wickedness (for it is not meet that those should be called wise who boast themselves in the bitterness of their wickedness), had passed on from this martyr, he lighted upon three young men of fine stature, and handsome in their person, and praiseworthy as to their souls, on account of their courage in worshipping God; and in order that he might afford amusement thereby, he sent them to the Ludus. Then he passed on from these, and delivered up an excellent and godly old man to be devoured by the wild beasts. Then the mad man passed on from this old man, and came to others, and commanded them to be castrated and turned into eunuchs. Then he left them also, and proceeded to those who appertained to Sylvanus, whose own lot also it was some time afterwards to become a martyr of God, and these he condemned to the mines of Phæno. Afterwards he passed on from these and came to others whom he insulted with tortures. Nor was the fury of his malice content with males, but he also threatened to torment the females, and delivered over these virgins to fornicators for the violation of their persons. Others again he sent to prison. Now all these things which we have described did this arrogant judge perpetrate in one hour.

And after all these things which I have described had been accomplished, that heavenly martyr of God, Pamphilus, a name very dear to me (p. 27), who was holy in all things, and adorned with every virtue, was tried in the conflict of martyrdom. He was indeed the most famous of all the martyrs in our time, on account of his accomplishments in philosophy, and his acquirements both in sacred and profane literature. Of this same man, admirable in all things, Urbanus first made a trial of his wisdom by questions and answers; and at last endeavoured to compel him by threats to offer sacrifice to dead idols; and when he had ascertained by trial that he was not to be persuaded by words, and also perceived that his threats were not heeded by him, he applied cruel torture, and lacerated him grievously on his sides. But he was not able to subdue him by this means, as he had expected. The wicked judge then considered that if he bound him in prison together with those confessors of whom mention has been already made, he might by this means subdue this holy martyr.

Now as to this cruel judge, who employed all these wicked devices against the confessors of God, what recompense and punishment must await him? For this is easy for us to know from what we are writing. For forthwith, and immediately, and without any long delay, the righteous judgment of God overtook him on account of those things which he had dared to do, and took severe and bitter vengeance upon him; and he that sat on the judgment-seat on high in his pride, and boasted himself in his soldiers that stood before him, and considered himself above all the people in Palestine, was in one night stripped of all his splendour and all his honours, and reduced to the condition of a private individual. And here, in our city of Cæsarea, where he had perpetrated all those crimes which have been written above, he was by the sentence of Maximinus, a wicked tyrant like himself, delivered up to a miserable death; and insult and humiliation, which is worse than all deaths, was heaped upon him, so that reproachful words from women, with dreadful imprecations from the mouths of all, were poured into his ears before he died [p. 28]. Wherefore, by these things we may perceive that this was a foretaste of that vengeance of God which is reserved for him at the last, on account of all his maliciousness and unmercifulness towards the servants of God.

These things we have related in a cursory manner for those believers, of whom some still remain unto this present time, omitting to relate many afflictions which passed over him, in order that we may arrange these things briefly, and in a few words, as a record for those who are to come after us; but there may come a time when we may recount in our narrative the end and fall of those wicked men who exerted themselves against our people.

THE CONFESSION OF PAULUS, AND VALENTINA, AND HATHA,

IN THE SIXTH YEAR OF THE PERSECUTION IN OUR DAYS IN CÆSAREA.

Up to the sixth year of the persecution which was in our days, the storm which had been raised against us was still raging; and great multitudes of confessors were in the mines which are called Porphyrites, in the country of Thebais, which is on one side of Egypt; and on account of the purple marble which is in that land, the name of Porphyrites has also been given to those who were employed in cutting it. This name, therefore, was also extended to those great multitudes of confessors who were under sentence of condemnation in the whole of the land of Egypt: for there were a hundred martyrs there all but three. And these confessors were sent, the men together with the women and children, to the governor in Palestine, whose name was Firmillianus. For he had superseded the governor Urbanus in his office, and he was a man by no means of a peaceful turn; indeed he even surpassed his predecessor in ferocity, having been a soldier that had been engaged in war, and had had much experience in blood and fighting. [p 29.]

There is a large city in the land of Palestine, teeming with population, of which all the inhabitants were Jews. It is called in the Aramaic tongue Lud, and in the Greek it is called Diocæsarea. To this city the governor Firmillianus went, and took thither the whole assembly of those hundred confessors. And this was a great sight which well deserves to be recorded in writing. And the Jews were spectators of this marvellous contest, having surrounded the place of judgment on all sides; and as if it were for a rebuke to themselves, they looked on with their own eyes at what took place, while the whole company of the confessors, with much confidence and immense courage, made their confession of belief in God's Christ. And they being Jews, to whom the coming of that Christ had been foretold by their prophets, whose coming their fathers looked for, had not received him when he was come; but these Egyptians, who had been of old the enemies of God, confessed, even in the midst of persecutions, their faith in God, the Lord of all, and in the Manifestation from him. And these Egyptians, who had been taught by their fathers to worship idols only, were at that time, from the conviction of their reason, undergoing this conflict, in order that they might avoid the worship of idols; while those Jews, who had always been accused by their prophets on account of their worship of idols, were surrounding them, standing and looking on, and listening as the Egyptians repudiated the gods of their own fathers, and confessed their faith in the same God as they also did; and bare witness for Him whom they had many times denied. And they were still more cut to the heart and rent, when they heard the criers of the governor shouting and calling Egyptians by Hebrew names, and addressing them with the names of the prophets. For the crier, shouting aloud, called to them and said: Elias, Isaiah, Jeremiah, Daniel, and other appellations similar to these, which their fathers had chosen from among the Hebrews, [p. 30.] in order that they might call their sons after the names of the prophets. Moreover, it also came to pass that their deeds corresponded with their names; and the Jews greatly wondered both at them and at their names, as well as at their words and their deeds, being rendered despicable themselves both by their own vice and infidelity. And I myself am convinced that these things were not done without the will of God. However, after this trial they were deprived of the use of their left leg, by having the muscles of the knee cauterized with fire, and then again they had their right eyes blinded with the sword, and then destroyed by fire. And not only were they men who endured these things, but really children and many women. And after this they were delivered over to the copper mines to see afflictions there.

And after a short time, the three men from Palestine, whom I mentioned a little while ago as having been for the moment handed over to the Ludus, were called to undergo similar sufferings, because they would not take the food from the royal provision, nor would give themselves up to that exercise and instruction which were requisite for pugilism; and they suffered many evils which we are not competent to describe: and at the end of all their afflictions they underwent this severe sentence. And others in the city of Gaza, being in the habit of assembling themselves for prayer, and being constant in reading the Holy Scriptures, were seized, and had to endure the same sufferings as their companions, being tortured on their legs and eyes. Others also had to contend in conflicts even greater than these, and after having been tortured both in their legs and eyes, were severely torn on their sides with combs. And others again more than these attained to this great excellence, and at the end of all contended with death itself.

And when he had turned himself away from these, he came to judge one who, although a woman in body, was a hero in the bravery of mind, which she possessed [p. 31]: she was also a virgin in her mode of life, and could not bear the threat of pollution which she heard, but at once gave utterance to harsh words against the tyrannical emperor, for having given authority to a vile and wicked judge. On this account, therefore, he in the first place bruised her body all over with stripes; then she was hung up and her sides were lacerated; and this not once only, but two and three times in one hour, and for a great while and also repeatedly, until those who inflicted the punishment became wearied and tired; then others succeeded them against her, and, at the commands of the furious governor, tortured her most severely. For these judges were barbarous in their manners, and enemies in their hearts. Moreover, it happened that while this furious judge was insulting this girl with his tortures, another young woman, small indeed in person, but courageous in soul—for she was possessed of a large mind, which supplied strength to the smallness of her person—being no longer able to tolerate the wickedness and cruelty of those things which were inflicted upon her sister, called out from the midst of the crowd of persons who were standing before the governor, and cried out complaining, and said: How long dost thou intend to tear my sister to pieces in so cruel and merciless a manner? And when the wicked Firmillianus heard this saying, he was bitterly incensed, and gave orders for the young woman who had complained to be brought before him. Her name was Valentina. Having therefore caught her up they brought her into the midst of the place of judgment. But she placed her trust in the holy name of Jesus. Then the murderous governor in his fury commanded her to offer sacrifice. But the maiden Valentina despised the word even of the threatener. Then he gave orders for those who were ministering to his will to lay hold upon the girl by force, and to take her up to the side of the altar, so that she might be polluted by the sacrifices. Then at that time of terror [p. 32.] the noble maiden shewed the courage of her mind, and gave the altar a kick with her foot, and it was overturned, and the fire that had been kindled upon it was scattered about; and because she did all these things without shewing any fear, the rage of the governor was roused like a wild beast, and he gave command for her to be tortured with the combs, without any mercy, so that no one man was ever torn to such a degree; and I think that, had it been possible, he would even have devoured the girl's flesh. And when at length his fury was satisfied with the sight of her blood, and he had learned, both by deeds and words, how divine is that invincible power which arms and strengthens even little girls with courage and valour, he caused both the young women, Hatha and Valentina, to be bound together, and gave sentence against them of death by fire. The name of the first was Hatha, and her father's house was in the land of Gaza; and the other was from Cæsarea, our own city, and she was well known to many, and her name was Valentina.

And after these things, Paul the confessor was called to the conflict. And he also endured it bravely, and in the same hour was condemned to be put to death, and his sentence was to be beheaded by the sword. When, then, this blessed man came to the place of execution where he was to be put to death, he besought the officer who was to behead him to have patience with him for a little while; and when the officer had granted him this desire, in the first place, with a mild and cheerful voice, he offered up thanksgiving, and worship, and glory, and supplication to God for having accounted him worthy of this victory. Then he prayed for tranquillity and peace for our people, and entreated God speedily to grant them deliverance. After this he offered up prayer for our enemies, the Jews, many of whom at that time were standing around him: then he went on in his supplication, and prayed for the Samaritans, and for those among the Gentiles [p. 33] who were without knowledge; he prayed that they might be converted to the knowledge of the truth. Nor was he unmindful of those who were standing around him, but prayed also for them. And oh, the perfection—which cannot be described—that he prayed even for that judge who had condemned him to death, and for all rulers in every place; and not only for them, but also for that officer who was then going to cut off his head. And as he was offering his supplications to God, the officers heard him with their own ears praying for them, and beseeching God not to lay to their charge that which they did to him. And as he prayed for all with a suppliant voice, he turned the whole multitude that was standing by and looking on to sorrow and tears; and then, of his own accord, he bent down his body, and put out his neck to be cut off by the sword. The conflict of this victorious martyr was consummated on the twenty-fifth of the month Thamuz.

THE CONFESSION OF ANTONINUS, AND ZEBINAS, AND GERMANUS, AND MANNATHUS (Gr. *Ennathas*),

IN THE SIXTH YEAR OF THE PERSECUTION IN OUR DAYS IN CÆSAREA.

AND when some time had elapsed after these things which I have related, another company of God's martyrs, amounting in number to one hundred and thirty, was sent from the land of Egypt into our country. And all of these had also undergone the same tortures in their eyes and legs as the former martyrs; and some of them were sent to the mines of Palestine, and some of them were delivered over to the judges in Cilicia to be chastised with injurious and insulting tortures. But from us the flame of the persecution ceased a little, the sword having been satiated with the blood of the holy martyrs; and a little rest and cessation threw some check upon the persecution which took place in our days. And continuously the scourge of God was sent upon Maximinus, the wicked tyrant, of all these evils, of which the governors of the countries were the instructors and cunning ministers, [p. 34], and that duke who was the general of the army of the Romans. And because of those things which took place, they urged the Logistæ of the cities, and the military commander, and the Tabularii to rebuild with diligence what was fallen of the temples of idols, and to compel all the men, together with their wives and children and slaves, and even the infants at the breast, to sacrifice and offer libations to devils, and also to force them to eat of the sacrifices. And a command was given that every thing that was sold in the market should be polluted with the libations and the sprinkling of the blood of the sacrifices. When these things, therefore, were done in this manner, these actions which were performed were abominated, even by the heathen who were without faith.

Great tumult, therefore, and consternation, such as there had never been the like before, overwhelmed all those who belonged to us in every place; and the souls of every one were set in affliction and trouble. But the Divine Power, on account of those things which had taken place, gave encouragement to such as belonged to Him, so that they were able to tread under foot the threats of the judges, and to depise their tortures.

But some servants of Christ's people, who in the stature of their bodies were only youths, but their soul was armed with the worship of God, both came of themselves, and when the governor was offering libations to idols in the midst of the city, suddenly rushed upon him, and called upon him to abandon his error, For there is no other God but one, the Maker and Creator of all things; and when they were asked who they were, they confessed they were Christians. No sooner, then, were these words uttered than they received sentence of death, and so passed on easily and without delay to Him in whom they made their confession. The name of the first of them was Antoninus, and the second was called Zebinas, and the third's name was Germanus; and these things were done on the thirteenth of Teshri the latter.

And they had at the same time a companion, a sister, one of the Lord's virgins, [p. 35] a chaste and courageous maiden, who came from the city of Baishan. She, however, had not acted in the same manner as those had done with whom she became confessor; for she had been brought by force from Baishan, and suffered insults and cruel tortures from the judge before she was condemned. But one of those who was set over the streets of the city was the originator of these evils. His name was Maxys, and he proved to all men that he was worse even than his name. This same blessed woman he stripped naked, and she was only left covered from the groin downwards, in order that he might indulge his lustful eyes in looking at the rest of her limbs; and he carried her about through the whole city, being tortured with straps; and afterwards took her before the tribunal of the governor, where with great boldness of speech she made the confession of her faith—that she was a Christian; and there also displayed her courage and patience under every kind of torture; and was afterwards delivered over by the governor to be burnt with fire. Moreover, the same judge became day by day more ferocious, displaying both his merciless disposition and cruelty, and he was carried away even beyond the laws of nature, so that he wreaked his vengeance and hatred even upon the lifeless corpses of the Christians, and forbade their burial. And of this same maiden of whom it has been just spoken, and of those who on the same day were consummated by confession, orders were issued that their bodies should be devoured by animals, and be carefully guarded night and day till they should be consumed by birds. Persons were therefore appointed to watch over this barbarous order from a distance, and to keep guard to prevent the bodies of the confessors from being carried away by us by stealth. So the beasts of the field, and the dogs, and the fowls of the heaven, were here and there tearing to pieces the flesh of men, so that men's bones and entrails were found even in the middle of the city; and all men were clad in sorrow on account of these things, because never before had such atrocities been done. [p. 35.] And great sorrow and grief came even upon those who were aliens from us in the faith, because of these things which their own eyes beheld; for even before the gates of the city was exhibited the dreadful spectacle of men's bodies devoured by wild beasts. When, therefore, things had continued in this manner for many days, there happened in the midst of the city a prodigy which will scarcely be believed. The atmosphere was perfectly calm and clear, when, all on a sudden, many of the columns of the porticos in the city emitted spots as it were of blood, while the market-places and the streets became sprinked and wet as with water, although not a single drop had fallen from the heavens. And it was declared by the mouth of every one, that the stones shed tears and the ground wept; for even the senseless stones and the ground without feeling could not endure this foul and barbarous deed; and that the blood which flowed from the stones, and the earth which without any rain emitted as it were tears from its body, rebuked all these godless folk. And perhaps it may seem to such as did not see with their own eyes the things which I have described, that what I have related must be attributed to a fable devoid of truth. Far from it, for these things which we have described were actually seen by those who were living at that time, some of whom are alive unto this very day.

Such then was the consummation of those holy martyrs of God, whose struggles and conflicts against error were exhibited before our eyes.

THE CONFESSION OF ARES, AND PRIMUS (Gr. *Promus*), AND ELIAS,

IN THE SIXTH YEAR OF THE PERSECUTION IN OUR DAYS AT ASHKELON.

In the month Canun the former, on the fourteenth of the same—on this day some Egyptian martyrs of God were seized before the gates of Ashkelon; and because, when they were questioned as to who they were, they acknowledged that they were Christians, [p. 38] and confessed that they had undertaken the journey, and were come from their own country for the purpose of taking sustenance to the confessors who were in Cilicia, they also were brought as malefactors before the judge. For the keepers of the gates of the city were cruel men, and laid hold upon these martyrs, and took them before Firmillianus the governor, because he was also, up to that time, still over the people of Palestine; and he decreed a cruel sentence against them: and some of them he ordered to have their eyes and their feet injured by fire and steel, and some of them to be delivered over to death by the sword; but one of them, whose name was Ares, was consummated in his confession by a fierce fire, and Primus and Elias were beheaded by the sword.

THE CONFESSION OF PETER, WHO WAS SURNAMED ABSALOM,

IN THE SEVENTH YEAR OF THE PERSECUTION IN OUR DAYS IN THE CITY OF CÆSAREA.

On the tenth day of the month Canun the latter, Peter, who was called Absalom, appeared, a famous confessor of the kingdom of God; and so manfully did he behave in his struggle for the worship of God, and so victorious was he in the conflict of his martyrdom, that he even excited admiration in the judge himself, and made those who were standing by him wonder greatly. Much, therefore, did they strive to induce him to have pity upon himself, to spare his own person, and save himself from the evils which were hanging over him; but he disregarded in his mind all that they said. And those who surrounded him—not those only who knew him, but those also who were not acquainted with him—urged him, and intreated him one after another, and besought the blessed man as if it were for their own lives. But some of them confirmed his good resolution; others, again, by what they said, suggested irresolution [p. 39], bidding him to regard with pity his own youth and person. Those of the same mind as himself called to his remembrance that hell fire which is to come, while others tried to make him afraid of the fire which was visible before him. Some endeavoured to terrify him by the mortal judge, while others reminded him of the Judge of all judges. Some called upon him to regard this transitory life, while others persuaded him to look to the kingdom of heaven. Those who belonged to the right hand invited him to turn towards them, while they who belonged to the left hand tried to persuade him to mind earthly things. But he was a young man, handsome in person, brave in mind, and active and able in body; and being such he proved his purity like gold in the furnace and the fire, and loved his confession in our Saviour better than the life of this time, which so soon passes away. And there was burned together with him in the same fire one who belonged to the heresy of Marcion, and called himself a bishop; and he gave himself up to this as in the zeal for righteousness, although he was not in true knowledge, and endured martyrdom by fire in company with this God's martyr. And this holy martyr of whom we have spoken came from Aia (Gr. *Anea*), a village which is on the confines of Beth Gobrin; and he contended in the consummation which we have described, and obtained in the conflict the crown of the glorious victory of the martyrs of Christ.

THE CONFESSION OF PAMPHILUS, AND VALES, AND SELEUCUS, AND PAULUS, AND PORPHYRIUS, AND THEOPHILUS (*Theodulus*), AND JULIANUS, AND ONE EGYPTIAN,

BEING IN NUMBER EIGHT, IN THE SEVENTH YEAR OF THE PERSECUTION IN OUR DAYS.

THE time now calls upon us to describe that grand spectacle which was displayed of the all-holy martyr Pamphilus, and of those [p. 39] who together with him were consummated by martyrdom; men admirable and brave, who exhibited, under many forms, contests for the sake of the worship of God. For indeed there are many whom we know to have been victorious in this persecution; but in none altogether like these whom we have just mentioned did we behold so completely all kinds of bodily stature, and of moral qualities of soul and education, and of deaths by different tortures, receiving the glory of the consummation of martyrdom by various triumphs. For all of the Egyptians who were with them appeared to be youths and boys; others were young men in the prime of life, among whom was Porphyrius; others again were in the full vigour both of mind and body, namely, those who were of the house of Pamphilus, that name dearly beloved by me; and Paulus, who came from Iamna; and Seleucus and Julianus, both of whom came from the country of Cappadocia. There were also among them some venerable seniors who were bent down with deep old age, as Vales, a deacon of the church of Jerusalem, and that other, whose conduct was conformable to his name, Theodulus. There was, likewise, a variety of bodily stature: and they differed too in their mental acquirements, for some of them were very simple-minded and ordinary like children, while others were possessed of profound understandings and courageous habits. There were also some among them who were also instructed in theology, and in all of them was their praiseworthy courage remarkable. But like the sun which giveth light to the day among the stars, so in the midst of them all shone forth the excellency of My Lord Pamphilus—for it is not meet that I should mention the name of that holy and blessed Pamphilus without styling him My Lord, for he indeed had no slight acquaintance with that learning which those among the Greeks admire; while there was no one in our time who was [p. 40] so well instructed in those scriptures which proceed from the Spirit of God, and also in the whole range of theology. And what is even greater than these acquirements, he was possessed of natural wisdom and discernment, that is, he received them by the gift of God. Moreover, Pamphilus was by birth of an illustrious family, and his mode of living in his own country was as that of the noble. Seleucus also had held a place of authority in the army. Some of them again were of the middle rank of life, and one also, who was called to this honour together with the rest, was a slave of the governor. Porphyrius too was reckoned the slave of Pamphilus, but in his love towards God and in his admirable confession he was his brother; and by Pamphilus himself he was considered rather as a beloved son; and, indeed, in every thing he closely resembled him who had brought him up. And were any one to say of this company of them all that they were a perfect representation of a congregation of the church, I should say that he did not go beyond the truth. For among them Pamphilus had been honoured with the presbytery, and Vales was in the orders of the diaconate, and others among them had the rank of readers; and Seleucus, even before the consummation of his confession, had been honoured as a confessor by the suffering of cruel scourgings, and had endured with patience his dismissal from his command in the army. And the remainder of the others who came after these were hearers and receivers (catechumens). And thus, under a small form, they completed the representation of a perfect church of many persons. And so this admirable selection of all these martyrs and such as these, while we looked upon them, although they were not many in number, lo! they still bore the semblance of a many-stringed harp, which consists of chords that do not resemble each other—the tenor and base, and flat, and sharp, and medial, all of which are well arranged together by the art of music. Like this resemblance, also, there were among them young men and old men together, and slaves and free, [p. 41] and clever and simple, and noble and common, and believers together with hearers (catechumens), and deacons with presbyters: all of which were variously harmonized together by one all-skilful—the Word—the only (begotten) of God. And they displayed each individually the excellency of the power within them by the endurance of tortures, and at the place of judgment produced the melody of a glorious confession.

It is also worthy of our admiration, when we look to their number, how they were twelve like the prophets and the apostles. Nor is it fit that we should omit the all-patient readiness of every one of them, each in his own part; the combs on their sides, and their incurable scourgings, and their tortures of every kind, and how they forced by violence these martyrs to do that which was abominated by them. And what necessity is there for our telling of the divine sayings which they uttered, as though stripes were reckoned by them as nothing, while with a cheerful and joyous countenance they answered the interrogatories of the judge, and jested with readiness under the very tortures themselves. And when he asked them over again whence they came, they avoided speaking of the city to which they belonged on earth, and spake of the city which in truth is theirs, and said that they were from Jerusalem which is above in heaven, confessing that they were hastening to go thither. And because of these things the judge became the more enraged at them, and prepared himself against them with cruel scourgings, in order that he might accomplish his will upon them; but when hefa iled in his expectations, he gave command that one of them should receive the crown of victory.

Moreover, the modes of their deaths also were of all kinds; for two of them were hearers (catechumens), and they were baptized at their deaths with the baptism of fire only, while others of them were delivered up to be crucified like our Saviour.

But Pamphilus, that name so especially dear to me—one who was a lover of God in truth, and a peacemaker among all men—[p. 42] received a triumph different from these. He was the ornament of the church of Cæsarea, because he also sat in the chair of the presbytery, both adorning it and being himself adorned thereby during his ministry in that place. In all his conduct too he was truly godly, being at all times in communion with the Spirit of God; for he was eminently virtuous in his mode of life, shunning wealth and honours, despising and rejecting them, and devoting himself entirely to the word of God. For every thing that he possessed from his parents he sold and distributed to the naked, and the sick, and the poor, and continued in private life without any possessions, and passed his time in the patient study of divine philosophy. He therefore quitted Beyrout, the city in which he had grown up in stature and learning together; and for the sake of his knowledge and understanding he attached himself to men seeking perfection. Human wisdom he abandoned, and loved the word of God. He also adopted the heavenly habit of the prophets, and was crowned with martyrdom.

The next after him that was brought to the conflict was Vales, a man venerable for his comely grey hairs, being in appearance a pure and respectable old man. Nor was he worthy of honour on this account only, but also for his great knowledge of the holy scriptures; for his memory was completely stored with the scriptures, so that he could repeat God's scriptures by rote like one in whose memory the whole scriptures were deposited. Moreover, he was a deacon of God's church.

And he that was reckoned third among them was named Paul, a man who was fervent in the Spirit of God; and he came from the city Iamna. And he also had previously to this his confession contended with the suffering [p. 43] of the cautery of confession.

And when they had endured affliction in prison for about two years, the immediate cause of their martyrdom was the arrival of those Egyptians who were also consummated in martyrdom at the same time together with them. For having accompanied those men who had been sent to suffer affliction in the mines of Cilicia, and being then on their way back to return to their own country, as they entered in at the gate of Cæsarea, they were questioned as to who they were and whence they came; and when they made no concealment of the truth, but said, We are Christians, they were at once seized, just as if they had been malefactors. And they were in number five. So when they were carried before the judge, and spake in his presence with openness of speech, they were forthwith committed to prison; and on the next day—the sixteenth of the month Shebat—they, together with those who appertained to Pamphilus, were brought before Firmillianus. First of all, then, the governor tried the Egyptians, and proved them by every kind of torture; and he brought forward the first of them into the midst, and asked him what was his name; but instead of his real name he heard from them the name of a prophet. Also the rest of the Egyptians who were with him, instead of those names which their fathers had given them after the name of some idol, had taken for themselves the names of the prophets, such as these—Elias, Jeremiah, Isaiah, Samuel, Daniel. And when the judge heard from the same martyrs some such name as these, he did not perceive the force of what they said, and asked them again what was the city to which they belonged. He then gave a reply similar to the former, and said, Jerusalem is my city; for he was acquainted with that city of which St. Paul spake, Jerusalem which is above is free, and our mother in whom we confess is the holy church. And the governor inquired diligently about this. Then he brought against them the combs and cauteries of fire. But he, when his hands had been bound behind him, and his feet were twisted in the stocks, sealed what he had said before, [p. 44.] and spake the truth. And again, when he questioned him many times as to what city and in what country was that Jerusalem which was said to belong to the Christians only, he replied, It is in the east, and on the side of the light of the sun, again making use of this artifice as it were in his own mind, while those who surrounded him continued to torture him with combs. Nor was he at all changed, but seemed as one who had no body. Then the judge grew furious in his mind, and imagined that perchance the Christians had built in some place a city for themselves; and so he became much more instant with tortures against them, making inquiries respecting this city, and the country in the east. When, therefore, he had punished this young man with scourging, and perceived that he varied not at all from what he had said to him at the first, he gave sentence of death against him that he should be beheaded. The rest then of the Egyptians he tried with tortures similar to his, and they likewise agreed in their confession with him who had preceded them.

And then, after these things he turned to those of the house of Pamphilus; and when he learned that they had been previously tried by many tortures, he thought that it would be folly in him to apply to them the same tortures again, and so labour in vain. He therefore only put to them the question whether they would now comply; and when he heard from them one after another the words of confession, he condemned them in the same manner as those who had preceded them, and gave sentence against them that they should be beheaded. And before the whole of the sentence was uttered, a youth from among the men, who was a slave of Pamphilus, cried out from the midst of the crowd which was standing round about the place of judgment; and then came forward into the midst, and cried out again with a loud voice to persuade the governor to grant permission for the bodies of the confessors to be buried. And he was no other than the blessed Porphyrius, the beloved disciple of Pamphilus, the mighty man of valour. [p. 45.] But Porphyrius himself was not yet eighteen years old; and he had been instructed in literature and writing, and for his modesty and manners was deserving of all praise. This youth then, who had been brought up by such a man, when he was informed of the sentence which had been issued against his master, cried out from the middle of the crowd, and begged the bodies of the confessors. Then that wretch, who is not worthy to be called a man, but rather a savage brute, not only refused to grant this becoming request, but also neither spared nor had pity upon one who in years was but a youth; and having learnt this one thing only, that he was a Christian, gave orders to those who applied the tortures to tear him with all their might: and after this, having commanded the blessed youth to sacrifice, and experiencing a refusal, he now applied the torture upon him, not as if it were upon a human body, but rather as if it were upon lifeless wood or stone, and commanded him to be torn even till they came to his bones and entrails. And when he had done this for a long while, he perceived that he was labouring to no purpose; and thus having exhibited his own cruelty and brutality upon this youth, he condemned him to be given up to a slow and lingering fire. Now, he was brought to the conflict before Pamphilus was consummated, and so departed from the body before his master who had brought him up. And thus Porphyrius exhibited himself as a warrior who was crowned with victory in all his conflicts; and although he was weak in body, he was of a cheerful countenance and courageous mind, and trod along the path of death without fear, and in truth he was full of the Holy Ghost. And when he arrived at the place where he was put to death, having put on his cloak like a philosopher, with his shoulder uncovered, he looked with his eyes up towards heaven, and in his mind looked down upon all the life of man, and approached the fire with a soul unmoved, like one who had no harm near him, and with a watchful mind, and undisturbed, he gave charge to his friends respecting his human affairs, and then was anxious to go speedily [p. 46] to the presence of God. When, therefore, the fire had been kindled at a distance around him, he caught at the flames here and there with his mouth, and his soul hastened to the journey which lay before him. Such was the conflict of Porphyrius.

Then Seleucus carried to Pamphilus a report of all these things which had been done to Porphyrius, and as the reward for this intelligence it was granted of God to Seleucus that he should become a martyr with Pamphilus. For immediately after he had given information to Pamphilus respecting the struggle and conflict of Porphyrius, as he saluted one of the martyrs with a kiss, the soldiers laid hold upon him and took him before the governor; and as Seleucus himself was anxious to go in company with the confessors, commandment was given for him to be beheaded. And this Seleucus came from the country of Cappadocia, and had acquired a glorious reputation by his military service, having held an important command in the ranks of the army. And not only this, but he also surpassed most men in stature by the size of his person and his prowess. His appearance, too, was very handsome. Moreover, at the commencement of the persecution he had been famous for his endurance of scourgings in confession; and after he had been dismissed from his military service on account of his religion, his zeal suffered not him to abstain from doing good, and so he was anxious to serve in the beloved ranks of Christ. As a visitor, therefore, of lonely orphans, and of destitute widows, and of those who were afflicted with poverty and sickness, he became a visitor and supporter of these, and, like a tender father, endeavoured to heal their afflictions. And after all these things, in which God delighteth more than sacrifices, and burnt-offerings, and incense, he was counted worthy of being consummated by confession. And this was the tenth combatant of those who have been mentioned above as having received all together on the same day their consummation and crown. And it seemed as if a great door of the kingdom of heaven had been opened by the confession of Pamphilus [p. 47], and an abundant entrance been effected for others as well as himself into the paradise of God.

The next that was brought forward after Seleucus was the pure and pious Theodulus; and he was one of the slaves of the governor, and the oldest of them all, and was much respected by them all, both on account of his manners and his years; and although he was the father of three generations, and had served his master with fidelity, still he had no mercy on him when he heard that he had saluted the martyrs in the same way as Seleucus. For after this had been told to his master, he was excited with fury against him much more than against the rest; and gave command that he should be put to death by the same mode of suffering as our Saviour, and suffer martyrdom on the cross.

But there was still one wanted after these to complete the number twelve; and so Julianus arrived from a journey, and, as if it were on purpose to make up the number of martyrs twelve, the moment he arrived, before he was yet entered into the city, immediately on the way he was told by some one respecting the matter of the confessors, and ran to have a sight of the confessors; and when he beheld the bodies of the saints lying upon the ground, he was filled with joy, and embraced them one after another with heavenly love, and saluted them all with a kiss. And while he was still visiting them, and lamenting that he himself had not suffered martyrdom with them, the officers seized him, and took him before the judge; and that judge commanded what his evil heart conceived, and delivered him also to a slow fire. So this Julianus, also, with joy and gladness praised God with a loud voice for having counted him worthy of this; and his soul ascended to his Lord with the company of the confessors. And this man was by family of Cappadocia, and in his soul he was filled with the fear of God, being a quiet and religious man, and diligent in the practice of every virtue. There was also in him a glorious savour of the Holy Spirit; and he was counted worthy to be associated with the company of these who received the consummation of confession together with the blessed Pamphilus. [p. 48.]

Four days and nights then were the bodies of the all-holy martyrs of God exposed to be devoured by wild beasts, by the command of the governor Firmillianus. When, therefore, nothing had touched them, not even the wild beasts, they were taken up whole without the permission of the governor, and with due reverence committed to an honourable burial; and were laid in the interior of the churches, and so consigned to a never-to-be-forgotten memorial in the temples of the house of prayer, that they might be honoured of their brethren who are with God.

THE CONFESSION OF HADRIANUS AND EUBULUS,

IN THE SEVENTH YEAR OF THE PERSECUTION IN OUR DAYS.

WHEN the consummation of Pamphilus and of those martyrs who were with him was published abroad by the mouths of all men, both Hadrianus and Eubulus, from a place which is called part of Batanea, had hastened to the rest of the martyrs at Cæsarea: and when they drew near to the gate of the city, they were interrogated as to the cause for which they were come, and having stated the truth, they were taken before Firmillianus; and he at once, without any delay, ordered them, in the first place, to have their sides torn with combs, and punished them in a peculiar manner, as if they had been enemies and were hated by him; and not being satisfied with this, he condemned them to be devoured by wild beasts. And after an interval of two days, the confessor Hadrianus was cast before a lion on the fifth of Adar, and bravely accomplished his conflict, and after having been torn by the beast, he was at last put to death by the sword. Eubulus, also, on the second day following, the seventh of Adar, when the judge had made many attempts with him, and said to him, If thou wilt sacrifice to devils thou shalt be set at liberty in peace, both despised the whole existence of this passing time, and chose for himself everlasting life rather than this fleeting and transitory life. He was then cast to a lion, and after [p. 49] he had been torn by the teeth of the lion, he suffered in the same manner as those who were gone before him. He was the last of all that suffered martyrdom and finished his conflict in Cæsarea.

THE CONFESSION OF PAULUS (Gr. *Peleus*) AND NILUS, AND PATRIMYTHEAS (Gr. *Patermutheus*) AND ELIAS,

IN THE SEVENTH YEAR OF THE PERSECUTION IN OUR DAYS.

It was the nineteenth day of Ilul, and during the same wonderful conflict of the martyrs of God, that a great spectacle was assembled in Phæno, in this same Palestine; and all the combatants were perfect, and in number they were about a hundred and fifty. Many of them, also, were Egyptians, amounting to more than a hundred. And the same in the first place had their right eyes and their left legs in their sinews destroyed by cautery of fire and by the sword. And then after these things they were delivered over to dig copper in the mines. Those, also, who belonged to Palestine had to endure afflictions in the same manner as the Egyptians; and they were all assembled together in a place called Zauara, as a congregation consisting of many persons. There was also much people with them, who came from other places to see them, and many others who ministered to them in their necessities, and visited them in love, and filled up their lack. And all the day they were occupied in the ministry of prayer, and in the service of God, and in teaching and reading; and all the afflictions which passed over them were esteemed by them as pleasures, and they spent all that time as if it had been in a festive assembly. But the enemy of God and wicked envier was not able to bear these things, so there was immediately sent out against them one of those generals of the Romans that is styled Dux; and first of all he separated them one by one from each other, and some of them were sent to that wretched place Zauara, and some not; and some of them to Phæno, the place where the copper is dug; [p. 50.] and the others went to different places. Afterwards he selected from among those in Phæno four of them who were of great excellence, in order that by them he might terrify the rest. Having, therefore, brought them to the trial, and not one of them having shewn any signs of dismay, this merciless judge, thinking that no punishment was so severe as that by fire, delivered up God's holy martyrs to this kind of death. When, therefore, they were brought to the fire, they cast themselves into the flames without fear, and dedicated themselves as an offering more acceptable than all incense and oblations; and presented their own bodies to God as a holocaust more excellent than all sacrifices. And two of these were Bishops Paulus and Nilus; and the other two were selected of the laity, Patermytheus and Elias; and by race they were all of them Egyptians. They were pure lovers of that exalted philosophy which is of God, and offered themselves like gold to the fire to be purified. But He who giveth strength to the weak, and multiplieth comfort to the afflicted, deemed them worthy of that life which is in heaven, and associated them with the company of angels.

THE CONFESSION OF SILVANUS, AND OF THOSE WITH HIM,

IN THE EIGHTH YEAR OF THE PERSECUTION IN OUR DAYS.

THIS blessed Silvanus came from Gaza, and he was one of the veteran soldiers; and when his freedom from service proved to be contrary to his habits, he enlisted himself as a good soldier of Christ. For he was a perfectly meek man, and of bright turn of mind, and used his faith with simplicity and purity. And he was a presbyter of the church in the city of Gaza, and conducted himself there with great propriety. And because the conflict for life was proclaimed against the soldiers of Christ [p. 51], he, an old man, of a noble person, went down to the Stadium, and there, in his first confession before the people of Cæsarea, he acquitted himself valiantly, being tried with scourgings. And when he had endured these bravely, he fought in a second conflict, in which the old man endured the combs on his sides like a young man. And at the third conflict he was sent to the copper mines; and during a life of much length he exhibited great probation. He was also deemed worthy of the office of the episcopate, and also rendered himself illustrious in this office of his ministry. But on the fourth day of Iyar the great gate of heaven was fully opened to him, and this blessed man went up with a company of martyrs, not being left alone, for a great assembly of brave men followed him. And suddenly a mandate of wickedness was issued, and command was given that all those in the mines who were become enfeebled through old age or sickness, and those who were not able to work, should be put to death by the sword; and God's martyrs, being all together forty in number, were beheaded all in one day. And many of them were Egyptians, but their leader and guide was this same martyr and bishop of martyrs, Silvanus, a man truly blessed and beloved of God.

Being now arrived at this place in our narrative, we will inform you how God in a short time took vengeance upon those wicked rulers, and they speedily experienced the punishment of their crimes. For he that was excited against these martyrs of God in a barbarous manner, like some fierce wild beast, suffered a wretched punishment; and by the command of him who possessed the power of the time, perished after the manner of a cruel wild beast. And all the rest perished by various kinds of deaths, and received that punishment which they deserved for their crimes.

So, then, we have described and made known the things which were done during the whole time of the persecution among the people in Palestine. And all these were blessed martyrs [p. 52] of God, who triumphed in our time; who made light of this temporary life, and prized the worship of God far above every other thing, and have received the hidden hope of those good things which are invisible to the bodily eyes.

Oh! the blessed confessors of the kingdom of Christ, who were tried like gold in the excellence of their righteousness, and obtained through the conflict in which they were set the heavenly life of angels, and laid hold upon the promises of the hidden good things of the victory of the high calling—For eye hath not seen nor ear heard, neither hath it entered into the heart of man, what God has prepared for them that love him.

Here end the chapters of the narrative of the victories of the holy confessors in Palestine.

NOTES.

P. ii. l. 18.—" Who shall separate us ..... slaughter." Rom. viii. v. 35. This passage varies slightly both from the Greek and the Peshito. There is nothing here to correspond with *της αγαπης* and *η γυμνοτης*; and also ܡܘܬܐ, "death," for *κινδυνος*.

l. 23.—"For him who loved us," v. 37: as if the Syriac translator had read *δια τον αγαπησαντα ημας*, or had mistaken the meaning of *δια* with a genitive.

l. 27.—v. 38. *ουτε αγγελοι, ουτε αρχαι* omitted.

l. 31.—Eusebius gives the account of the martyrdom of Peter and Paul at Rome in his Eccl. Hist. book ii. ch. 25.

P. iii. l. 6.—"As for those conflicts." Eusebius makes a similar statement, book viii. ch. 13, on which passage Valesius has the following note:—(c) " He means doubtless his book *concerning the Martyrs of Palestine.* For no other book but that can be found, wherein Eusebius relates the conflicts of the Martyrs which he himself had seen. The opinion of Christophorson is from this passage further disproved, who supposed the book *concerning the Martyrs of Palestine* was a part of this eighth book." In speaking here of Christophorson, Valesius alludes to a note immediately preceding, which runs thus—" (b) To wit, in the book *concerning the Martyrs of Palestine,* which is placed after this eighth book. For in that Eusebius at large declares the martyrdom of Pamphilus, as may there be seen. Moreover, from this place it appears that that book *concerning the Martyrs of Palestine* was written by Eusebius after his *Ecclesiastical History,* and after his books *concerning the life of Pamphilus the Martyr.* Christophorson, who had inserted the whole Appendix before this chapter, was forced to omit these words of Eusebius here, lest Eusebius should seem to have forgot himself." See English Translation of Eusebius's Ecclesiastical History in "*The History of the Church*: fol., London, 1709, p. 148. I shall cite this in the following notes as *Eng. Trans.*

l. 18.—"Procopius." There is an antient Latin copy of these Acts, as they stand here, published by Valesius in his notes upon the first chapter of the Martyrs of Palestine as they exist in the Greek at the end of the eighth book of the Eccl. Hist. of Eusebius. Respecting these, he writes thus:—"The same relation is in the *Acts of the Passion of Procopius the Martyr*, which begins thus: '*The first of the Martyrs that appeared in Palestine was Procopius*,' &c. From whence it is evident that those acts were translated out of the Greek copy of Eusebius into Latin. To make this more apparent, it will in no wise be unuseful to insert here the entire acts. For many things worth our knowledge are contained in these which neither Baronius nor Molanus happened to have a sight of."

Passio Sancti Procopii Martyris, qui passus est sub Fabiano judice 4 Nonas Augusti.

Primus martyrum qui sunt in Palæstina, apparuit Procopius, vir cœlestis gratiæ, qui et ante martyrium sic suam vitam disposuit, ut etiam a parva ætate castitati semper et morum virtutibus studeret. Corpus quidem suum sic confecit, ut pæne mortuum putaretur, animam vero ejus sic verbis confortabat divinis, ut etiam corpori virtutem ex hujus refectione ministraret. Cibus et potus ei panis et aqua fuit. Solis his utebatur, cum post biduum triduumque, diem interdum etiam post septimam ad cibum rediret. Sacrorum quoque meditatio sermonum ita mentem ejus obstrinxerat, ut nocte ac die in hoc infatigabilis permaneret. Clementiæ autem et mansuetudinis tanquam ceteris inferior documentum sui præbebat copiam. In verbis divinis ei tantum studium erat. Illa vero quæ extrinsecus sunt, mediocriter attigerat. Igitur genere quidem Æliensis, conversatione autem vel habitatione Scythopolitanus erat. Ibi ecclesiæ tria ministeria præbebat, unum in legendi officio, alterum in Syri interpretatione sermonis, et tertium adversus dæmones manus impositione consummans. Cumque ab Scythopoli una cum sociis in Cæsaream transmissus fuisset, ab ipsis portis ad præsidem ducitur, et priusquam carceris vel vinculorum experiretur angustias, in ipso ingressu suo a judice Flaviano ut diis sacrificaret impellitur. At ille magna voce non esse deos multos sed unum factorem omnium opificemque testatus est. Judex autem plaga sermonis ictus et conscientia saucius, consensit ejus sermoni. Atque ad alia se rursum argumenta constituit, ut vel regibus sacrificaret. Sanctus autem Dei martyr sermonem ejus despiciens, Homeri, inquit, versum dicens: non est bonum multos dominos esse. Unus dominus est, unus rex. Itaque hoc verbo ejus audito, quasi qui infausta in regibus deprompsisset, jussu judicis ducitur ad mortem, et capite amputato ingressum vitæ cœlestis, vel compendium beatus invenit: Desii septima Julii mensis, quæ Nonas Julias dicitur apud Latinos, primo anno quo adversus nos fuit persecutio. Hoc primum in Cæsarea martyrium consummatum est, regnante Domino nostro Jesu Christo, cui honor et gloria in sæcula sæculorum. Amen.

And in a note following this Latin copy he writes (r)—"Many things are omitted in the Greek text of Eusebius, which must be made perfect by these Acts in Latin. For when Eusebius had here said expressly, that Procopius upon his first arrival was brought before the judge, he adds nothing concerning the place from whence he came, where he was apprehended, or to what place he was brought: nothing of which ought to have been omitted. Besides, Eusebius does accurately relate the descent and country of other Martyrs mentioned in this book; and if any of these had attained to any Ecclesiastical honour, he does usually take notice of that also. But of this person, who was the chief and leader of all the Palestine Martyrs, we see no such relation made. This, it is probable, was not the fault of Eusebius, but of his exscribers; for in the Latin Acts, which, as we before evinced, were translated out of Eusebius, all these circumstances are manifestly declared." See Ecc. Hist. *Eng. Trans.*, p. 154. This Latin version is also printed by Th. Ruinart, p. 353, *Acta primorum*

Martyrum Sincera et Selecta, fol. Amstel. 1713. There is also another Syriac version of these Acts taken from Cod. Nit. Vat. 1. (See Assemani, *Bibl. Orient.* vol. 1. p. 56); and published with a Latin translation and notes, by S. E. Assemani, in *Acta SS. Martt. Orient. et Occident.*, 2 vol. fol. Romæ, 1748, part ii. p. 169. I have collated it with this version. It is not of importance to note the variants, which seem to be chiefly due to separate translations.

l. 20.—"The first year of the persecution in our days." The preface to the account of the *Martyrs of Palestine*, in the eighth book of *Ecc. Hist.*, says this was the 19th year of Diocletian, or A. D. 303. See Ruinart *Acta primorum Martt.* p. 316.

P. iv. l. 2.—"His family was from Baishan." The Latin has—"Igitur genere quidem Æliensis, conversatione autem vel habitatione Scythopolitanus erat," with which the other Syriac agrees in reading, ܓܢܣܗ ܕܝܢ ܡܢ ܐܘܪܫܠܡ ܐܝܬܘܗܝ܆ ܗܘܐ ܘܡܥܡܪܗ ܒܡܕܝܢܬܐ ܒܝܫܢ ܗܘܐ—"But his family was from Jerusalem, and he dwelt in the city Baishan." Scythopolis was the Greek name of Baishan, and Ælia occupied the scite of Jerusalem. See, respecting Baishan, S. E. Assemani, *Ibid*, not. p. 171.

l. 4.—"In the second order he translated from Greek into Aramaic." He was an interpreter; on which passage S. E. Assemani observes—"Ad munus interpretis recte adnotat Valesius, apud Syros olim Divinas Scripturas Græce fuisse lectitatas, quas deinde Interpres Syriacus redderet," *Ibid.* p. ii. p. 171. I should feel much disposed to question this assertion without greater proof. Doubtless before this time the Scriptures were translated into Syriac. The meaning of the passage may also imply that Procopius was engaged in translating other ecclesiastical works into Syriac from the Greek. This very copy of Eusebius was transcribed only 108 years after the Martyrdom of Procopius. *Ibid.* p. 166. S. E. Assemani gives his opinion in these words:—"Imo vero quum S. Procopius Sanctorum librorum a Græco in Syriacum sermonem in ecclesia Scythopolitana Interpres dicatur, plane inde colligitur, Syriacum seu Chaldaicum idioma Palæstinis tunc vernaculum fuisse, atque adeo ejusdem Procopii, quemadmodum et aliorum martyrum in Palæstina coronatorum, Acta Syriace seu Chaldaice ab Eusebio fuisse primum exarata, eademque ipsa esse, quæ præ manibus habemus, omnino tenendum est. Neque enim verisimile est, Eusebium, quam in usum popularium suorum; et in ovium sibi concreditarum solatium scribebat, martyrum historiam iis literis consignasse, quas omnes non callerent." *Ibid.* p. 166.

l. 12.—"Flavianus." The other Syriac has ܦܘܠܝܢܘܣ, Paulinus, evidently a mistake of the scribe.

l. 21.—"Greatest of the poets of the Greeks." The Latin has "Homeri inquit versum, dicens;" and the other Syriac, ܗܘܡܪܘܣ ܡܫܡܗܐ ܕܦܘܐܝܛܐ ܕܝܘܢܝܐ, "Homer, the celebrated of the poets of the Greeks." Those words of Homer, *Iliad* ii. 24, were often cited by the early Christians, and do not therefore prove that Procopius was acquainted with his poems. See *Heinichen's note.*

l. 19.—"The Emperors, who were four in number." These were Diocletianus, Maximianus, Constantius, and Galerius. See Eusebius *Ecc. Hist.* b. viii. c. 13; and supplement to same book; and Valesius's notes, *Eng. Trans.* pp. 148. 153.

l. 27.—"On the seventh day of the month Heziran." See Valesius's note on this passage in the Greek; *Eng. Trans.* p. 157.

l. 31.—"The confession of Alphæus, Zacchæus, and Romanus." Their festival is celebrated on the 18th of November. See Baillet, *Vies des Saints.* There is also a Syriac version of these Acts published by S. E. Assemani in *Acta SS. Martt.* part ii. p. 177.

l. 35.—"Festival—on the twentieth year." That is, Diocletian's Vicennalia. See Valesius's note on this place, *Eng. Trans.* p. 158; and also on Life of Constantine, *ibid.* p. 529.

P. v. l. 9.—"Of Gadara." So in the other Syriac. This is not in the Greek, but Valesius has supplied the fact in the following note (e):—"He was of Gadara, concerning whom we have this passage in the Menology at 18th of November—*The comme-*

moration of the holy Martyrs, Michæus, Zacchæus, deacon of Gadara, and Alphæus, ibid. p. 158. See also Ruinart, n. 4. p. 317, *Acta prim. Martt.*

l. 22.—"Four holes of the rack." Valesius has the following note on Eusebius, *Ecc. Hist.* b. v. c. i.—"The fashion of this engine for punishment, and the manner how persons were punished in it, seems to have been this. It was a piece of timber wherein five pairs of holes were made at a certain distance one from the other. Into these holes, as it were into boots, they put the feet of the offenders, and fastened them therein with cords and fetters. The meaning of *their feet being strained to the fifth hole* is, they forced them to straddle so wide as to put their feet into the last pair of holes, which posture (those holes being at the greatest distance one from the other) was the sharpest degree of torture in this engine."—*Eng. Trans.* p. 71. See also *Gallonius De SS. Martt. cruciatibus*, Parisiis, 1659.

l. 25.—"Exorcist." Valesius has this note on Exorcists (*):— "There was in former times a twofold use of the *Exorcists* in the Church; for their business was to cleanse both those possessed with devils, and also the *catechumens*, who were exorcised more than once; for after every examination in their catechism they were brought to the Exorcist ungirt and with their shoes off, that they might be purged by him. See Cyril Hierosol. in *Procatechesi ad Illuminandos*, and Chrysostom in his first Homily *ad Illuminandos.*" *Eng. Trans.* p. 158. See also Bingham, *Antiquities of the Christian Church*, book iii. ch. 4. Respecting Readers or Lectors, see *ibid.* ch. v.

P. vi. l. 16.—"Combs." See Gallonius de *SS. Martt. Cruciat.* ch. v.

l. 33.—"Romanus." There are other Acts of Romanus, in Syriac, giving a much longer and fuller account than this. *British Museum Cod. Add.* 12,174, fol. 300 b. In these the day of his martyrdom is given the 19th of Teshri the latter. See L. Surius, *de Probatis Sanctorum vitis*, at the 18th of November, and Baillet, *Vies des Saints*, at the same day. See a further account of him from Eusebius *de Resurrectione*; Prudentius *περι στεφανων*, &c., collected and published by Ruinart. *Acta prim. Martt.* p. 357 seq.

P. vii. l. 7.—“The judge.” His name was Asclepiades. See Prudentius *Hymn περι στεφανων*, l. 687, in Ruinart, *Acta prim. Martt.* p. 361. S. E. Assemanni also observes:—“Hunc Asclepiadem vocant *Acta* apud Mombritium et Prudentius in *Hymno.*” See *Acta SS. Martt.* ii. p. 182, and the other Syriac Acts, *Mus. Brit. Cod. Add.* 12,174.

l. 24.—“The officers,” ܩܣܛܘܢܪ̈ܐ, “Quæstionarii.” They were the persons who inflicted the punishment, as appears from the following passage of the acts of Trypho:—“Præfectus autem admirans tantam eorum perseverantiam, jussit eos manibus post tergum ligatis nudos cædi: et cum acerrime cæderentur, quæstionarii deficiebant, Præfectus ira repletus jussit ungulas et lampades eorum lateribus applicari. Quæstionarii accedentes jussa complebant.” See Ruinart, *Act. prim. Martt.* p. 163. He also has this note, *ibid.* p. 172.—“Quæstionis nomine designat tormenta, quæ ad confessionem eliciendam adhibentur: vox etiam nunc ad eandem rem significandam usurpata est. Ab ea *Confessores quæstionati et torti* dicuntur apud Cyprian, *Epist. ad Florentium*, 66.

l. 34.—“The emperor Diocletian.” The name is not given in the Greek. It appears from this that Valesius was mistaken when he wrote,—“I suppose he means Galerius Cæsar, for Diocletian made his abode then at Nicomedia.” See *Eng. Trans.* p. 158. The other Syriac Acts, however, give the name ܡܟܣܝܡܝܢܘܣ ܚܬܢܗ ܕܕܝܘܩܠܛܝܢܘܣ, “Maximinus, the son-in-law of Diocletianus.” *Mus. Brit. Cod. Add.* fol. 304.

P. viii. l. 8.—“Then did great wonder.” The miraculous part of this narrative, which savors so strongly of the superstitious, is omitted from the Greek; and that passage added which, in the Syriac, commences the account of Zacchæus, but is not found at that place in the Greek. The story of Romanus having spoken after his tongue was cut out is, however, repeated in the other Syriac Acts, and is also told in the Greek *Menæum.* See Valesius, note (*) *Eng. Trans.* p. 158. Ruinart has the following note:—"Omittit miraculum Romani, etiam abscissâ linguâ loquentis, quod alias adeo exaggerat. Hinc patet non omnia isto libello contineri." p. 318. Eusebius himself also, in his book *de Resurrectione*, affirms the miracle. See Ruinart, *Acta prim. Martt.* p. 359; and Chrysostom, *Orat.* 43 et 48. *Ibid.* See also S. E. Assemani's note, *Act. SS. Martt.* p. ii. p. 182.

l. 20.—"Upon the rack." The other Syriac version adds here, "to five holes," ܒܚܡܫܐ ܢܩܒ̈ܝܢ. *Ibid.* p. 181.

l. 22.—"Strangling instrument." ܒܚܢܘܩܝܬܐ. Greek, τῷ ξύλῳ βρόχῳ. The other Acts have, "He was strangled in Prison," fol. 304.

l. 30.—"Confession of Timotheus." These Acts are also given in the other Syriac Translation by S. E. Assemani, *Act. SS. Martt.* p. ii. p. 184. See Surius, at the 19th of August, and Baillet, at the same day.

P. ix. l. 2.—"Edicts from the Emperors." Respecting these Edicts Valesius has the following note on the Ecc. Hist. b. viii. c. vi. (*)—"By the first Edict of the Emperors against the Christians it was ordered that the churches should be ruined and the scriptures burnt, and that those who were honoured with any preferment (if they refused to sacrifice) should be deprived of their dignity. The meaner sort were to lose their liberty. See chap. 2. Another Edict soon followed this, that Bishops, Priests, and Deacons should be imprisoned, and by all ways compelled to sacrifice. The third Edict comprehended all sorts of Christians, as well those of the laity as the clergy; which Edict was proposed (says Eusebius in the chap. 3 of his book *concerning the Martyrs of Palestine*) in the second year of the Persecution. But this seems rather to have been the fourth Edict: for the second and third concerned the Presbyters only. By the second it was ordered they should be imprisoned, and by the third it was enjoined that they should by tortures be compelled to sacrifice." *Eng. Trans.* p. 143.

l. 25.—"The people of the city of Gaza were accursed in their heathenism." See the account given by Theodoretus, book iii.

c. 6 and 7; and S. E. Assemani, *Acta SS. Martt.* p. ii. p. 186, note (4).

P. x. l. 9.—"Theckla (she of our days)." There were several martyrs of this name. S. E. Assemani has published the Acts of two others. See *Acta SS. Martt.* vol. i. pp. 101, 123; but Eusebius seems especially to draw the distinction with reference to Theckla, the companion of St. Paul, so celebrated in the early ages of Christianity. See Grabe, *Spicilegium*, vol. i. p. 95 Jer. Jones, *New and Full Method,* vol. ii. p. 353; Tischendorf, *Acta Apost. Apocr. Lips.* 1851, p. 40. There are also antient copies in Syriac of the Acts of Theckla, brought from the Nitrian Convent, now in the British Museum. The account of Theckla is in one or two instances found in a volume containing also the Books of Ruth, Esther, and Judith, and called in Syriac "The Book of Women." See *Cod. Add.* 12,174; 14,641; 14,652.

l. 15.—"Timotheus." The Greek has *Τιμολαος*. See Surius, at March 24th, and Baillet, at the same day.

l. 16.—"Paesis." The Syriac is ܦܠܣܝܣ, "Plasis," which I have corrected here from the reading below, where it is ܦܐܣܝܣ, Paesis, or Pausis, for some Greek MSS. read *Παησις* and others *Παυσις*. Valesius notes (c)—"In the *Maz.* and *Med.* MSS. his name is *Paesis.* In the *Greek Menology* (which *Canisius* published) at the 5th of March, instead of *Paesis* he is called *Publius.*" *Eng. Trans.* p. 159. The variation in the Syriac doubtless arose from confounding *Α* with *Λ* in the word *ΠΑΗϹΙϹ* or *ΠΛΗϹΙϹ.*

l. 27.—"The Phrygians." There is no mention of Phrygians in the Greek; but in *Ecc. Hist.* book viii. ch. 11, Eusebius speaks of the destruction of a whole city of Christians in Phrygia. These, perhaps, were some of them who had been reserved for a spectacle in the theatre.

P. xi. l. 35.—"A subdeacon." Syriac ܦܪܝܩܐ, evidently a blunder for ܦܕܝܩܐ. Greek *υποδιακονος*.

P. xii. l. 5.—"A sudden change." See respecting this, Eusebius, *Life of Constantine,* book i. ch. 18, *Eng. Trans.* p. 537, where Valesius has the following note(a):—"This place is highly remarkable, for from it this conclusion may be made, that the persecution began in Dioclesian's eighth, and Maximian's seventh consulate, and not on the foregoing year, as Baronius will have it. Concerning which matter I have spent many words in my notes on Eusebius, *Ecc. Hist.* book viii. c. 2, note ([c]). For whereas Eusebius affirms that the Emperors Dioclesian and Maximian divested themselves of their purple in the year after the persecution was begun; and whereas it is manifest that they did that on the year of Christ 304; what I have said does necessarily follow, that Dioclesian's persecution was begun in the year of Christ 303." Ruinart has this note:—"Diocletianus scilicet prope Nicomediam, Herculius Mediolani, cogente Galerio Maximinano, non autem sponte, uti hactenus putabatur. Totam hunc historiam egregie describit Lactantius in lib. de *Mortibus Persecut.* cap. 18 seq. *Acta Prim. Martt.* p. 319.

l. 16.—The Greek adds a passage, "But we will give an exact account of these matters at a more opportune place and time," referring perhaps to the Life of Constantine.

l. 18.—"Epiphanius." Syriac, ܐܦܝܦܢܝܘܣ; but the Greek reads *Απφιανος*; the other Syriac version published by S. E. Assemani, *Acta SS. Mart.* P. ii. p. 189, ܐܦܝܢܘܣ; and an Arabic account cited by him, امفيانوس, "Amphianus." In Latin he is called *Apianus, Apphianus,* and *Amphianus. Ibid.* See Surius and Baillet, at the 2d of April.

l. 33.—"He was sprung from one of the most illustrious families in Syria." For which the Greek is, *ει τις αρα Παγας επισταται της Λυκιας, ουκ ασημον πολιν, εντευθεν ορμωμενος.* On this Valesius has the following note ([e]):—"In the *Med.* MS. this city is called *Arpagas;* in the *Maz.* MS. *Arapagas,* in the *Fuk* MS. *Harpagas;* but in the margin a notice is given that it should be *ἀραγας* with an aspirate. I never met with any thing concerning *Aragas,* a city of Lycia.—In the *Menæum* of the Greeks, Amphianus is said to have been born in Lydia."—*Eng. Trans.* p. 160. There seems, therefore, to have been some mistake in the copies in this place at an early period.

l. 36.—"Educated at Beyrout." ([c]) "At Berytus there was a

school of civil law, as many have taken notice from Gregory Thaumaturgus, Eunapius, Nonnus, and others. Gregorius Nazianzenus calls Berytus *Φοινικης κλυτον αστυ, νομων εδος Αυσονιηων, a famous city of Phœnicia, the seat of Ausonian laws.*" See Valesius, *ibid.*

P. xiii. l. 20.—"This our city." The Greek has *την Καισαρεων πολιν.*

l. 23.—"Pamphilus." His name is not mentioned in the Greek, and Valesius has this note on the passage (ᶠ):—"Simeon Metaphrastes, who professes that he transcribed the Martyrdom of *Apphianus* (or, as he calls him, Amphianus), out of Eusebius, has altered this passage thus:—*And having been conversant with us in divine studies, and instructed in the sacred scriptures by the great Martyr Pamphilus, he obtained no mean habit of virtue; by which he opened a passage for himself, whereby he procured the crown of Martyrdom.*" See *Eng. Trans.* p. 160. And in note (ᶜ), on the same page, Valesius writes:—"In the Menologies of the Greeks at the 2d of April, Amphianus, with his brother Ædesius, is mentioned to have been instructed in the Christian religion by Pamphilus the Martyr, at Berytus;" but not having the knowledge of the fact that Pamphilus himself had been educated at the same place—supplied in the Syriac, but omitted in the Greek—Valesius supposed the Menologies to be mistaken. See note (ᶠ), *Ibid.* It is evident from this that Simeon Metaphrastes, and the compilers of the Menologies, read these Acts as in the Syriac.

P. xv. l. 12.—"His bones and entrails became visible." The same thing is said of the Martyr Alexander, whose Acts were published by Ruinart:—"Ita enim laniatum fuerat corpus crudelitate verberantium, ut carne soluta costarum, patefactisque visceribus, secreta animæ panderentur." *Acta Prim. Martt.* p. 77.

l. 28.—"Was hung up at a great height." See, respecting the various modes of suspension in torture, Gallonius *de SS. Martt. cruciatibus*, p. 6.

P. xvii. l. 30.—After the Martyrdom of Apphianus the Greek adds the following account of Ulpianus:—"At the same time, and almost on the same day, a young man in the city of Tyre, by name Ulpianus, after he had been cruelly scourged, and endured most grievous stripes, was sewn up in the raw hide of an ox, together with a dog and a venomous serpent, and cast into the sea. Wherefore we thought it agreeable to make mention of this person at [this place wherein we have related] the Martyrdom of Apphianus."—*Eng. Trans.* p. 161. On this Valesius has the following note (ᵉ):—"*Διο μοι δοκει κ.τ.λ.*: that is, *Although Ulpianus suffered not in Palestine, but in Phœnicia, yet because he suffered martyrdom at the same time, and died by the same sort of punishment that Apphianus had inflicted on him, we judged it not unfit to make mention of him here.* It is therefore apparent from these words that Eusebius in this book designed to give an account of the Martyrs of the Province of Palestine only."—*Ibid.*

l. 33.—"Alosis." In the Greek Ædesius, *Αιδεσιος*, the variation has doubtless arisen from the similarity of the names *ΑΛΟCΙΟC* and *ΑΔΕCΙΟC* in a MS. partly effaced. The other Syriac published by S. E. Assemani has ܐܕܣܝܣ. See *Acta SS. Martt.* P. ii. p. 195. The account of this martyrdom is given by Baillet, at the 2d of April.

l. 36.—"Both on the father's and the mother's side." And so also in the other Syriac.—*Ibid.* p. 195. The Greek has here *ομοπατριος αδελφος* only. Valesius has this note (ᵈ):—"In the *Greek Menæum*, at the second day of April, Ædesius is styled Apphianus's brother by the mother's side."—*Eng. Trans.* p. 161. Hence it appears they both followed a text like this, each omitting one part of it.

P. xviii. l. 12.—"In the society of the martyr Pamphilus." There is no mention of this or of Pamphilus in the Greek; but in the *Menæa* and in the *Menology* Apphianus, with his brother Ædesius, is said to have been instructed by Pamphilus. See Valesius, note (ᶠ), *Eng. Trans.* p. 160.

l. 20.—"Hierocles." His name is also omitted in the Greek, but it is given in the Menæum of the Greeks, which Valesius quotes in explanation of the passage, otherwise obscure, as it is found in the Greek, but plain enough from the facts supplied in the Syriac. "The explanation of this place is to be had from the Menæum of the Greeks, where Ædesius is said to have struck Hierocles, Prefect of Egypt, with his fist. The words there are these:—*But Ædesius, who was condemned to work in the mines of brass, having seen (at Alexandria in Egypt) Hierocles, the president, punishing the Christians, he accounted him a despicable person, and struck the president with his own hand.*—Epiphanius and Lactantius mention this Hierocles, Prefect of Egypt, who was famous for the great slaughter he made amongst the Christians. This was the Hierocles against which our Eusebius wrote a book." See *Note* ([d]) p. 161, *Eng. Trans.* See also *Acta SS. Martt.* S. E. Assemani, p. 1, p. 197. The last and best edition of Eusebius *Against Hierocles* was published by the late most excellent and learned Dr. Gaisford, Dean of Christ Church: *Eusebii Pamphili contra Hieroclem et Marcellum* libri, 8vo., Oxonii, 1852.

P. xix. l. 15.—"Agapius." The Syriac is ܐܓܦܘܣ, which would be more correctly transcribed "Agapus;" but the other Syriac, published by S. E. Assemani, *Acta SS. Martt.* P. ii. p. 198, has ܐܓܦܝܣ. The omission of the vowels causes frequently great discrepancy in the transcription of Greek proper names in the Syriac character. The Acts of Agapius are given by Baillet, at the 19th of August.

P. xx. l. 10.—"In another chapter." See above, p. 10. Valesius was mistaken in supposing that this was a different Agapius from the one there mentioned. For it is distinctly stated here, that although he had been condemned by the Judge Urbanus to be devoured by wild beasts two years before, the sentence had not yet been put into execution, but was kept back till now, when Maximinus was present. See note ([b]) p. 162. *Eng. Trans.* He is called in the Greek the *second Agapius*—*Αγαπιος ουτος ο δευτερος*—because, although he had been condemned before, he was not put to death till after the other Agapius mentioned above, p. 11, who was beheaded.

l. 12.—Concerning the leading about in the Stadium Valesius has this note on the *Ecc. Hist.* b. v. c. 1 ([r]):—"The Gladiators and the Bestiarii, before they began the encounter, were wont to be led about in the presence of the spectators. See Lucian, in *Toxari.* This was usually done, not only with those who let themselves out to play prizes, but also with those offenders, which were condemned to the sword and to the wild beasts. So Martial, "Traducta est gyris, nec cepit arena nocentes." *Eng. Trans.* p. 72.

l. 25.—"Maximinus." The Emperor's name is not mentioned in the Greek; but the following passage, not found in the Syriac, is added:—"The Emperor himself being then present, being reserved as it were on set purpose for that opportunity, that that saying of our Saviour's which, by his divine knowledge, he foretold his disciples might be accomplished in him, *that they should be brought before kings for their testimony of him.* See *Eng. Trans.* p. 162.

P. xxi. l. 3.—"That Light which he had caused to arise." Syriac, ܠܕܢܚܐ ܕܡܢܗ; and again below, P. xxvii. l. 20.—"The manifestation from him." Eusebius's work, *Περι Θεοφανειας*, which having been long lost, was discovered in this same MS., and has been published both in Syriac and English by the late lamented Dr. Lee, bears the Syriac title, ܕܥܠ ܕܢܚܐ ܐܠܗܝܐ, On the "Divine Manifestation," or, more literally, on "The Divine Sunrise," the *Ανατολη*; which is the Septuagint version of צמח of Zech. vi. 12. *ιδου ο ανθρωπος ῳ ονομα Ανατολη.* In our English translation, "Behold the man whose name is the Branch." So in Luke i. 78, *ανατολη εξ υψους*; and Matt. iv. 16, *φως ανετειλεν*; Epist. to Heb. vii. 14, *εξ Ιουδα ανατεταλκεν ο Κυριος ημων*: all referring to the coming of Christ.

P. xxii. l. 1.—"Theodosia." There is another Syriac version of these Acts, published by Assemani in *Acta SS. Martt.* P. ii. p. 203. Ruinart notes:—"Celebris est ejus memoria apud Latinos et Græcos die 2 Aprilis. Alii tamen aliis diebus ejus festum peragunt. Ejusdem Martyris Acta prolixiora vidimus in multis codd. MSS. sed aliquatenus amplificata. Ipsius vero sacrum corpus in Monasterium Dervense allatum ab ipso S. Berchario fuisse dicitur. Vide Mabillon, sæc. 2; Bened. p. 848; et

Bolland, ad diem 2 April." See *Acta Prim. Martt.* p. 323. Her martyrdom is given by Baillet, at the 2d of April.

l. 10.—"One of the virgins of the Son of God." The other Syriac has "*Christian* virgins," ܟܪܣܛܝܢܝܬܐ; the Greek, *παρθενος, πιστον και σεμνοτατον κορασιον.*

l. 18.—"Urbanus." The name of the Governor is omitted in the Greek.

P. xxiii. l. 19.—"Copper mines in Palestine." The Greek adds the name of the place Phæno, which occurs also in the Syriac below. See P. xxiv. l. 35; P. xlvi. l. 9, and note thereon.

l. 28.—"The first day of the week." The Greek has *εν αυτῃ κυριακῃ ημερᾳ της του Σωτηρος ημων αναστασεως*, upon which Valesius has a note (a):—"In the MS. Acts of the passion of Theodosia, she is said to have suffered, not on Easter-day, but only on a Sunday.—*Eng. Trans.* p. 162.

P. xxiv. l. 1.—"Confession of Domninus." In the Greek mention is made of Sylvanus before him, and the account of both much abridged. See Surius and Baillet, at the 4th of October.

l. 28.—"Ludus." "Munera seu ludi, pugnæ cum bestiis appellabantur, quod in populorum vel militum delectationem darentur. Dicebantur autem ludi castrenses, si in castris fierent. Sermonem in *die Munerum* habuit Augustinus in *Basilica Restituta,* qui est in nova edit. 19, tomi v. vide notas ibi appositas." See Ruinart, *Acta Prim. Martt.* p. 96, in not.; also p. 111. The Greek, however, has in this place, *και τρεις μεν εις το μονομαχειν επι πυγμῃ καταδικαζει*, on which Valesius has this note (c):—"See the following chapter; from whence we are informed that those who were condemned to such combats were delivered to the procurators of Cæsar, who caused them to practise exercise daily, so that at last they might be fit to engage in combat." *Eng. Trans.* p. 163.

l. 29.—"An excellent and godly old man." The Greek gives his name "Auxentius." See Baillet, at the 13th of December.

l. 33.—"Silvanus." A further account is given of him below, p. 47. The Greek adds here—"who was then a Presbyter and a Confessor, but some time after was honoured with a Bishopric."—*Eng. Trans.* p. 162.

P. xxv. l. 26.—"Without any long delay." For this the Greek has, *και ουκ εις μακρον τοις κατα Παμφιλου τετολμημενοις.*

l. 31.—"Considered himself above all the people of Palestine." The Greek adds here—"Who also was companion of the tyrant himself, for he was his chief favourite, and did usually eat at the same table with him." *Ibid.* p. 163.

P. xxvi. l. 8.—"The servants of God." The Greek more boldly, "against us," *καθ' ημων*; and so at line 15 below. Instead of "There may come a time ..... against our people," the Greek has, "There may happen a seasonable opportunity, wherein we shall be more at leisure to relate the exits and calamitous deaths, by which those impious wretches (especially Maximinus and those about him who were his advisers) that were the greatest sticklers in the persecution against us, finished their lives." See *Eng. Trans.* p. 163. This account is given in the Appendix to the Eighth Book of the *Ecc. Hist.* *Ibid.* p. 153. See also *Ecc. Hist.* b. viii. c. 16; and Valesius, note (b) *Eng. Trans.* p. 151, and b. ix. c. 9, *Ibid.* p. 177.

l. 19.—"Hatha." The Greek gives no name, but only *η αδελφη*, "The Sister." The word *Hatha* means "Sister." *Hathai* ܚܬܝ was not an uncommon woman's name.—See S. E. Assemani, *Acta SS. Martt.* P. i. p. 101, &c. In the Greek Menology she is called *Thea.* Valesius gives this note (c):—"This virgin's name is wanting here, but we will supply this defect from the *Grecian Menology;* where this passage occurs at the 15th of July. *On the same day the holy Martyrs* Valentina *and* Thea, which were Egyptians, *being brought to the city* Dio Cæsarea, *before* Firmillianus *the judge, made confession of Christ's name, who is our God; after which, their left feet being burnt and their right eyes pulled out, they were killed with a sword, and their bodies burnt.* But this account disagrees with Eusebius's relation here. For he says the one was born at Gaza and the other at Cæsarea; and he makes no mention of the burning of their feet or the pulling out of their eyes." See *Eng. Trans.* p. 164. The mistake in the Menologium perhaps arose from the compiler having read that the Egyptians, who are spoken of in the beginning of this same chapter, had their eyes put out and their feet burnt, and therefore concluding that these two virgins, mentioned immediately afterwards, were Egyptians, and had suffered like the rest. See Surius and Baillet, at the 25th of July.

P. xxvii. l. 6.—"Lud:" and in the Greek it is called *Dio Cæsarea.*" Lydda is the same as Diospolis. It seems, therefore, that Dio Cæsarea, which is the same as Sepphoris, is a mistake for Diospolis. See Van de Velde, *Memoir to accompany the Map of the Holy Land*, p. 331 and 347. If, however, it be a mistake, it has been copied into the Greek Menology. See the preceding note.

l. 31.—"Calling Egyptians by Hebrew names." Eusebius refers to this in his Commentary on Isaiah as a fulfilment of the prophecy contained in ch. 44, v. 5:—"One shall say, I am the Lord's, and another shall call himself by the name of Jacob, and another shall subscribe with his hand unto the Lord, and surname himself by the name of Israel." Eusebius's words are—*Θαυμασαι δε εστι, και καταπλαγηναι αληθως την των προφητικων λογων δυναμιν, ως αυτοις εργοις τα αποτελεσματα παρειληφαμεν· εν γουν τοις καθ' ημας αυτους γενομενοις διωγμοις, πολλους των αλλοφυλων εθνων εθεασαμεθα, προσαρπαζοντας εαυτοις τας των αγιων ανδρων προσηγοριας. ων ο μεν εαυτον Ιακωβ εκαλει, και ετερος Ισραηλ, αλλος δε Ιερεμιαν, και Ησαιαν ετερος, και Δανιηλ παλιν αλλος. τοιαυτα γουν επιγραφομενοι ονοματα επι το μαρτυριον του Θεου συν πολλῳ θαρσει και παρρησιᾳ παρῃεσαν· α δη σημαινουσα η προφητεια φησιν, Ουτος ερει, του Θεου ειμι.* Hoc est: Mirari plane subit prophetiæ vim et efficaciam, et quam vere rei eventum oculis perceperimus. Nam in persecutionibus nostro tempore concitatis, multos ex alienigenis gentibus vidimus, qui sanctorum virorum nomina usurpabant; alius quippe sese Jacobum appellabat, alius Israelem, alius Jeremiam, hic Hesaiam, iste Danielem. Etenim his sibi adscriptis nominibus, ad martyrium pro Deo subeundum cum fiducia et constantia accedebant. Quæ prophetia indicat dum ait, Hic dicet, Dei Sum, &c. See

Eusebius's *Comm. in Hesaiam*, in *Collectio Nova Patt.*, edited by Montfaucon, vol. ii. pp. 353 et 527.

P. xxviii. l. 17.—"Food from the Royal provision —— pugilism." The Greek is *επει μητε τας εκ του βασιλικου ταμειου τροφας, μητε μην τας επιτηδειους τη πυγμη μελετας υπεμενον*; and also adds, which is not in the Syriac, *ηδη δε ουκ επιτροποις αυτο μονον οι δηλουμενοι, αλλα και αυτῳ Μαξιμινῳ τουτου γε ενεκεν παρασταντες*: on which Valesius observes (e):—"He means, as I judge, the Procurators of the company of gladiators and of the morning exercises; of whom there is frequent mention in the inscriptions. For the gladiators that were maintained by stipends paid out of the imperial exchequer, were committed to their care, and they gave them their allowances out of the treasury." *Eng. Trans.* p. 163, note.

P. xxx. l. 8.—"Our own city." Omitted in the Greek; and so probably for the same purpose below, *υπερ των ομοεθνων* instead of "for our people." l. 20.

P. xxxi. l. 8.—"Mannathus." The Greek has *Ενναθας* below, on which Valesius remarks (f)—"In the Greek Menology she is called Manatho." *Eng. Trans.* p. 165. Ruinart observes—"Hoc ipso die memorantur (*i.e.* Antoninus, Zebinas, et Germanus) cum Ennatha virgine in Martyrol. Romano, ac Menologio Basilii Imp., sed in magnis Menæis et Menologio Canisii die præcedenti. Porro hæc omnia Menologia *Nicephorum* tribus his martyribus adjiciunt, et pro Ennatha habent *Manatho.*" *Acta Prim. Martt.* p. 327. See Baillet, *Vies des Saints*, at the 13th of November.

l. 23.—"And continuously —— Romans." This passage is evidently corrupt, and it is difficult to understand it. I subjoin the corresponding Greek:—*αθροως δ' ουν αυθις Μαξιμινου διαφοιτᾳ καθ' ημων πανταχου γραμματα κατ' επαρχιαν. ηγεμονες τε και προσετι ο των στρατοπεδων αρχειν επιτεταγμενος, κ. τ. λ.*

l. 28.—"They urged the Logistæ of the cities, and the military commander, and the Tabularii." On this Valesius notes (a)—"I judge he means the Prefect of the Prætorium. For at that time they took care of the military matters. Indeed, Eusebius's following words are a sufficient evidence that the Prefect of the Prætorium is meant here. For he speaks of the injunctions and public orders given to the Curators, Magistrates, and Tabularii of every city: which orders were issued out by the Prefect of the Prætorium only; as might be made to appear from several places. See Book 9, ch. 1 & 9, where Eusebius speaks of Sabinus, Prefect of the Prætorium to Maximin." *Eng. Trans.* p. 165. Concerning the Logistæ or Curators he writes ([b])—"The *Curator* of the city was he, who looked after the Treasure and whatever else belonged to the revenue of the city: this is manifest from the *Pandects of the Law.* He is also called *Logista* (from the Greek word λογιστης, which is the term here in the original) in Lege 3, *Cod. de modo mulctandi.* Hence λογιστευειν was used to signify *the performance of the Curator's office.*" See *Ecc. Hist.* b. viii. c. 9; *Eng. Trans.* p. 146. Respecting the Tabularii he writes ([c])—"These officers had in their custody the public tables or rolls of the cities, and looked after the accounts of the tribute. They were first called *Numerarii.* Afterwards Valens made a law that they should be called Tabularii." He then refers for further information to his observations on Ammianus Marcellinus, *ibid.* p. 165, which Heinichen has incorporated into his notes at this place.

P. xxxii. l. 18.—"They received sentence of death." The Greek says this was passed upon them by Firmillianus. It also adds that Zebinas was from Eleutheropolis.

l. 20.—"Antoninus." Valesius ([e]):—"In the Greeks' Menology this man is called Antonius, where, besides Zebinas and Germanus, there is a fourth companion of their's named, to wit, Nicephorus. For the 12th day of November this passage occurs:—*The birthday of the holy Martyrs Antonius and his fellows, who were in the times of Maximinus. Antonius was an old man, Nicephorus, Zebinas, and Germanus were in the flower of their age. They were taken at Casarea, and after they had boldly confessed Christ, were slain.* Here you see the author of the Menology has rendered πρεσβυτερος an *old man,* and *not a Presbyter.*" *Ibid.* p. 165.

l. 23.—"A sister, one of the Lord's virgins, a chaste and courageous maiden." For this the Greek has *τις γυνη παρθενιας στεμματι και αυτη κεκοσμημενη*; and also adds the name *Ενναθας*, omitted here in the Syriac.

l. 30.—"Maxys." Greek *Μαξυς*. Ruinart, *Acta Martt.* p. 327, has this note:—"Hæc vox Græca non est. An a Syris repetenda, apud quos *mochos* est pulicanus a *casas* increpare?" That is ܡܟܣܣ from ܟܣܣ; but the form here is ܡܟܣܘܣ, which seems rather to follow the Greek.

P. xxxiii. l. 33.—"The stones shed tears," &c. This, which doubtless was produced by natural causes, seemed miraculous to Eusebius, more especially if he looked upon it as fulfilling a prophecy of our Lord—Luke xix. 40: "I tell you, that if these should hold their peace, the stones would immediately cry out." See also Habak. ii. 11. Compare note p. 55 above.

P. xxxiv. l. 12.—"Primus." The Greek is *Προμος*, on which Valesius observes (a)—"In the Greek this man's name is Promus; but I suppose it should be Probus, for I have never met with such a proper name as Promus. This mistake rose from hence: in antient MSS. *Beta* is usually written like *My*. In the *Fuk.* and *Sav.* MSS. it is *Probus*." *Eng. Trans.* p. 166.

P. xxxv. l. 1.—"Peter, who was surnamed Absalom." In the Greek he is called *Πετρος ασκητης, ο και Αψελαμος*. Valesius has this note: (b)—"Mention is made of this person in the *Greek Menæa* at the 14th of October, although Eusebius says he suffered on the 3d of the Ides of January. In the Menæum he is called *Auselamus*, but in the Menology *Anselamus* is, by a mistake, put for *Auselamus* or *Abselamus*. The import of the passage there is this:—'On the same day is the commemoration of the holy Martyr Petrus Anselamus of Eleutheropolis, who, being in the flower of his age and of a vigorous mind, behaved himself most admirably in the conflicts he underwent for religion; and having despised earthly things, was by fire offered up as a victim well pleasing to God in the sixth year of Dioclesian's and Maximian's empire. In which passage this is observable, that the sixth year of Dioclesian's empire is put for the sixth year of the Persecution." See *Eng. Trans.* p. 166. Ruinart has published *Passio Sancti Petri Balsami,* who, although some have doubted the fact, can hardly be a different person from the one here described as "as Peter, who was surnamed Absalom." See *Acta Prim. Martt.* p. 501. The account is given by Baillet in the *Vies des Saints* at the 3d of January.

P. xxxvi. l. 1.—"One who belonged to the heresy of Marcion." The Greek gives the name *Asclepius,* omitted here.

l. 6.—"Aia, a village which is on the confines of Beth Gobrin."—The Greek has *Ανεας, κωμης των ορων Ελευθεροπολεως.* The other Syriac version published by S. E. Assemani has ܐܢܐܐ, which he renders—"Ex agro Eleutheropolitano in vico Anea." *Acta SS. Martt.* P. ii. p. 207. See Van de Velde—*Eleutheropolis: Betogabra* (Ptolemy xvi. 4), *Betogabri, Bethgebrim;* also *Geberin* of the Crusaders, identified with great care by Robinson and Smith (*Bib. Res.* 404—420, 642, seq.), with the Modern Beit-Jibrin. *Memoir to accompany the Map of the Holy Land,* p. 309.

l. 11.—"The Confession of Pamphilus," &c. This account is considerably abridged in the Greek. Valesius has the following, note (*):—"Symeon Metaphrastes has transcribed this whole relation of the Martyrdom of Pamphilus and his companions, out of our Eusebius, adding some things and altering others, as he usually does. But he seems to have been furnished with more perfect copies of Eusebius, than those we now have; which will manifestly appear to the reader, who may meet with Metaphrastes' account hereof in the Latin version of him, which Lipomannus and Surius put forth, Tome the third, at the 1st of June, p. 139, Edit. Ven. at 1581." *Eng. Trans.* p. 166. This account of Pamphilus and his companions still exists entire in Greek. It was first printed from a Medicean MS. by D. Papebrochius in the *Acta Sanctorum,* June, vol. i. p. 64. J. A. Fabricius reprinted it in his edition of Hippolytus' works, vol. ii. p. 217. Both of these learned men supposed it to have been an extract of Eusebius' *Life of Pamphilus,* to which he frequently refers in his Ecclesiastical History, and of which Jerome speaks. See note, p. 78 below. It is quite evident that Metaphrastes had before him the same copy of the Martyrs of Palestine as this Syriac, with some very slight variations. I have thought that it would be useful, for the sake of comparison, to copy here the whole of Lipomannus' Latin version after Metaphrastes in Surius, *De Probatis Sanctorum Vitis*, at the 1st of June:—

Certamen SS. Martyrum Pamphili et Sociorum ex Symeone Metaphraste.

I. "Tempus invitat ad omnibus enarrandum magnum et gloriosum spectaculum Pamphili et sociorum, virorum admirabilium, cum eo consummatorum, et qui ostenderunt multiplicia certamina pietatis. Atque cum plurimi in nobis cognita persecutione se fortiter gesserint, eorum de quibus agimus rarissimun certamen quod nos cognovimus, conscripsimus, quod in se simul omne genus ætatis et corporis et animi vitæque diversorum studiorum est complexum, variis tormentorum generibus, et diversis in perfecto martyrio coronis exornatum. Licebat enim videre quosdam adolescentes et pueros, atque adeo plane infantes, ex illis qui erant ex ipsis, alios autem pubescentes, cum quibus erat Porphyrius, corpore simul vigentes et prudentia, nempe mihi carissimum Jamnitem Paulum, Seleucumque et Julianum, qui ambo orti erant ex terra Cappadocum. Erant autem inter eos sacris quoque canis et profunda ornati senectute, Valens quidam diaconus ecclesiæ Hierosolymitanæ, et cui verum nomen obtigerat, Theodulus.

II. Atque hæc quidem fuit in eis ætatum varietas. Animis autem inter se differebant. Nam alii quidem erant rudiores, utpote pueri, et quibus erat ingenium adhuc tenerius et simplicius, alii vero severi et morum gravitate præditi. Erant autem inter eos quoque nonnulli disciplinarum sacrarum non ignari. Aderat vero omnibus congenita, insignis et admirabilis animi fortitudo. Veluti autem quoddam in die resplendens luminare in astris fulgentibus, in medio eorum eminebat meus Dominus, non est enim fas mihi aliter appellare divinum et plane beatissimum Pamphilum. Is enim et eruditionem, quæ habetur apud Græcos in admiratione, non modice attigerat, et in divinorum dogmatum et divinitus inspiratarum scripturarum eruditione, si quid audacius, sed verum dicendum est, ita erat exercitatus, ut nullus æque ex iis qui erant suo tempore. Quod autem erat his longe majus et præstantius, habebat donum, nempe domi natam, vel potius ei a Deo datam, intelligentiam et sapientiam.

III. Et quod ad animum quidem attinet, omnes ita se habebant. Vitæ autem conditionis et conversationis erat inter eos plurima differentia, cum Pamphilus quidem duceret genus secundum carnem ex iis qui erant honesto loco nati, fuisset autem insignis in republica gerenda in patria sua; Seleucus vero fuisset insigniter ornatus militiæ dignitatibus; alii autem nati essent ex mediocri et communi loco. Non erat eorum chorus nec extra servilem conditionem. Nam et ex præsidis domo in eorum numerum relatus erat Theodulus, et Porphyrius, qui specie quidem erat Pamphili famulus; is autem ipsum affectione habebat loco fratris, vel germani potius filii, ut qui nihil omitteret, quo minus imitaretur dominum. Quid aliud? Si quis dixerit in summa, eos ecclesiastici cœtus typum esse complexos, is non procul abfuerit a veritate, cum inter eos presbyterio quidem dignatus esset Pamphilus; Valens vero diaconatu, et alii sortiti essent locum eorum, qui e multitudine consueverunt legere, et confessionibus per fortissimam flagrorum tolerantiam diu ante in martyrio præclarissime se gessisset Seleucus, et militaris dignitatis amissionem fortiter excepisset, et reliqui deinde per catechumenos et fideles reliquam implerent similitudinem innumerabilis ecclesiæ, ut in parva imagine.

IV. Sic adspexi admirabilem tam multorum et talium martyrum electionem, qui etsi non essent multi numero, nullus tamen aberat ex iis ordinibus, qui inveniuntur inter homines. Quomodo autem lyra, quæ multas habet chordas, et ex chordis constat dissimilibus, acutis et gravibus, remissisque et intensis, et mediis, arte musica concinne adaptatis omnibus, eodem modo in his adolescentes simul et senes, servi simul et liberi, eruditi et rudes, obscuri generis homines, ut multis videbatur, et gloria insignes, fideles simul cum catechumenis, et diaconi simul cum presbyteris. Qui omnes tanquam a sapientissimo musico, nempe Dei verbo unigenito, varie pulsati, et quæ erat in ipsis potentiæ unusquisque per tormentorum tolerantiam, hoc est confessionem, ostendentes virtutem, et clarissimos numerososque, et concinnos sonos edentes in judiiciis, uno et eodem fine in primis piam et longe sapientissimam, per Martyrii consummationem, Deo universorum impleverunt melodiam.

V. Opera pretium autem est admirari virorum quoque numerum, qui significat propheticam quamdam et apostolicam gratiam. Contigit enim omnes esse duodecim, quo numero patriarchas et prophetas et apostolos fuisse accepimus. Non est autem prætermittenda uniuscujusque singulatim laboriosa fortitudo, laterum lacerationes, et cum pilis caprinis laceratarum corporis partium attritiones, et flagella immedicabilia, multiplicia que et varia tormenta, gravesque et toleratu difficiles cruciatus, quos, jubente judice, manibus et pedibus infligentes satellites, vi cogebant martyres aliquid facere eorum quæ prohibita.

VI. Quid opus est dicere memoriæ perpetuo mandandas voces virorum divinorum, quibus labores nihil curantes, læto et alacri vultu respondebant judicis interrogationibus, in ipsis tormentis ridentes viriliter, et bonis moribus ludificantes ejus percontationes? Cum enim rogasset undenam essent, mittentes dicere, quam in terris habebant civitatem, ostendebant eam, quæ vere est eorum patria, dicentes se esse ex Hierusalem. Indicabant vero eadem sententia Dei quoque cælestem, ad quam tendebant, civitatem, et alia quæ sunt ejusmodi, ignota quidem et quæ non possunt perspici ab iis, qui sacras literas non gustarunt, eis autem solis qui a fide divina sunt incitati, aperta adducebant. Propter quæ judex indignatus, et valde animo cruciatus, et plane quid ageret dubius, varia, ne vinceretur, in eos operabatur. Deinde cum a spe cecidisset, concessit unicuique auferre præmia victoriæ. Erat autem varius modus eorum mortis, cum duo quidem inter eos catechumeni, consummati sint baptismo ignis, alius vero fuerit traditus figuræ salutaris passionis, qui autem erat mihi carus, fuerit diversis braviis redimitus.

VII. Atque hæc quidem dixerit quispiam, horum magis faciens universam mentionem, singulatim autem unumquemque persequens, merito beatum pronuntiarit eum, qui in choro primum locum obtinet. Is autem erat Pamphilus, vir revera pius, et omnium, ut semel dicam, amicus et familiaris, re ipsa nomen sibi impositum verum esse ostendens, Cæsariensium ecclesiæ ornamentum. Nam presbyterorum quoque cathedram, cum esset presbyter, honestabat, ut qui simul ornaret ministerium et ex eo ornaretur. Quinetiam aliis quoque erat divinus et divinæ particeps inspirationis, quoniam tota sua vita fuit maxime insignis virtute, multum quidem jubens valere delicias et copiam divitiarum, cum se totum dedicasset Dei verbo, renuntians quidem iis quæ ad ipsum redibant a majoribus, nudis, mancis, et pauperibus omnia distribuit. Ipse autem degit in vita, quæ nihil possidebat, per valentissimam exercitationem, divinam persequens philosophiam. Atque ortus quidem erat ex Berytensium civitate, ubi in prima ætate educatus fuerat in illis, quæ illic erant, studiis litterariis. Postquam autem ejus providentia ad virilem pervenisset ætatem, transiit ab iis ad sacrarum litterarum scientiam. Assumpsit vero mores divinæ et propheticæ vitæ, et ipse se verum Dei martyrem exhibuit etiam ante ultimum vitæ finem. Sed talis quidem erat Pamphilus.

VIII. Secundus autem post ipsum accessit Valens ad certamen, qui senili, et quæ decet sacerdotem, erat ornatus canitie, ipsoque aspectu venerandus et sacro-sanctus senex; qui etiam divinarum scripturarum sciens, ut si quis alius, eas quidem certe ita erat complexus memoria, ut a lectione nihil discreparent, quæ memoriæ mandatæ ab eo conservabantur, sacrosanctorum discipulorum promissiones. Erat autem diaconus, etsi esset hujusmodi, ecclesiæ Eliensium.

Tertius in eorum numerum relatus erat Paulus, qui, vir acerrimus et spiritu fervens, agnoscebatur ex civitate Iamnitarum: qui etiam in martyrio per cauterii tolerantiam susceperat certamen confessionis.

IX. His in carcere duobus annis contritis, martyrii occasio fuit Ægyptiorum adventus, qui etiam cum eis fuêre consummati. Ii autem cum vel sic valde afflicti, in metallis usque ad loca pervenissent, domum revertebantur. Qui, cum in ingressu portæ Cæsariensium interrogati essent a custodibus, quinam essent et unde venirent, et nihil veri celassent, dixissent autem se esse Christianos; perinde ac malefici in ipso furto deprehensi, vincti sunt et comprehensi: erant vero quinque numero. Ad Præsidem autem adducti, et coram eo libere locuti, in vincula quidem statim conjiciuntur: die autem sequente, qui erat sextus decimus mensis Peritii, more vero Romano quartus decimus Calend. Martii, hos ipsos cum Pamphilo et sociis adducunt ad Firmillianun. Ille autem Ægyptiorum solum periculum fecit ante tormenta, omni ratione eos exercens. Atque eorum quidem principem, quum adduxisset in medium, rogavit quisnam esset, et unde? Qui cum pro proprio nomine quoddam propheticum audisset (hoc autem fiebat ante alia, ut qui pro patriis eis impositis idolicis nominibus sibi prophetica nomina impossuissent, ut qui Eliam, et Hieremiam, Esaiam, Samuelem et Danielem ipsi seipsos nominarent, et qui est in occulto, Judæum et germanum Israelitem, non solum factis, sed etiam vocibus proprie enunciatis judicarent).

X. Cum tale ergo Judex audivisset a martyre, vim autem nominis non attendisset, secundo rogavit, quænam esset ejus patria? Ille vero cælestem Hierusalem dixit esse suam patriam, illam intelligens de qua dictum est Paulo. 'Quæ sursum est Jerusalem est libera, quæ est mater nostra.' Et 'accessistis ad montem Sion et civitatem Dei viventis, Hierusalem cælestem.' Et hic quidem hanc cogitabat: ille autem humi suam abjiciens cogitationem, quænam hæc esset, et ubi terrarum sita esset, accurate perscrutabatur, atque adeo ei etiam inferabat tormenta, ut verum fateretur. Hic vero dum torqueretur, se verum dixisse affirmabat. Deinde eo hæc rursus et sæpe sciscitante quænam esset, et ubi sita esset dicta civitas Hierusalem? solum dicebat eam esse patriam Christianorum; nullos enim alios præter eos esse ejus participes, sitam autem esse ad orientem et ad ipsam lucem et solem. Atque hic quidem rursus per hæc mente sua philosophabatur, nihil sentiens eos, qui circumcirca ipsum tormentis afficiebant. Tanquam autem carnis expers et incorporeus, nihil videbatur pati molestum. Judex vero animi dubius, odio cruciabatur, et existimans Christianos hanc sibi civitatem, quæ esset infesta Romanis, constituisse, valde urgebat tormentis, et curiose scrutabatur eam, quæ dicta fuerat, civitatem, et quæ est in Oriente, inquirebat regionem. Cum autem adolescentem, diu cæsum flagellis, videret non posse dimoveri ab iis, quæ prius dixerat, statuit in eum ferre sententiam capitis.

XI. Et in eum quidem res hoc modo processit: reliquos autem Ægyptios cum simili palæstra exercicuisset, similem quoque in eos fert sententiam. Deinde cum ab his transisset ad Pamphilûm, accepit quod ii jam prius essent plurima experti tormenta. Absurdum autem esse arbitratus, eosdem iisdem rursus afficere tormentis, et frustra laborare, hoc solum est percontatus, an nunc saltem obedirent? Cum vero ab unoquoque eorum andiisset ultimam vocem martyrii, in eos similiter fert sententiam capitis.

XII. Nondum autem dictum universum absolverat, et alicunde exclamat quidam adolescens ex familia Pamphili, et ex media turba accedens in medium eorum, qui circumsidebant judicium, alta voce corpora eorum petiit sepulturæ. Is autem erat beatus Porphyrius, Pamphili germanum pecus, nondum totos octodecim annos natus, recte scribendi scientiæ peritus, modestia vero morum has laudes celans, ut qui a tali viro fuisset institutus. Is, postquam adversus dominum latam cognovit sententiam, exclamavit ex media multitudine, Corpora rogo, ut humi mandentur. Ille autem non homo, sed fera, et quavis fera agrestior, neque honestam et rationi consentaneam admittens petitionem, neque juvenili ætati dans veniam, cum hoc solum intellexisset, eum fateri se esse Christianum, jubet tortoribus ut totis viribus in eum uterentur. Cum vero, eo jubente, sacrificare recusasset vir admirandus, non utique tanquam carnem hominis, sed tanquam lapides et lignum, aut aliquid aliud inanimum usque ad ipsa ossa et ima viscera jubet eum torquere et corpus ejus cædere. Cum autem hoc diu fieret, agnovit se hoc frustra aggredi, cum propemodum mutum et inanimum effectum esset corpus generoso Martyri. Perseverans vero Judex in sævitia et inhumanitate, iubet latera tormentis exagitata, pilorum textis amplius atteri. Deinde cum sic eum cepisset satietas et furore esset exsatiatus, pronunciat sententiam ut tradatur lento et molli igni. Atque hic quidem, cum ante Pamphili consummationem postremus accessisset, prior e corpore excessit ad Dominum.

XIII. Licebat autem videre Porphyrium, non secus affectum quam victorem in sacris certaminibus, qui in omnibus pugnis evaserat superior, corpore pulverulentum, vultu lætum, audenter et exultando ad mortem progredientem, re vera plenum divino spiritu. Philosophico autem habitu suo indumento amictus instar superhumeralis, rursum aspiciens et omnia humana despiciens, sicut vitam mortalem, quieto animo accedit ad rogum. Cum jam flamma ei appropinquaret, et tanquam nihil ei adesset molestum, sana mente et nulla affecta perturbatione de rebus suis mandavit suis necessariis, adhuc vultum et universum corpus lætum conservans et immutatum. Postquam autem notos suos satis allocutus, eos valere jussit, jam de cætero contendebat ad Dominum. Cum vero rogus, satis longo spatio disjunctus, circa eum esset accensus, hinc et illinc ore flammam arripiebat, se ipsum incitans ad iter propositum. Hoc autem faciebat nihil aliud quam Jesum invocans. Tale est certamen Porphyrii.

XIV. Cum ejus autem consummationis Pamphilo nuncius fuisset Seleucus, dignus habetur, cui sors eadem cum eis obtingeret. Cum primum itaque renuntiasset Pamphilo exitum Porphyrii, et uno osculo salutasset Martyres, comprehendunt eum milites et ducunt ad Præsidem. Ille autem perinde ac urgens, ut ipse abiret simul cum prioribus, jubet eum affici supplicio capitis. Is erat ex regione Cappadocum, cum autem militia se præclare gessisset, ad non parvos gradus dignitatum pervenerat in Romano exercitu. Quin etiam statura, viribusque et magnitudine corporis, reliquos omnes longe superabat: ipso quoque aspectu erat omnibus suspiciendus, et tota forma corporis plane admirabilis, tam propter magnitudinem quam propter pulchritudinem. Atque in principio quidem persecutionis, per flagellorum perpessionem clarus extitit in certaminibus confessionis. Postquam autem fuerat liberatus a militia, seipsum constituens æmulatorem eorum, qui se exercent in pietate, efficitur Christi germanus miles, orphanorum desertorum et viduarum, quæ carebant præsidio, eorumque qui paupertate opprimebantur et imbecillitate, tanquam episcopus quispiam et procurator, curam gerens et instar diligentis et soliciti patris, omnium, qui abjecti erant, labores recreans et affectiones. Quamobrem merito Deo his magis lætante quam quæ per fumum et sanguinem fiunt, sacrificiis, dignus fuit habitus consummatione, quæ fit per martyrium. Hic decimus athleta cum iis, qui dicti sunt, consummatus fuit uno eodemque die: in quo, ut est consentaneum, maxima Pamphili martyrio porta cœlorum aperta, facilis et expeditus ei fuit aditus regni cœlorum.

XV. Seleuci institit vestigiis Theodulus quidam, venerandus et pius senex, qui primum honoris locum obtinuerat inter servos præsidis, et morum et ætatis gratia, et quod trium filiorum esset pater, et maxime propter benevolentiam quam conservabat in suos. Is autem, cum similiter fecisset atque Seleucus, et quendam ex martyribus salutasset osculo, adducitur ad dominum. Quem cum magis ad iram irritasset quam alii, salutaris passionis cruci traditus, subiit martyrium.

XVI. Cum post hos unus adhuc restaret, qui inter eos, qui dicti sunt, numerum impleret duodecimum, eum impleturus aderat Julianus. Is, cum ea ipsa hora rediisset ex peregrinatione, ne ingressus quidem civitatem, ita ut erat ex itinere, hoc audito profectus ad videndos martyres, postquam adspexit sanctorum corpora humi jacentia, gaudio repletus, unumquemque amplectitur, omnes salutans osculo. Eo autem adhuc agente, eum comprehendunt lictores et adducunt ad præsidem. Impius vero suo instituto faciens consentanea, eum quoque tradit lento igni. Sic itaque Julianus lætans et exultans, et magna voce Deo, qui tantis bonis eum erat dignatus, agens gratias, assumptus fuit in choros martyrum. Erat autem is quoque genere quidem Cappadox, moribus plenus quidem pietate, plenus et fide, vir mitis et mansuetus, et alioqui vir bonus, et spirans bonum odorem Sancti Spiritus. Tanta turba comitatus, dignatus fuit consummatione martyrii cum beatissimo Pamphilo.

Et quatuor quidem dies et totidem noctes jussu Firmilliani sanctissima martyrum corpora exposita fuerunt bestiis carnivoris.

Cum autem Dei providentia nihil ad eos accessisset, non fera, non avis, non aliquid aliud, sed sana permansissent et integra, justum et convenientem honorem consecuta, consuetæ mandata sunt sepulturæ, reposita in pulchris templorum ædibus, et sacris traditæ oratoriis ad perpetuam memoriam, ut honorarentur a populo, ad gloriam Christi, veri Dei nostri."

P. xxxvi. l. 13.—"Theophilus." An error of the scribe for Theodulus. It is given correctly in the narrative below.

l. 15.—"Being in number eight." And so the names enumerated above are eight; but there were really twelve. See pp. 38 and 44. The Greek, which is here a good deal abridged, has at the beginning, δωδεκα δ' ησαν οι παντες.

l. 28.—"Youths and boys." Papebrochius corrects here the error of Lipomannus—"*Adolescentes et pueros atque adeo plane infantes.*" See *Hippolyti Opera*, curante J. A. Fabricio, vol. ii. p. 217. I have not the *Acta Martyrum* at hand, and therefore cite the reprint of the Acts of Pamphilus and his companions by Fabricius. When I use the term *the other Greek*, I mean these Acts, in contradistinction to *the Greek*, which I have used in these notes to signify the abridgement found in the Ecclesiastical History of Eusebius.

l. 29.—"Porphyrius." The Syriac has by mistake here ܦܘܪܦܘܢ, "Porphon."

l. 32.—"Iamna." "Jamnia sive Jamna urbs maritima Palæstinæ, haud procul a Joppe, sed totis 20 leueis horariis dissita a Cæsarea, cujus Archiepiscopo subest: etiam urbs maritima in confiniis Phœniciæ." Papebrochius. *Ibid.* p. 218.

l. 36.—"Conformable to his name, Theodulus." That is, *Servant of God.*

P. xxxvii. l. 7.—"But like the sun ..... My Lord Pamphilus." Eusebius speaks of him several times in his Ecc. Hist. Book vi. chap. 32, he says:—"But what necessity is there at present to write an exact catalogue of this man's works, which requires a work itself, which we have also written in our *History of Pamphilus's life*, the blessed martyr of our times.

In which, endeavouring to prove how great Pamphilus's care and love towards sacred learning was, we have published the catalogue of Origen's works, and of several other ecclesiastical writers which he collected." *Eng. Trans.* p. 107. And in the next chapter:—"But what things concerning him are necessary to be known, may be read at large in that *Apology* for him which was written by me and Pamphilus, the holy martyr of our times, which we conjointly composed." *Ibid.* In book vii. ch. 33. "In this man's (Agapius) times we knew Pamphilus, a most eloquent man and a true philosopher in the practices of his life, honoured with a presbytership of that church (Cæsarea). To declare what a person this man was, and whence descended, would be a copious subject. But all things relating to his life, the school he founded, the conflicts which, during the time of persecution, he underwent in several confessions, and lastly, the crown of martyrdom with which he was encircled, we have fully declared in a peculiar work. Indeed, this Pamphilus was the most admirable person of all that lived here." Valesius's note (ʳ). Christophorson takes these words to signify one book only. But Eusebius wrote three books of the life of *Pamphilus,* which Hieromynus attesteth in his book, *De Scriptoribus Ecclesiasticis,* and in his *Apology against Ruffinus.* *Ibid.* p. 138. Book viii. c. 13—"Amongst which number we must in no wise omit the mention of *Pamphilus* the Presbyter, the most admirable person in our age, and the greatest ornament of the Church of Cæsarea, whose fortitude and courageous exploits we will declare at a fit and convenient opportunity." Valesius remarks (ᵇ)—"I must indeed confess that in the *Maz., Med., Fuk.,* and *Savil* MSS, the reading is (*αvεγαψαμεv, we have declared*); but if that reading be true, Eusebius must mean his Books *concerning the life of Pamphilus the Martyr,* which, as we before observed, he wrote before his *Ecclesiastical History, Ibid.* p. 148. See the former part of this note which I have quoted above, p. 49. See also what Eusebius says in the *Confession of Domninus,* p. 25, above. The Greek, in the account of Pamphilus, here adds:—"This person's other virtues and egregious performances, which require a larger relation, we have already comprised in *three Books*, being a particular work which we wrote concerning his life. On this Valesius remarks (⁴):—"Moreover, hence we make this manifest conclusion, that the *Book concerning the Martyrs of Palestine* was Eusebius's own work, written by him after his Books concerning Pamphilus's life, and after his Ecclesiastical History." *Eng. Trans.* p. 166. We must bear in mind that this observation of Valesius applies to the *abridged* form of the Martyrs of Palestine, and not to the original copy; for the passage upon which he founds his conclusions does not exist, either in the Syriac or the other Greek. It therefore affirms that the *abridgment* was made by Eusebius himself. The Confession of Pamphilus is given by Baillet, *Vie des Saints*, at the 1st of June.

l. 10.—"Without styling him My Lord." Upon referring to the Syriac here it is seen that Simeon Metaphrastes, whom Lipomannus followed in translating "*non est mihi fas aliter appellare*," had *ετερον* correctly; and that the reading *εταιρον* of the *other Greek* is wrong. See Papebrochius' note in *Hipp. Oper.* vol. ii. p. 218.

l. 23.—"Porphyrius." His martyrdom and that of those who suffered with him is given by Baillet, *Vie des Saints*, Feb. 17.

l. 36.—"His dismissal from his command in the army." Lactantius speaks of the order of Diocletian respecting the dismissal of soldiers who professed Christianity thus:—"Tunc ira furens, sacrificare non eos tantum qui sacris ministrabant, sed universos qui erant in palatio, jussit, et in eos, si detractassent, verberibus animadverti; datisque ad Præpositos litteris, etiam milites cogi ad nefanda sacrificia præcepit, ut qui non paruissent, militia solverentur." See *De Mortibus Persecutorum*, ch. x.

P. xxxviii. l. 6.—"They bore the semblance of a many-stringed harp." Eusebius uses the same comparison in his Theophania, bk. i. ch. 28:—ܗܘ ܗܟܝܠ ܟܠܗ ܥܠܡܐ ܡܬܬܩܢܢܐ ܒܙܡܘܪܬ ܩܝܢܪܐ ܗܘ ܥܡ ܩ̈ܢܝܐ ܕܡܬܩܝܡ ܡܢ ܩ̈ܢܝܐ ܕܠܐ ܕܡܝܢ ܠܚܕܕܐ ܡܢ ܡܫܠܡܢܘܬܐ ܘܚܬ̈ܝܬܘܬܐ ܘܢܘܚܡ ܙܢܝܬܐ ܘܡܢ̈ܝܚܘܬܐ ܘܡܙܪ̈ܩܬܐ ܕܢܩܫ

ܡܪ̈ܟܒܢ ܟܠܗܘܢ ܒܐܘܡܢܘܬܐ ܕܡܘܣܝܩܘܬܐ ܐܟܘܬܗ̇
ܕܝܢ ܕܗܕܐ ܐܦ ܗܢܐ ܕܐܬܝܘܗܝ، ܡܢ ܡ̈ܢܐ ܘܡܢ
ܪ̈ܘܟܒܐ ܘܩܪܝܪܘܬܐ ܐܟܚܕܐ ܘܚܡܝܡܘܬܐ ܕܠܘܩܒܠܗ̇
ܪ̣ܛܝܒܘܬܐ ܘܝܒܝܫܘܬܐ ܕܐܘܣܝܐ ܠܚܕ ܪܘܟܒܐ ܐܬܟܢܫ
ܘܡܐܢܐ ܐܝܬܘܗܝ، ܪܒܐ ܘܥܒܕܐ ܕܐܠܗܐ ܕܟܠ

which Dr. Lee translates as follows:—

"This sensible world is therefore, not unlike the lyre of many strings, consisting of many dissimilar portions: of acute and grave, lax and intense; and of others between these, all well combined together by the art of the musician. Such, then, is also this (universe), collected (as it is) into one compound, consisting of many parts, and many compositions; of cold at once, and warm its opposite; and of matter, wet and dry. It is, moreover, a mighty vessel, and is the work of the God of all." See *Eusebius, Bishop of Cæsarea, on the Theophania*, translated by S. Lee. 8vo. *Cambridge*, 1843, p. 18.

l. 19.—"Like the prophets." He means the Twelve Minor Prophets.

l. 20.—"Nor is it fit that we should omit." So also the Latin version of Lipomannus. The other Greek is corrupt here, reading *ου περυ ετερων*.

P. xxxix. l. 6.—"The baptism of fire." Martyrdom for the sake of Christ was held in antient times to supply the place of baptism to those who had not yet received that sacrament. It was generally called the "Baptism of Blood." Thus Cyprian, *letter* 57, to Cornelius:—"Qui martyrium tollit, sanguine suo batizatur." Edit. *Dodwell*, Amst. 1691, p. 118. And 73, to Jubaianus:—"Sanguine autem suo baptizatos et passione sanctificatos consummari, et divinæ pollicitationis gratiam consequi; declarat in Evangelio idem Dominus." *Ibid.* p. 208. *Exhort. ad Mart.*:—"Nos tantum, qui, Domino permittente, primum baptisma credentibus dedimus, ad aliud quoque singulos præparemus, insinuantes et docentes hoc esse baptisma in gratia majus, in postestate sublimius, in honore pretiosius: baptisma in quo angeli baptizant, baptisma in quo Deus et Christus ejus exultant, baptisma post quod nemo jam peccat, baptisma quod fidei nostræ incrementa consummat, baptisma quod nos de mundo recedentes statim Deo copulat. In aquæ baptismo accipitur peccatorum remissa, in sanguinis corona virtutum. *Ibid.* p. 168. See also *Bingham Antiquit.* Book 10, ch. 2, s. 20, and other passages cited by him. St. Cyril of Jerusalem, Cat. 3, ch. 10:—*ει μη τις λαβοι το βαπτισμα, σωτηριαν ουκ εχει, πλην μονων μαρτυρων, οι και χωρις του υδατος λαμβανουσι την βασιλειαν.* Eusebius speaks also of Herais, a catechumen, receiving *baptism by fire,* Book 6, ch. 4:—*και γυναικων δ' Ηραϊς ετι κατηχουμενη το βαπτισμα, ως φησιν που αυτος, το δια πυρος λαβουσα τον βιον εξεληλυθεν.*

l. 8.—"But Pamphilus, that name ..... different from these." The other Greek varies here from the Syriac. See Lipomannus's Translation above, vii.

l. 14.—"In communion with the Spirit of God." The other Greek, *Θειας μετεχων εμπνευσεως.*

l. 24.—"Men seeking perfection." Other Greek, *τελειους ανδρας.*

l. 26.—"Martyrdom." The other Greek adds here, *αλλ' ο μεν Παμφιλος τοιουτος ην.*

l. 27.—"Vales." There is added here in the Greek, "a deacon of Ælia." This had been stated of him before in the part omitted from the Greek, "a deacon of the Church of Jerusalem." See p. 37, l. 35, above.

P. xl. l. 4.—"In prison." The other Greek has *επι της κρητης,* which Papebrochius has corrected after Metaphrastes from Lipomannus's translation *in carcere,* to *της ειρκτης.*

l. 33.—"Our Mother in whom we confess is the Holy Church." The Greek here, as in Gal. iv. 26, *ητις εστιν μητηρ ημων*; and adds, Heb. xii. 12, *προσεληλυθατε Σιων ορει, και πολει Θεου ζωντος, Ιερουσαλημ επουρανιῳ,* and so the other Greek and Lipomannus' version. See p. 74 above.

P. xli. l. 3.—"In what country was that Jerusalem." At the time when these events took place, there was no city known to the Romans by the name of Jerusalem; otherwise, as Valesius observes, Firmillianus, president of Palestine, would never have been so earnest in his inquiries of the martyrs where Jerusalem was situated. Eusebius writes, Book 4, ch. 6:—"From that time the whole nation was altogether interdicted to enter into the country about Jerusalem, the law, edict, and sanctions of Adrian having commanded them that they should not so much as from afar off behold their paternal soil. Ariston of Pella relates this. Thus the city being destitute of the Jewish nation, and wholly cleared of its old inhabitants, was possessed by foreigners, who dwelt there, and afterwards made a Roman city; and changing its name, was, in honour of the Emperor *Ælius Adrianus*, called *Ælia*." Valesius, in his note on this place, says (°):—"Eusebius is here doubly mistaken; both in that he says Jerusalem was wholly destroyed in Adrian's time; and also because he thought Ælia Capitolina was built by the same Adrian after the siege of Betthera.—*Ælia Capitolina* was built long before; to wit, in the second year of Adrian: from whose times to those of Constantine the Great it was always called *Ælia*. But from the time of Constantine the Great it recovered again the name of Jerusalem, both upon account of the honour of that name, and also because of its prerogative, being the first episcopal seat." See *Eng. Trans.* p. 52.

P. xlii. l. 7.—"Wretch —— savage brute." Such epithets as this, and others—"that bitter viper," p. 12, "fierce wild beast,' p. 49, when applied to the persecutors of the Christians, are not peculiar to Eusebius. Cyprian calls Nero, *execrabilis ac nocens tyrannus, bestia mala;* and Decius, *execrabile animal:* also he calls Diocletianus, Maximinianus Herculius, and Galerius Maximinianus, *tres acerbissimæ bestiæ.* See *De mortt. Pers.* ch. 4, 9, 16, &c.

l. 24.—"Weak in body." Syriac, ܒܦܓܪܗ ܡܚܝܠ. The other Greek, κεκονιμενον το σωμα, and Lipomannus, *corpore pulverulentum.* Perhaps originally the translation was ܡܚܝܠ, afterwards altered by a transcriber.

l. 28.—"Having put on his cloak like a philosopher, with his shoulder uncovered." Valesius has this Note on Book 6, ch. 19 of Ecc. Hist. (ᵖ):—"The philosophic habit was the pallium or cloak, which was the usual badge of the Greek philosophers, different from that which was worn by the ordinary Greeks, which those Christians still kept to, who, before their conversion, were philosophers."—See *Eng. Trans.* p. 101. And on this place (*):—"This garment is in the Greek termed *εξωμις*: see its description, A. Gellius, Book 7, ch. 12." *ibid.* p. 168.

P. xliv. l. 2.—"The father of three generations." The Greek, *τῳ τριγονειας πατερα καθεσταναι*, and the other Greek, *διο τριγονειας αυτον πατερα καθεσταναι.* On which Papebrochius observes:—"Trium filiorum patribus præmia apud Romanos fuisse proposita notius est quam ut hic moneri debeat, atque id hic dici credo *τριγονειας πατερα.* Valesius, tamen aliter vertit *quod tertiæ jam stirpis nepotes haberet.*" See *Hippol. Opera*, vol. ii. p. 224.

l. 19.—"Officers," here "Quæstionarii," as above, p. 55. The Greek is, in this place, *οι των φονων διακονοι.*

l. 27.—"There was also in him a glorious savour of the Holy Spirit." Greek, *πνεων αυτου αγιου πνευματος*; and the other Greek, *πνεων ευωδιας αγιου πνευματος*.

l. 36.—"Without the permission of the Governor." Omitted in the Greek.

P. xlv. l. 1.—"And were laid in the interior of the Churches ..... with God." This passage is not found in the abridged Greek, but it is in the *other Greek.* Upon which Papebrochius has the following note: "Deest hæc clansula in historia: quam tamem Eusebio abjudicare nihil nos cogit, qui vitam Pamphili æque ac Historiam Ecclesiasticam scripsit, cum jam Constantinus lege lata permisisset Christianis sacras ædes condere et Martyrum corpora eis inferre." See *Hippol. Opera.* vol. ii. p. 224.

l. 13.—"Of Batanea." ܕܒܬܢܝܐ. Greek, *απο Μαγγανειας*.

l. 32.—"He was the last ..... in Cæsarea." The Greek here adds the account of Firmillianus having been put to death by the sword; and then a chapter concerning what happened to the prelates of the Church.

P. xlvi. l. 1.—"The confession of Paulus," &c. The name in the Greek is *Πηλευς*, both in this place and in Ecc. Hist., Book 8, ch. 13.

l. 9.—"Phæno." Eusebius has described this place thus in his book, *De locis Hebraicis*:—*Φινων, ην κατῳκησεν Ισραηλ επι του ερημου· ην δε και πολις Εδωμ. αυτη εστι Φαινων, ενθα τα μεταλλα του χαλκου, μεταξυ κειμενη Πετρης πολεως και Ζουρων.* And Athanasius:—*μεταλλον ουχ απλως, αλλα εις το του Φαινω, ενθα και φονευς καταδικαζομενος ολιγας ημερας μογις δυναται ζησαι.* See Reading's Note on Eusebius at this place.

l. 18.—"Zauara." This is *Ζουρα*, mentioned by Eusebius in the preceding note, now Zara, Zora, or Zoara. See Van de Velde, *Memoir to Map of the Holy Land*, p. 354.

P. xlvii. l. 8.—"Patermytheus." Above, *Patrimytheas*, with the usual inconsistency in writing proper names in Syriac.

l. 10.—"Lovers of that exalted philosophy which is of God." That is, the Christian religion. See Ecc. Hist. passim.

l. 25.—"Presbyter of the Church in the city of Gaza." The Greek has, *ων ηγειτο εκ της Γαζαιων επισκοπος ορμωμενος Σιλβανος.* And in the Ecc. Hist. Book 8, ch. 13:—*επισκοπος των αμφι την Γαζαν εκκλησιων.* And in the Greek of the Mart. Palest., ch. 7, he gives the same account of him as in this place, that he was at that time presbyter of Gaza, and afterwards was promoted to the episcopate:—*Σιλβανον ετι δη τοτε οντα πρεσβυτερον, ομολογησαντα, ον ουκ εις μακρον επισκοπῃ τιμηθηναι συνεβη.*

P. xlviii. l. 5.—"And suddenly a mandate of wickedness was issued." The Greek states that this order was given by Maximinus.

l. 9.—"Forty in number." The Greek says "thirty-nine."

l. 10.—"Many of them were Egyptians." The Greek adds in this place the account of one John, who had learned the Scriptures so thoroughly by heart, that Eusebius states, that when he saw him standing up and repeating portions of the Scripture to the congregation, he supposed that he had been reading, till he drew near, and discovered that he was quite blind.

l. 16.—"For he that was excited against us ..... perished after the manner of a cruel wild beast." It does not appear to whom this applies. Probably he means Firmillianus, of whose savage disposition and extreme cruelty he had spoken above in such strong terms, see p. 27, 29; some account of whose death he gives in the Greek, although omitted here. See note above, on P. xlv. l. 32, p. 84. Or he may mean the Maximinus whose death he describes in the Ecclesiastical History, b. xi. ch. 10.

W. M. WATTS, CROWN COURT, TEMPLE BAR.

ERRORS IN THE SYRIAC TEXT.

P. ܗ. l. 8. for ܡܬܬܪܝܡ read ܡܬܬܪܝܡ

P. ܝܘ. l. 20. „ ܬܗܕܐ „ ܬܗܪܐ

P. ܝܚ. l. 6. „ ܠܚܡܪܐ „ ܠܚܡܐ

P. ܟܘ. l. 24. „ ܒܘܠܛܠܐ „ ܒܘܠܛܝܐ

P. ܕܠ. l. 20. „ ܡܫܘܐ „ ܡܚܘܐ

P. ܗܠ. l. 18. „ ܕܗܘܢ „ ܘܕܗܘܢ

ܢܒ. ܕܟܠ ܡܘܕܝܢܐ ܕܟܠܘܛܝܢܐ ܕܐܡܝܪ ܠܐܘܩܘܡܘܣ ܡܣܪܐ.

ܠܦܬܝܐ ܕܐܠܗܐ ܕܒܪܒܢ ܐܬܒܪܝܘ. ܦܘܩ ܕܡܢ ܫܢܐ ܕܐܒܢܐ
ܡܫܬܐܠܝܢ ܗܘܘ ܘܠܡܛܪܬܐ ܕܐܠܗܐ ܠܦ ܡܢ ܟܠ ܡܕܡ ܡܥܡܪ
ܗܘܘ. ܘܗܒܪܐ ܚܘܫܐ ܕܠܦܬܐ ܕܠܐ ܡܬܚܝܡ ܚܬܢܐ ܦܓܪܐ ܡܢ
ܐܠܗܐ ܦܬܠܘ. ◦ ◦ ◦

ܐܘ ܡܘܕܝܢܐ ܠܦܬܝܐ ܕܦܠܚܘܬܗ ܕܡܫܝܚܐ. ܦܘܩ ܕܒܪܡܘܬ
ܕܡܟܐ ܒܡܚܘܪܬܐ ܕܐܬܡܘܬܗܘܢ ܐܬܚܝܪܘ. ܘܫܢܐ ܥܫܝܢܐ
ܕܫܠܝܡܐ ܠܐܝܓܘܢܐ ܕܡܒܟܐ ܚܘ ܡܘ. ܘܟܬܝܒܬܐ ܕܠܦܬܐ
ܒܚܬܬܐ ܕܐܫܘܬܐ ܕܡܪܝܢܐ ܕܠܟܠ ܢܗܘܐ. ܚܢܢܐ ܓܒܪ ܠܐ ܒܝܬ
ܡܐܕܝܢܐ ܠܐ ܥܡܟܬ. ܘܟܠ ܠܟܐ ܕܒܪ ܐܢܫܐ ܠܐ ܗܘܠܝ. ܡܕܡ
ܕܠܦܝܢ ܐܠܗܐ ܠܗܘܢ ܕܐܫܬܡܥ. ◦ ◦ ◦

ܫܠܡܘ ܬܘܪܝܐ ܕܐܬܩܛܠܬܐ ܕܠܚܫܝܗܘܢ ܕܡܘܕܝܢܐ
ܩܕܝܫܐ ܕܟܠܘܛܝܢܐ. ◦.

ܗܘܬ. ܗܟܢܐ ܗܕܝܢ ܒܡܫܡܫܢܘܬܗ ܠܐܘܦܠܝܢ ܚܝܠܬ. ܘܡܫܡܫܢ ܒܡܫܡܫܢܘܬܗ ܡܫܡܫܢܝܬܐ ܡܢ ܒܢܝܐ ܕܥܕ̈ܬܐ ܐܬܚܫܒ ܘܡܫܡܫܢܘܬܐ ܐܬܚܝܒ. ܘܟܕ ܗܟܢ ܗܠܝܢ ܚܙܝܐܝܬ ܒܐܘܪܚܐ ܕܬܪܝܢ ܐܬܚܒܠ. ܘܗܪܟܐ ܒܫܒܩܗ ܦܘ ܗܟܢܐ ܐܝܟ ܒܠܒܟܐ ܗܟܝ ܗܘܬ. ܘܒܐܘܪܚܐ ܕܬܠܬܐ ܠܥܠܡܐ ܕܫܘܪܝܗ، ܕܫܡܝܐ. ܘܩܝܡܐ ܕܐܒܢܐ ܦܘܠܚܐ ܒܡܫܚܐ ܙܒܢܐ ܫܘ، ܘܠܬܫܡܫܬܐ ܕܐܦܝܣܩܘܦܘܬܐ ܚܕܐ. ܘܐܬܚܝܒ ܚܫܝܫܐܝܬ ܐܦ ܒܗ ܒܡܫܡܫܢܘܬܗ. ܘܒܝܘܡ ܐܪܒܥܬܐ ܒܐܝܕ ܬܪܝܢܐ ܙܒܢܐ ܕܡܫܒܢܐ ܡܠܝܐܝܬ ܐܬܚܬܡ ܠܗ. ܘܒܗ ܒܢܝܐ ܕܥܕ̈ܬܐ ܦܘ ܦܘܠܚܢܐ ܐܘܬܠܝ ܘܠܐ ܗܘܬ ܒܠܫܘܕܗ، ܢܦܩ ܗܘܐ ܠܗ ܒܪ ܒܢܝܐ ܦܠܚܐ ܕܫܠܝܚܐ ܘܡܢ ܥܠܝܐ ܗܡܕܝܢܐ ܕܪܥܝܐ ܐܬܥܬܕ ܕܢܦܩܘܢ ܕܒܡܫܒܚܬܐ ܘܡܫܪܪܢܐ ܐܬܚܙܝܘ ܒܡܬܠܘܢ ܗܢܝܢ ܕܠܒܒܐ ܠܐ ܫܚܝܩ ܕܐܬܦܬܠܘܢ ܒܡܫܐ ܐܬܥܒܕ ܠܗܘܢ ܐܚܫܒܐ ܐܪ̈ܒܥܝܢ ܒܡܫܝܚܐ ܗܕ̈ܪܐ ܕܐܠܗܐ ܒܣܪ ܡܘܫܐ ܪ̈ܫܡܘܢ ܐܬܦܫܛܘ. ܘܦܢܝܘܗܝ ܕܡ ܕܗܠܝܢ ܐܬܚܙܝܘ ܗܘܘ ܐܬ̈ܦܠܝܐ ܪ̈ܫܡܘܢ ܕܡ ܘܡܫܪܪܝܢܘܢ ܕܗܠܝܢ ܐܬܘܗܝ، ܗܘܬ ܦܘ ܗܠܝܐ ܗܕܪܐ ܐܦܘܡܦܐ ܕܗܕ̈ܪܐ ܘܠܘܐܘ ܦܠܒܢܐ ܒܪ̈ܝܬܐ ܘܟܕ ܐܬܐ ܫܒܚܐ ܕܐܠܗܐ ○ ○ ○ ○ ○

ܘܡܛܠ ܕܦܠܝܢ ܚܕܡܐ ܠܗܘܝܐ ܒܡܠܬ݀ ܢܘܕܥܘܢ ܕܠܐܒܢܐ ܘܒܘܪܐ ܡܢ ܗܠܝܢ ܡܕܒ̈ܪܢܐ ܪ̈ܥܝܢܐ ܐܠܗܝܐ ܐܬܚܙܝ. ܘܡܛܠ ܒܢܝܐ ܕܫܠ̈ܝܚܘܗܝ ܡܗܝܡܢܘܬܐ ܡܠܘ. ܦܘ ܒܪ ܕܟܠ ܗܠܝܢ ܡܕ̈ܒܪܢܐ ܕܐܠܗܐ ܒܪܚܡܬܗ ܐܝܟ ܚܘܬܐ ܒܒܬܐ ܡܫܬܚܝܢ ܗܘܬ. ܘܡܛܠ ܒܢܝܐ ܗܟܝ ܗܘܐ ܘܒܡܫܒܬ ܐܘܒܒܐ ܕܫܘܬܐ ܦܪܬܐ ܒܡܫܒܢܐ ܕܦܘ ܕܠܒܝܠ ܗܘܐ ܒܠ ܕ̈ܒܢܐ ܐܒܕ ܘܦܪܟܐ ܕܠܗܘܢ ܒܡܫ̈ܒܬܐ ܕܐܝܟ ܚܘܢ ܡܠܘܬ. ܘܡܛܠ ܒܢ̈ܝܐ ܕܕܡܝܢ ܗܘܘ ܠܡܫܠ̈ܡܢܘܬܗܘܢ ܦܠܘ. ○ ○ ○

ܗܠܝܢ ܗܟܠ ܕܐܘܬܒܪ ܒܠܘ ܐܟܢܐ ܕܐܪܕܘܦܐ ܒܒܡܟܐ ܕܠܘܩܒܢܐ ܠܬܒ ܡܐܘܕܡ. ܘܗܠܝܢ ܠܗܘܢ ܐܬܘܗܝܢ ܗܕ̈ܪܐ

ܕܡܬܘܡܪ ܡܢܗ ܢܒܥܐ ܘܡܟܝܠܘܢ ܠܐܬܪ̈ܘܬܐ ܐܚܪ̈ܢܐ ܟܠܗ̇.
ܘܗܕܝܢ ܡܢ ܦܘܢ ܕܟܡܘܢ ܟܒܫ ܐܪ̈ܒܥܐ ܡܢܗܘܢ ܦܘܢ
ܕܗܟܢ ܒܡܢܝܢܘܬܐ ܐܬܡܢܝܘ ܗܘܘ. ܡܛܠ ܕܗܢܘܢ ܢܦܠ
ܠܐܚܪ̈ܢܐ ܘܒܗ ܒܢܘܣܚܐ ܡܢܗ ܠܗܘܢ. ܘܟܕ ܡܢܗܘܢ ܠܐ
ܡܬܐܡܪ ܗܘܐ ܐܬܟܢܫ ܕܢܗܐ ܕܠܐ ܕ̈ܡܝܐ. ܕܠܗ ܡܢܗܘܢ ܒܢܝܐ
ܕܡܢܐ ܐܝܟ ܕܢܗܪܐ. ܘܠܗ ܠܡܢܐ ܡܗܘܬܐ ܠܗܕ̈ܝܐ ܡܕ̈ܢܝܐ
ܕܐܠܗܐ ܐܝܠܟ ܗܘܐ. ܘܟܕ ܠܐܠܗܘܬܐ ܐܬܦܪܫ ܦܘܢ ܠܒܠ
ܡܢ ܐܠܗܘܬܐ ܢܦܩܘܢ ܟܕ ܕܠܐ ܕܝܠܐ. ܘܩܠ ܡܢ ܒܘܠܛ
ܠܒܘܬܐ ܘܟܠ ܡܘ̈ܪܒܝܢ ܢܦܩܘܢ ܡܡܠܠܬܐ ܡܕܡ. ܘܬܘܒ ܡܢ
ܟܠ ܕܩ̈ܝܢ ܦܓܪ̈ܝܗܘܢ ܠܐܠܗܐ ܚܠܦܐ ܕܟܠ ܕܒܝܫܐ ܥܠܡܐ
ܐܝܟܢܐ. ܬܪ̈ܝܢ ܕܝܢ ܡܢܗܘܢ ܐܬܚܙܝܘ ܗܘܘ ܐܦܣܩܘܦܐ ܦܘܠܘܣ
ܘܢܠܗ ܘܬܪ̈ܝܢ ܟܬ̈ܒܐ ܕܟܬܒܐ ܦܠܓܘܬܗܘܢ ܡܠܟܐ ܝܘܣܛܝܢܐ
ܕܠܗܘܢ ܐܓܪ̈ܬܐ ܗܘܘ. ܡܢܩܕ̈ܝܢ ܗܘܘ ܒܬܪ ܕܩܢ̈ܝܐ ܕܗ̇
ܦܠܘܣܘܦܘܬܐ ܒܠܘܬܐ ܕܡܢ ܐܠܗܐ. ܘܦܘܢ ܒܟܡܘܬ ܕܗܘܐ
ܢܦܫܗܘܢ ܠܢܗܪܐ ܐܒܠܘ ܕܢܬܦܫܩܘܢ. ܗܘ ܕܝܢ ܩܡ ܕܢܗܘܐ ܚܠܝܐ
ܠܚܝ̈ܠܐ ܘܠܡܫܐܠ ܒܐܝܕܐ ܐܝܟܢ ܒܟܝܢܐ ܠܗ̇ ܒܗܘܕܪܐ
ܥܡܢܐ ܐܝܟ ܗܝ ܐܢܘܢ. ܘܟܡ ܒܢܝܐ ܕܩܠܐܟܐ ܫܠܡ ܐܢܘܢ . ܘ .

ܡܬܢܝܬܐ ܕܫܠܘܡܗ ܘܕܘܢ ܕܒܟܡܘ. ܒܫܢܬ ܬܡܢܝܢ
ܕܪܘܦܐ ܕܒܢܝܡܬ.

ܡܢ ܒܬܪ ܕܝܢ ܢܚܡ ܗܘܐ. ܦܘ ܗܢܐ ܫܠܘܡܗ ܓܡܝܢܐ.
ܐܬܬܘܗ ܗܘܐ ܕܝܢ ܚܕ ܡܢ ܩܠܝܣܐ ܒܟܘܡܪܐ. ܘܟܕ ܐܬܬܦܠܛ
ܫܪܘܬܐ ܠܒܡܕܝܢ. ܦܘ ܠܢܡܘܣ ܗܠܝܐ ܓܒܪܐ ܕܡܫܝܚܐ ܒܒܕ
ܒܪ ܐܢܫܐ ܗܘܐ ܒܪ ܡܕܡܐ ܒܟܠ ܘܒܙܒܢܘܗܝ ܢܓܝܫܐ ܗܘܐ
ܘܒܡܬܢܘܬܗ ܗܢܝܓܬ ܘܕܒܝܫܘܬ ܐܬܬܐܢܣ. ܐܬܬܘܗܝ ܗܘܐ
ܕܝܢ ܡܢܝܢܐ ܕܒܢܝܢ ܕܟܪܐ ܡܕܝܢܬܐ. ܘܬܘܒ ܗܟܝܠ ܐܬܬܕܢ
ܗܘܐ. ܘܡܛܠ ܕܐܝܟܘܬܐ ܕܫܢܐ ܠܥܠܡܘܗܝ ܕܡܫܝܚܐ ܐܬܬܢܝ

ܕܡܢ ܐܪܥܐ ܐܬܐܟܠ. ܐܝܟ ܗܢܘܢ ܕܡܢ ܡܕܡܘܬܗ، ܚܙܐ. ܘܗܘܝܐ ܕܟܠܗܘܢ ܗܢܘܢ ܕܒܡܘܬܐ ܐܘܡܢ ܗܘܐ. ܘܐܬܟܠܝܘ ܥܠܡ ○ ○ ○

ܡܕܝܢܬܐ ܕܟܠܗ ܘܕܝܠܗ ܘܕܐܬܪ̈ܘܬܗ ܘܕܐܠܗܐ ܥܒܝܕ ܥܒܕ ܕܐܪܘܣܐ ܕܥܘܡܪܗܘܢ

ܫܢܬܐ ܬܫܥܡܐܐ ܒܐܝܠܘܠ ܐܬܘܗܝ، ܗܘܐ. ܘܗܘ ܒܫܢܐ ܐܝܟܢܐ ܬܡܘܗܐ ܕܗܘܐ ܕܐܠܗܐ ܘܚܙܬܐ ܕܢܬܐ ܐܬܟܫܦܬ ܒܫܢܐ ܕܗܘ ܒܠܘܩܝܢܐ. ܘܟܠܗܘܢ ܐܢܛܠܝܐ ܗܘܘ ܠܡܕܝܢܬܐ. ܐܬܡܗܘܢ ܗܘܘ ܕܝܢ ܒܡܕܝܢܬܐ. ܐܝܟ ܡܟܐ ܘܚܙܝܢ. ܦܓܪ̈ܐ ܕܝܢ ܡܢܗܘܢ ܐܢܛܠܝܐ ܗܘܘ. ܘܟܠ ܡܟܐ ܬܘܒ ܚܙܝܢ ܗܘܘ. ܗܘܝܘ ܗܢܘܢ ܠܗܘܢ ܚܝܘܗܝ ܕܡܢܝܢܐ ܘܦܓܠܝܘܗܝ ܕܗܘ̈ܠܐ ܒܡܩܒܘܠܗܘܢ ܒܒܥܐ ܕܐܘܪܐ ܘܡܘܫܐ ܐܬܚܒܠ. ܘܬܘܒ ܒܬܪ ܗܠܝܢ ܠܡܠܠܘ ܕܫܡܥܘ ܢܚܫܐ ܐܬܓܠܝܘ. ܘܗܢܘܢ ܬܘܒ ܟܠܗ ܠܝܠܝܐ ܒܝܘܡܬ ܐܢܬܠܝܐ ܒܢܫܐ ܗܘܝܘ. ܒܬܪ ܕܝܢ ܗܠܝܢ ܐܬܚܙܝ ܒܪܘܒܬܐ ܕܡܬܕܪܐ ܗܘܬ ܠܡܘܒܠܐ ܐܝܟ ܒܥܝܬܐ ܕܐܡܪܐ ܦܓܪ̈ܐ ܐܬܐܡܪܘ. ܘܒܡܟܐ ܦܓܪ̈ܐ ܐܚܝܬ ܗܘܐ ܒܫܡܝܢ: ܗܢܘܢ ܕܡܢ ܐܬܪ̈ܘܬܐ ܐܚܪ̈ܢܐ ܠܚܝܬܗܘܢ ܐܬܘ ܗܘܘ. ܘܦܓܪ̈ܐ ܐܚܪ̈ܢܐ ܐܝܠܝܢ ܕܡܬܡܚܝܢ ܗܘܘ ܠܗܘܢ: ܒܡܟܐ ܕܚܙܝ ܗܘܐ ܠܗܘܢ ܘܡܝܬܝܢ ܗܘܘ ܠܗܘܢ ܒܫܘܩܐ ܘܒܦܘܪ̈ܫܝܗܘܢ ܡܬܟܠܝܢ ܗܘܘ. ܘܟܠܗ ܫܢܬܐ ܒܝܠܘܬܐ ܘܟܬܫܬܫܬܐ ܕܐܠܗܐ ܘܐܠܐܠܝܢ ܘܒܫܘܠܛܢܐ ܘܡܛܪܢܐ ܡܬܡܚܝܢ ܗܘܘ. ܘܫܠܗܘܢ ܐܢ̈ܫܝܐ ܕܒܟܪܐ ܒܠܚܘܕܘܗܝ ܐܝܟ ܒܗܘܡܐ ܫܟܝܚܝܢ ܗܘܘ ܠܗܘܢ: ܗܐܝܟ ܕܟܕܟܕܐ ܗܐܝܟ ܕܟܢܫܐ ܗܠܝܢ ܟܠܢܐ ܗܘ ܡܬܕܒܪܝܢ ܗܘܘ. ܘܢܫܐ ܕܡܢ ܕܐܠܗܐ ܘܫܘܡܟܐ ܒܫܐ ܠܡܫܬܡܥܘ ܗܠܝܢ ܠܐ ܐܫܟܚ ܗܘܐ ܘܟܢܫܟܬܘ ܐܫܬܪܝ ܟܠܗܘܢ ܦܫܝܠܐ ܗܘ ܕܡܬܕܪܐ ܕܘܟܐ ܕܦ̈ܘܪܡܟܐ ܘܠܗܘܢ ܦܪܫ ܐܝܢܘܢ ܚܝ ܡܢ ܚܝ ܘܡܟܝܢܘܢ ܠܐܘܟܘܡܪܐ ܕܒܟܬܐ ܒܝܬܐ ܐܬܝܕܥܘ. ܘܡܟܝܢܘܢ ܠܐ ܘܡܟܝܢܘܢ ܠܗܘܢ ܕܒܟܬܐ ܗܝ،

ܛܘܒܢܐ ܒܫܘܡܠܝܐ ܕܣܗܕܘܬܗ ܥܒܕ ܕܢܬܠܘܐ. ܐܪ̈ܒܥܐ ܗܘܝܠ
ܐܢ̈ܫܝܢ ܩ̈ܠܝܠܬܗܘܢ ܒܥܘܡܪܐ ܕܦܘܠܚܢܗܘܢ ܗܓܡܘܢܐ ܦܓ̈ܪܐ
ܦܩ̈ܕ ܒܗܘܠ ܕܗܘ̈ܝܐ ܕܐܠܗܐ ܡܐܟܘܠܬܐ ܠܚܝ̈ܘܬܐ ܗܘܡܝܢ
ܗܘܘ. ܘܟܕ ܕܝܢ ܠܐ ܡܕܡ ܦܪܫ ܠܗܘܢ ܘܐܦܠܐ ܚܝܘܬ ܥܒܕ
ܐܬܬܠܝܘ ܟܕ ܥܠܝܗܘܢ ܕܠܐ ܡܢ ܡܣܟܢܘܬܐ ܕܗܓܡܘܢܐ. ܘܠܐܢܫܪܐ
ܕܦܪܚܝܢ ܗܘܘ. ܘܠܡܟܘܪܐ ܡܣܝܒܪܐ ܐܝܟ ܕܫܘܡ ܐܬܡܟܪܘ.
ܘܟܬ̈ܒܐ ܕܐܝܟ ܗܠܝܢ ܐܬܬܗܝܒܘ ܘܟܬ̈ܝܒܐ ܕܐܝܬ ܠܒܠܬܐ ܠܡܕܝܢܬܐ
ܕܠܐ ܡܬܝܕܥܐ ܕܢܬܦܪܣܘܢ ܡܢ ܐܢܫܝܢ ܐܝܠܝܢ ܕܐܬܦܪܣܘܢ ܒܗܘܢ
ܕܐܠܗܐ ܐܫܬܠܡܘ. . . .

ܡܘܕܝܢܘܬܐ ܕܗܕܪܝܢܘܣ ܘܕܐܘܒܘܠܘܣ ܒܝܘܡ ܥܣܪ ܕܐܕܪ ܕܒܩܣܪܝܐ
ܕܒ̈ܩܣܛܝܢ. . . .

ܟܕ ܫܘܡܠܝܗ ܕܡܣܬܝܟܠܘܬܐ ܘܕܝܢܘܗܝ ܗܘܐ ܕܒܝܬ ܒܩܘܡܐ
ܕܥܠ ܐܝܟ ܡܬܦܪܝ ܗܘܐ. ܗܕܪܝܢܘܣ ܘܐܘܒܘܠܘܣ ܡܢ ܕܒܬܪܐ
ܕܡܬܩܪܝܐ ܕܒܛܢ̈ܐ ܠܘܬ ܥܕܬܐ ܕܡܕ̈ܝܢܬܐ ܐܬܦܪܣܘ ܠܩܣܪܝܐ.
ܘܟܕ ܠܬܪܥܐ ܕܡܕܝܢܬܐ ܦܪܩܘ. ܕܡܛܠ ܐܝܕܐ ܥܠܬܐ ܐܬܝܐ ܐܬܘ
ܐܫܬܐܠܘ. ܘܟܕ ܐܫܪܪܘ ܥܘܕ̈ܬܐ ܠܦܘܠܚܢܗܘܢ ܦܪܩܘ ܐܢܘܢ. ܗܘ
ܕܝܢ ܒܡܕܡ ܠܐ ܐܬܟܢܝ. ܘܠܩܕܡ ܗ̈ܘܟܐ ܕܥܠ ܪ̈ܓܠܝܗܘܢ ܦܩܕ
ܘܐܝܟ ܕܒܬܠܬܒܟܐ ܘܐܝܟ ܕܒ̈ܣܝܢܐ ܦܢܝܐܝܬ ܐܬܬܣܪܩܘ ܒܗܘܢ
ܘܟܕ ܠܐ ܗܦܟܘ ܒܗܠܝܢ ܠܡܗܝܡܢܘܬܐ ܕܣܝܒܘܬܐ ܣܓܝ ܐܢܘܢ ܘܟܕ ܕܝܢ
ܬܪ̈ܝܢ ܝܘܡ̈ܝܢ ܒܬܪܗ ܗܕܪܝܢܘܣ ܡܕܝܢܬܐ ܒܡܣܟܢܘܬܐ ܒܩܕܡ ܠܚܝܘܬܐ
ܐܫܬܕܝ. ܘܒܣܝܦܐ ܠܡܓܡܘܪܗ ܓܡܪ . ܘܟܕ ܡܢ ܝܘܡܬܐ ܐܬܬܢܝܚ.
ܠܝܘܡܬܐ ܒܗܘܢ ܐܬܦܠܠ ܘܐܘܒܘܠܘܣ ܠܘܬܗ ܐܘܪܚܐ ܒܫܒܬܐ
ܒܩܕܝ ܟܕ ܐܡܪ ܠܗܘܢ ܘܡܓܪܬܐ ܗܘ ܕܢܬܐ ܘܐܬܦܢܝ ܠܗ. ܕܐܢ
ܠܟ̈ܘܪܐ ܬܩܒܠ ܒܡܫܟܐ ܬܫܬܪܐ. ܘܗܘ ܠܐ ܠܟܘ ܒܡܟܪܐ ܕܟܒܐ
ܒܩܘܪܐ ܐܫܟܚܪ ܗܘܐ. ܦܩܕܐ ܠܗ ܚܝܐ ܕܠܟܠܗ ܦܠܓ ܡܢ ܗܠܝܢ
ܚܝܐ ܫ̈ܐܠܬܐ ܘܒܩܘܪܐ. ܘܗܘ ܕܝܢ ܠܬܪܥܐ ܐܫܬܕܝ. ܘܟܡ ܒܬܪ

ܐܬܦܬܚ ܘܡܕܒܪܢܘܬܐ ܕܠܐ ܚܘܣܟ ܒܗܘܢ ܠܦܪܢܣܐ ܕܐܠܗܐ ܗܘܬ
ܐܦ ܠܡܣ̈ܟܢܐ. ܘܡܢܗܘܢ ܕܝܢ ܕܬܠܡܝܕܘܗܝ ܬܫܡܫܬܗ ܕܥܒܐ
ܘܫܘܒܚܐ ܕܐܠܗܐ ܐܬܦܪܥ. ܐܬܬܘܗܝ، ܗܘܐ ܕܝܢ ܗܟܐ ܕܟܠܗܘܢ
ܒܒ̈ܢܝܐ ܕܡܫܡܫܢܐ. ܕܥܡ ܟܠܗܘܢ ܡܛܠ ܐܘܟ̈ܡܘܗܝ ܘܫ̈ܩܘܗܝ
ܚܡܪ ܗܘܐ. ܘܡܛܠ ܕܐܡܟܐ ܕܬܠ̈ܬܐ ܕܝ̈ܢ. ܐܬܬܘܗܝ، ܗܘܐ ܘܬܘܒ
ܡܛܠ ܕܫܪܪܐ ܠܡܪ̈ܝܘܗܝ، ܢܛܪ ܗܘܐ. ܠܐ ܐܚܕ ܒܠܘܗܝ، ܥܠ ܕܫܩܒ
ܒܠܘܗܝ، ܕܡܠܟܐ ܕܥܘܬ̈ܪܐ ܒܥܡܟܬ ܫܠܡܘܗܝ ܫܩܠ ܗܘܐ.
ܘܟܕ ܐܬܟܢܫ ܠܡܪ̈ܝܘ ܡܬܪ̈ܐܬ ܒܠܘܗܝ، ܒܡܫܟܬܐ ܓܠܒ ܡܢ ܕܟܠ
ܐܢ̈ܫܝܐ ܐܬܢܝܚ. ܘܦܓܪ ܒܠܘܗܝ، ܕܠܡܘܬܐ ܕܝܫܘܥ ܦܪܘܩܢ ܡܬܠܒ
ܠܡܕܝܢܘܬܐ ܕܟܢܫ ܘܫܦܟܐ ܟܬܪ ܗܘܠܝ ܕܝܢ ܚܕ ܚܡܫܪ ܗܘܐ
ܕܡܣܟܢܐ ܕܐܬܒܗܪ ܢܠܡ ܗܘܐ. ܡܠܝܢܘܗܝ ܓܒܪ ܡܢ ܐܘܪܚܐ ܐܬܐ
ܗܘܐ. ܘܟܕ ܕܢܠܡܘܗܝ ܗܘܐ ܠܡܣܟܢܐ ܕܐܬܒܗܪܬܐ ܕܗܘ̈ܐ
ܘܟܕ ܒܥܠܬܐ ܕܐܬܬܐ ܒܗ ܒܫܒܠ ܠܡܣܟܢܘܬܐ ܠܐ ܓܠ ܗܘܐ.
ܒܫܒܬܗ ܡܢ ܐܘܪܚܐ ܡܢ ܐܚܕ ܠܒܟ ܗܘܐ ܥܠ ܥܪܒܐ ܕܡܣ̈ܟܢܐ.
ܘܪܗܛ ܗܘܐ ܠܣܘܬܐ ܕܡܣ̈ܟܢܐ. ܘܟܕ ܚܙܐ ܕܠܬܘܬ ܥܠ ܐܘܪܚܐ
ܦܬ̈ܘܪܘܗܝ ܕܡܣ̈ܟܢܐ ܦܬܝܚܝܢ ܗܘܘ. ܐܬܩܒܠ ܫܪܘܬܐ ܘܠܒܫ ܚܕ
ܡܢܗܘܢ ܒܫܘܟܐ ܫܟܝܢܐ ܒܥܡ ܗܘܐ. ܘܒܡܫܡܫܬܐ ܒܠܒܫܐ
ܕܒܠܘܗܝ ܫܩܠ ܗܘܐ. ܘܟܕ ܒܫܒܠ ܗܠܝܢ ܗܟܢ ܗܘܐ.
ܘܟܕ ܒܥܡܠܗܘܢ ܠܐ ܐܫܬܘܕܝ ܚܒܐ ܗܘܐ. ܠܡܫܡܫܘܗܝ، ܘܦܠܘܛܐ ܘܠܚ̈ܢܐ
ܦܪܡܘܗܝ. ܘܐܦ ܕܝܢܐ ܡܕܡ ܕܐܬܚܫܒ ܗܘܐ ܚܝܪܘ ܒܥܐ ܦܩܕ
ܘܠܚܡܪܐ ܝܗܒܬܐ ܐܦ ܠܗܢܐ ܐܫܟܚ ܗܘܐ. ܗܟܢܐ ܗܟܝܠ ܐܦ
ܗܢܐ ܡܠܝܢܘܗܝ ܒܗ ܕܐܢܝ ܗܘܐ ܘܡܫܐ ܒܚܠܐ ܦܪܫܐ ܠܐܠܗܐ ܗܘ
ܕܠܗ̇ܪܐ ܐܫܬܡܥ ܡܫܬܒܚ ܗܘܐ. ܘܟܡ ܒܢܝܐ ܕܡܣ̈ܟܢܐ ܢܫܡܗ
ܠܘܬ ܡܪܗ ܐܫܬܠܡܬ ܐܢܬܘܬܗ، ܗܘܐ ܕܝܢ ܒܚܫܐ ܕܗܢܐ ܡܫܬܕܪܢܐ.
ܘܟܢܫܘ ܕܝܠܬܐ ܕܐܠܗܐ ܡܠܐ ܗܘܐ ܘܟܪ ܐܡܬܐ ܗܘܐ ܡܫܬܟܚܐ
ܘܚܒܘܫܐ ܘܟܠܗܘܢ ܡܠ̈ܬܐ ܫܒܝܩܬܐ ܗܘܐ. ܘܐܝܬ ܗܘܐ ܒܗ
ܐܢܫ ܥܡܠܐ ܕܪܘܚܐ ܡܫܬܥܐ. ܘܡܥܠܝܐ ܗܘ ܕܝܢ ܫܡܥܠܘܗܝ

ܡܫܪܘܒ ܗܘܐ. ܘܟܕ ܢܦܩ ܡܢ ܪܘܡܐ ܚܪܘܗܝ، ܡܬܓܘܪܐ
ܗܘܬ. ܡܟܐ ܘܡܟܐ ܠܠܡܠܟܘܬܐ ܒܗܘܡܘܣ ܚܠܦ ܗܘܐ. ܘܢܟܣܘ
ܠܗ̇، ܡܢܪܕܘܬܐ ܕܡܕܡܘܗܝ، ܡܫܪܘܒܐ ܗܘܬ ܐܝܟ ܗܢܐ ܗܘܐ
ܗܟܝܠ ܬܫܬܘܡܣ ܕܐܪܢܣܘܣ ܓܒܪܐ ܕܝܢ ܕܩܠܝܠ ܦܠܘܣ ܕܐܬܗܬܪ
ܒܐܪܢܣܘܣ ܐܘܒܠ ܗܠܘܢܘܣ ܠܡܟܝܠܘܣ. ܘܡܓܪܐ ܕܗܒܪܬܗ
ܕܗܠܘܢܘܣ ܡܢ ܐܠܗܐ ܐܬܝܗܒ ܕܐܦ ܗܘ ܒܝܬܗ ܕܡܟܝܠܘܣ
ܢܗܘܐ ܗܘܐ. ܡܢ ܕܐܬܬܗ ܓܒܪ ܕܐܫܬܒܝ ܠܡܟܝܠܘܣ ܥܠ
ܐܓܘܢܐ ܘܬܫܬܘܡܣ ܕܐܪܢܣܘܣ. ܡܛܠ ܒܠܡܟܐ ܕܚܕ ܡܢ ܗܘܕܐ
ܒܢܟܣܬܐ. ܠܟܠܗܘܢ ܐܘܓܪܓܐ ܘܦܪ̈ܟܘܗܝ ܠܡܓܢܘܢܐ ܗܘ ܕܝܢ
ܗܠܘܢܘܣ ܐܝܟ ܗ̇ܘ ܕܡܬܗܦܟ ܗܘܐ ܕܒܝܬ ܡܟܪ̈ܝܢܐ ܢܐܪܠ
ܒܠܘܬܐ ܘܕܒܬܗܠ ܪܗܛܐܬܗܝ ܒܠܘܗܝ. ܐܬܬܘܗܝ، ܗܘܐ ܕܝܢ ܗܘܐ
ܗܠܘܢܘܣ ܡܢ ܐܪܟܐ ܕܡܣܕܘܡܐ ܘܡܢܚܐܬ ܒܠܘܬܗ ܡܬܬܒܥ
ܗܘܐ. ܘܡܕܢܚܐ ܕܐܘܓܪܓܘܢܐ ܦܠܓܢܐ ܪܒܐ ܐܝܟ ܐܢܫ ܗܘܐ.
ܘܠܐ ܒܠܚܘܕ ܐܠܐ ܐܦ ܗ̇ܘ ܗܘܡܬܗ ܒܪܟܘܬܐ ܕܦܓܪܐ
ܘܫܠܝܛܘܬܐ ܠܡܓܪܐ ܕܐܡܬܐ ܒܝܢ ܗܘܐ. ܘܫܬܗ ܠܟܠ ܐܢܫ
ܦܐܪܐ ܗܘܬ. ܘܒܥܘܪܗ ܕܪܕܘܦܝܐ ܒܡܡܠܟܘܬܐ ܕܬܓܪ̈ܐ
ܕܡܕܒܪܢܘܬܐ ܐܬܦܢܝ ܘܡܢ ܒܬܪ ܕܐܫܬܪܝ، ܡܢ ܦܠܚܘܬܐ ܡܛܠ
ܡܡܒܪܢܘܬܗ ܓܢܘܢ ܬܘܒ ܕܢܦܠܐ ܡܢ ܓܒܪ̈ܐ ܠܐ ܒܥܘܢ ܗܘܐ.
ܘܓܒܪܐ ܪܘܫܟܐ ܕܡܩܕܫܐ. ܕܢܦܠ ܐܬܓܪܓܙ ܗܘܐ. ܘܐܝܟ
ܡܒܘܪܐ ܕܬ̈ܠܡܟܐ ܡܫܘ̈ܬܐ ܘܕܐܪ̈ܡܠܬܐ ܡܓܪܬܐ ܘܕܗ̈ܘܝܐ
ܕܡܟܒܢܘܬܐ ܘܡܒܘܪܗܐ ܚܣܝܢ ܗܘܘ. ܐܝܟ ܡܒܘܪܐ ܘܒܝܠ
ܓܒܢܐ ܒܝܫ ܗܘܐ. ܘܫܟܝܚܬ ܐܢܫܐ ܡܪܘܡܢܐ ܒܐܪ̈ܥܐ ܕܟܗܘܢ
ܡܐܬܐ ܗܘܐ ܘܒܬܪ ܗܠܝܢ ܗܠܝܢ ܕܒܗܘܢ ܚܙܐ ܐܠܗܐ ܓܒ
ܡܢ ܕܒ̈ܢܝܐ ܘܡܩ̈ܪܐ ܘܓܠܝܐ ܕܒ̈ܡܟܐ ܕܡܬܡܟܠܐ ܒܡܒܕܢܘܬܐ
ܥܒܪ. ܘܗܢܐ ܗܘ ܐܬܠܛܠܐ ܒܗܪܝܐ ܕܦܘܪܢܘܣ ܕܡܢ ܠܟܠ ܚܬܡܝܢ.
ܕܟܡܐ ܒܗܘܡܟܐ ܒܟܡܐ ܘܣ ܐܫܬܒܠ ܘܐܬܟܠܠ ܘܐܝܟ ܕܕܡܝܐ
ܬܪܝܢܐ ܪܟܐ ܕܢܝܠܗܘܬܐ ܕܫܡܝܢܐ ܒܡܒܕܢܘܬܗ ܕܡܟܝܠܘܣ

ܣܠܩܐ. ܗܘ ܕܝܢ ܦܪܨܘܦܗ ܐܦ ܠܐ ܒܪ ܬܫܒܘܚܬܐ ܫܦܝܪ ܗܘܐ.
ܗܘܐ. ܘܒܢܘܠܡܢܐ ܘܒܡܬܘܡܝܘܬܐ ܡܟܣܐ ܗܘܐ ܘܒܡܣܟܢܘܬܗ
ܘܒܐܘܟܡܗ. ܒܟܠ ܬܫܒܚܬܐ ܐܝܬܘܗܝ ܗܘܐ. ܗܘ ܗܟܝܠ ܓܠܝܐ ܕܡܢ
ܗܘܐ ܒܥܝܢܐ ܐܚܪܢܐ ܗܘܐ. ܟܕ ܝܕܥ ܒܪܘܚܐ ܕܢܦܩ ܒܗ ܡܢܗ.
ܡܢ ܡܕܝܢܬ ܒܝܬܐ ܡܢܐ. ܘܦܓܪܐ ܕܡܘܪܝܐ ܫܩܠ. ܗܘ ܕܝܢ
ܠܡܫܟܚܐ ܐܝܟܐ ܕܐܦ ܠܐ ܒܪ ܐܢܫܐ ܙܕܩ ܕܢܬܩܪܐ. ܐܠܐ ܫܘܬܐ
ܒܪܝܪܬܐ ܠܐ ܒܡܘܬܐ ܕܙܕܩܐ ܗܘܬ ܡܛܠ. ܐܦ ܠܐ ܒܠ ܗܘ
ܕܡܢܗ ܓܠܝܐ ܗܘܐ ܣܘ ܘܪܘܫ ܘܟܕ ܐܠܦ ܗܕܐ ܒܠܫܢܗ
ܕܒܪܘܓܙܐ ܗܘ. ܦܩܕ ܠܗܘܢ ܕܢܪܩܘܡ ܕܡܢ ܒܠܗ ܣܠܝܩܘܢ
ܢܪܘܡܘܢܗ. ܘܟܕ ܕܝܢ ܕܢܬܒܥ ܠܗܘ ܓܠܝܐ ܠܡܟܢܐ ܦܩܕ ܗܘܐ ܘܠܐ
ܐܫܬܡܥ ܠܗ ܐܝܟ ܕܡܦܩܢܐ ܕܒܪ ܐܢܫܐ ܐܫܬܡܥ ܗܘܐ. ܐܠܐ
ܐܝܟ ܕܡܫܘܕܐ ܘܐܝܟ ܕܡܫܐܠܐ ܕܠܐ ܢܩܫܐ. ܘܡܕܡܕܐ ܕܠܗܘܢ
ܠܥܒܕܐ ܘܠܦܘܠܚܢܐ ܢܦܠܘܢ ܕܢܬܪܘ ܦܩܕ ܗܘܐ. ܘܟܕ ܢܦܩܐ
ܗܠܝܢ ܒܝܬ ܗܘܐ. ܝܕܥ ܕܪܘܫܐ ܐܚܪܬܐ. ܘܟܕ ܦܪܣܬܗ ܘܫܢܝܘܬܗ
ܒܓܠܝܐ ܗܝ ܗܘܐ. ܠܗܘܢ ܐܝܟ ܟܢܘܫܬܐ ܘܦܫܝܛܐ ܕܡܛܠ ܒܪ ܟܠܗܘܢ.
ܗܘܐ ܗܟܝܠ ܡܢ ܕܡܟܝܠܗ ܢܬܡܟܠܐ ܠܬܫܡܫܬܐ ܡܪܢ.
ܘܒܫܘܢܗ ܕܡܢ ܦܓܪܐ ܠܡܢܘܗ ܘܡܢܟܝܢܗ ܡܕܡ ܗܘܐ. ܡܬܚܙܝܐ
ܗܘܐ ܕܝܢ ܦܪܨܘܦܗ ܒܕܡܘܬ ܚܠܝܡܐ ܕܡܘܠ ܬܬܘܠܢ ܒܕܡܘܬܐ
ܐܬܠܝܛ. ܘܟܕ ܒܦܓܪܗ ܡܫܠ ܗܘܐ. ܒܥܪܝܘܬܗ ܦܪܝܫ ܗܘܐ.
ܘܒܪܝܫܐ ܠܒܢܝܐ ܕܠܐ ܕܚܠܐ ܒܐܘܪܚܐ ܕܡܘܬܐ ܙܕܐ ܗܘܐ.
ܘܫܦܝܪܐ ܪܘܚܐ ܕܡܘܕܥܐ ܡܓܠܐ ܗܘܐ. ܘܟܕ ܠܕܘܟܬܐ ܗܝ ܕܡܢ
ܡܘܬܐ ܡܓܝܠ ܗܘܐ. ܐܙܠ. ܒܕܡܘܬ ܦܠܘܣܦܐ ܢܟܠܝܗ ܒܪ ܒܬܪܗ
ܟܠܝܐ ܗܘܬ ܓܠܝܦ ܗܘܐ ܘܟܠ ܒܣܡܐ ܒܫܘܡܗ ܫܢܝ ܗܘ.
ܘܟܠ ܒܗܠܝܢ ܒܗܡܪܐ ܐܢܫܐ ܒܪܝܫܗ ܦܫܐ ܗܘܐ. ܘܒܝܫܐ
ܕܠܐ ܡܬܝܕܥܐ ܠܗܘ ܢܘܪܐ ܐܬܦܪܥ ܗܘܐ. ܐܝܟ ܐܢܫ ܕܡܕܡ
ܒܡܬܐ ܠܐ ܡܪܝܐ ܠܗ. ܘܒܪܝܫܐ ܒܢܝܐ ܕܠܐ ܡܕܝܢ ܒܠ
ܐܝܬܘܗܝ ܠܡܘܬܗ ܦܘܫ ܘܡܟܝܠ ܠܗܘ ܐܠܗܐ ܕܥܕܠ ܢܟܠ

ܫܠܡܘܬܗ ܡܫܡܠܝܬܐ ܣܟܡ ܡܣܪܪܐ ܐܡܪ. ܘܬܘܒ ܟܕ ܕܒܬܪܗ
ܦܘܠܚܢܬܐ ܓܡܝܪܬܐ. ܕܦܢ ܗܘ ܘܡܫܝܚܐ ܐܡܪܐ ܐܬܘܗܝ. ܗܘܐ
ܐܘܪܫܠܡ ܡܫܝܚܬܐ ܕܐܬܬܩܪܒܬ ܕܫܠܡܘܢ ܗܘ ܫܠܡܘܬ ܕܡܫܡܠܝܘܬܐ
ܐܡܪ ܘܡܫܝܚܐ ܠܟ ܡܠܠ ܠܢܒ ܢܘܗܪܐ ܕܢܡܟܐ ܐܬܘܗܝ.
ܘܦܘ ܗܢܐ ܬܘܒ ܒܗ ܗܠܝܢ ܐܝܟ ܕܡܡܠܟܐ ܕܠܗ ܐܬܝܗܒ. ܟܕ
ܦܝܘ ܕܫܪܘܗܝ ܒܗܘܢܐ ܐܬܝܠܕܘ ܒܗ. ܘܠܐ ܒܡܟܝܢ ܗܦܟܝ.
ܘܐܝܟ ܦܘ ܕܕܠܐ ܦܓܪ ܐܬܘܗܝ ܗܘܐ ܗܡܬܦܪ ܗܘܐ. ܗܘ ܕܝܢ
ܕܢܐ ܒܪܝܫܗ ܐܬܝܗܒ. ܘܗܦܪ ܕܟܒܪ ܡܫܝܚܐ ܒܕܘܟܐ ܒܗ
ܠܗܘܢ ܒܪܘܚܢܐ. ܘܗܟܢ ܐܬܬܐܡ ܒܗܘܢ ܒܥܕܬܐ. ܡܛܠ ܒܠ
ܗܕܐ ܡܫܝܚܬܐ ܘܒܠ ܐܬܪܐ ܕܡܫܝܚܐ. ܟܕ ܕܝܢ ܠܒܠܝܡܐ ܦܘ
ܒܡܫܘܬܐ ܢܦܫ ܗܘܐ. ܘܫܐ ܕܡܢ ܡܫܬܚܬܐ ܕܐܡܪ ܠܐ ܡܬܬܝܠܘ
ܗܘܐ. ܠܒܪ ܕܒܢܐ ܕܡܘܬܐ ܦܓܪ ܒܠܗܘܢ ܕܪܫܡ ܫܬܐܠ. ܠܥܪܒܐ ܕܝܢ
ܕܐܬܩܛܠܐ ܒܬܫܘܒܐ ܕܕܡܢ ܠܕܘܟܐ ܒܣܪ ܘܠܦܘ ܡܫܡܫܘܢ
ܒܡܫܝܚܘܬܗܘܢ ܫܠܡܘܢ. ......

ܘܗܟܢ ܡܢ ܒܬܪ ܗܠܝܢ ܒܠ ܕܟܠܗ ܒܡܫܠܡܘܬ ܥܠ. ܘܠܐ ܕܐܟ
ܡܢ ܡܟܡ ܗܢܐ ܕܟܢܐ ܒܥܒܕܐ ܦܓܪܐ ܐܬܢܬܘܢ ܘܐܬܝܪܒ
ܕܗܠܝܢ ܗܘ ܕܗܘܢ ܟܕ ܗܘܢ ܥܒܕܐ ܣܓܝܐ ܫܠܡܘܢ ܘܠܐܐ
ܦܢܝܐܬ. ܘܗܕܐ ܫܠܡܘܬ ܥܐܠ ܐܝܟ ܕܐܢ ܡܬܦܠܓܝܢ ܗܘܐ.
ܟܕ ܡܢ ܣܝ ܡܫܡܫܘܢ ܒܪܬ ܘܠܐ ܕܡܫܡܠܝܘܬܐ ܥܡܕ ܗܘܐ ܐܝܟ
ܕܠܦܘܢ ܕܡܢ ܡܫܡܫܘܢ ܣܒܪ ܐܝܟܢ ܦܓܪ ܕܢܐ ܕܫܬܐܠ
ܢܦܫܘܢ ܦܓܪ ܫܠܡܘܢ ܘܟܕ ܕܝܢ ܦܘܠܚ ܫܠܡܘܬ ܠܐ ܐܬܬܩܪܒܬ
ܗܘܬ. ܡܢ ܦܢܝܢ ܐܡܟܐ ܦܠܓܐ ܣܝ ܓܒܪܐ ܕܡܫܠܡܘܢ ܡܢ ܡܝܬܒ
ܒܡܟܐ ܗܦ ܕܠܒܫܬ ܕܢܐ ܣܡܪ ܗܘܐ ܦܓܪܐ. ܘܠܡܝܬܒܬܐ ܬܘܒ
ܦܪܢ ܗܘܐ. ܘܡܠܟܐ ܢܦܫܐ ܬܘܒ ܡܟܐ ܗܘܐ. ܐܝܟ ܕܢܫܘ
ܦܓܪܢܐ ܕܬܫܡܪܘܢ ܦܓܪܘܢ ܕܡܘܪܢܐ. ܐܬܘܗܝ ܗܘܐ
ܕܡ ܗܢܐ ܦܢܝܢܘ ܠܦܓܪܐ ܦܢܝܬܗ ܣܝܒܬܐ ܕܡܫܠܡܘܢ ܠܒܪ

ܕܟܐ̈ܒܐ ܕܟܘܪܗܢܘܬܗ ܐܬܒܛܠ. ܘܟܕ ܒܗܠܝܢ ܟܠܗ ܚܘܫܒܢܐ ܐܝܟ
ܬܪ̈ܬܝܢ ܥܡܝ ܐܬܚܫܒܘ ܒܠܒܐ ܕܟܘܪܗܢܘܬܗܘܢ ܗܘܐ ܗܘܬ.
ܡܫܬܐܠܐ ܕܐܬܝܗ̈ܠܢܐ ܗܘܘ ܕܐܦ ܦܘܩܘ ܒܥܒܕܘ ܒܟܘܪܗܢܘܬܐ
ܐܬܬܣܝܡܘ. ܟܕ ܠܗܘ ܚܙܐ ܠܗܘܢ ܕܠܡܬܠܠܘܢ ܕܡܠܝܚܐ
ܐܬܕܪܘ. ܕܒܝ̈ܬܐ ܢܘܟܪ̈ܝܐ ܗܘܘ. ܘܟܠܗܘ ܐܝܟ ܕܢܐܡܠܘܢ
ܠܐܬܪܗܘܢ ܘܟܕ ܚܠܡ ܒܬܪܟܐ ܕܗܘܪܐ ܡܕܝܢܬܐ ܕܡܢ ܐܝܟ
ܘܡܢ ܐܢܫܐ ܐܚܪܢܐ ܐܬܬܣܝܡ. ܘܠܐ ܦܠܓܘ ܥܠܝܗܘܢ. ܐܠܐ
ܐܦܪܘ ܕܒܪܗܦܠܐ ܐܢܫܝ. ܘܡܐܗܡܢܐ ܕܝܢܐ ܒܝ̈ܬܐ ܠܒܝܬ
ܐܝܟ ܐܬܚܫܒܘܢ ܗܘܘ ܕܝܢ ܒܡܫܝܚܐ ܫܒܝܚܐ. ܘܟܕ ܐܬܦܪܩܘ
ܠܗܝܢ ܘܡܕܡܘܗܝ ܒܦܪܘܩܐ ܡܠܠܘ. ܒܪܫܝܬܗ ܠܒܝܬ ܫܒܘܚܐ
ܐܬܬܠܝܡ. ܠܒܬܪܗ ܕܝܢ ܕܗܘܡܐ ܒܬܒܗܘܪܐ ܒܢܝܢ ܫܡܠ ܠܗܘܢ
ܠܗܠܝܢ ܒܢ ܕܒܝܬ ܦܫܝܠܘܬܗ ܡܢܢ ܦܘܪܩܢܘܗܝ ܡܪܗ. ܗܘ ܕܝܢ
ܦܚܡܘܢܐ ܠܐܬܚܦܠܝܐ ܠܗܘܕܢ ܝܘ. ܗܘܘܐ. ܘܟܠ ܕܫܘܡ ܕܫ̈ܘܢܐ
ܒܢܪ ܐܝܟ. ܘܠܡܕܡܘܗܝ ܐܢܬ ܠܡܝܬܘܬܐ. ܘܕܐܡܒܢܐ ܗܘ
ܫܒܚ ܫܠܘ. ܘܝܠܦ ܗܘ ܫܒܚܐ ܫܪܪܐ. ܫܒܚܐ ܕܢܒܝܐ ܫܒܚ
ܡܢܗܘܢ. ܐܦ ܗܘܝܘ ܫܪܒܐ ܕܐܬܦܠܓܐ ܕܥܒܕܗ ܝܠܦ ܗܘܝܘ
ܫܒ̈ܚܬܐ ܕܟܠ ܫܪ ܦܬܓܡܐ ܗܘܘ ܠܗܘܢ ܐܡܫܝܚܘܢ ܗܘܝܘ
ܫܒ̈ܚܬܐ ܕܢܒ̈ܝܐ ܠܢܒܝܘܢ ܗܘܘ. ܐܝܟ ܗܠܝܢ ܫܒ̈ܚܬܐ ܐܠܗܐ
ܐܪܡܝܐ ܐܫܟܚܐ ܫܒܚܘܗܝ ܕܢܚܐܠ ܘܟܕ ܐܝܟ ܗܢܐ ܫܒܐ
ܡܢܗܘܢ ܕܗܘ̈ܕܝܐ ܕܢܒܐ ܫܒܚ ܗܘܐ. ܠܐ ܐܬܟܢܫ ܒܝܘܡܐ
ܕܡܠܬܗܘܢ ܘܕܬܪ̈ܬܝܢ ܐܬܥܝܢ ܕܡܢ ܗܝ ܡܕܝܢܬܗܘܢ ܫܒܩ ܐܝܟܢ
ܦܘ ܕܝܢ ܡܠܬܐ ܕܕܡܢܐ ܠܗ ܡܕܡܬܐ ܐܡܪܬ. ܘܐܡܪܬ ܕܐܘܪܫܠܡ
ܗܝ ܡܕܝܢܬܗ. ܠܗ ܒܪ ܡܕܝܢܬܐ ܢܕ ܗܘܐ. ܗܝ ܕܐܡܪܬ ܥܠܝܗ
ܗܠܝܢ. ܕܗܝ ܐܘܪܫܠܡ ܥܠܝܗ ܫܪܬܐ ܗܘ. ܘܦܝ ܐܝܟ ܕܐܘܕܝܢ
ܒܗ ܒܪܬܐ ܡܕܝܢܬܐ. ܘܡܠܠܝܢܢ ܦܘ ܡܦܩܢܘܬܐ ܥܠ ܗܢܐ
ܒܝܬܗ. ܘܗܕܝܢ ܐܢܬ ܒܠܝܗܘܢ ܦܘܪܩܢܐ ܘܦܓܪܐ ܕܢܦܪܐ. ܦܘ ܕܝܢ
ܒܪ ܐܢܕܘܗܝ ܠܟܬܝܒܘܗܝ ܐܬܦܩܪ ܘܬܠܟܘܗܝ ܒܟܪܝܗܘܢ ܐܬܦܩܦ. ܥܠ

ܘܒܒܪ̈ ܫܠܡܐ ܒܗ ܥܠ ܐܢܫ. ܗܘ ܕܐܝܬܘܗܝ ܗܘܐ ܓܒܝܬܐ
ܕܒܝܬܐ ܕܡܥܘܢܐ. ܡܛܠ ܕܐܦ ܥܠ ܟܘܪܣܝܐ ܕܡܫܝܚܘܬܐ ܢܬܒ
ܗܘܐ ܘܢܬܟܬܫ ܘܐܬܢܨܚ ܡܢܗ ܒܬܫܡܫܬܐ ܕܬܘܢ. ܐܦ ܒܟܠܗܘܢ
ܕܥܒܪܘܗܝ، ܐܠܗܐ ܐܝܬܘܗܝ، ܗܘܐ. ܘܠܪܘܚܐ ܕܐܠܗܐ ܥܠ ܒܢܝ̈ܗܘܢ،
ܡܫܘܬܦ ܗܘܐ. ܡܛܠ ܕܒܘܚܪܢܗ ܡܬܚܪܐܝܬ ܐܬܬܠܝܓ ܗܘܐ.
ܐܢܫ ܓܒܪ ܘܐܬܚܠ ܡܫܪܐ ܒܟܬܪܐ ܦܓܐܘܬܐ ܘܢܚܡ ܠܡܠܬܐ
ܕܐܠܗܐ ܢܦܩ ܗܘܐ. ܥܠ ܡܕܡ ܓܒܪ ܕܡܢ ܐܒܗ̈ܘܗܝ، ܐܬܗܡܟ
ܠܗ. ܐܦ ܗܘܐ ܘܠܒܝ̈ܬܐ ܘܠܒܢܝ̈ܢܐ ܘܠܡܩܕܫܐ ܦܠܚ ܗܘܐ. ܗܘ
ܕܡܢ ܒܛܘܪܐ ܡܫܘܚܐ ܕܠܐ ܡܚܝܠܐ ܗܘ. ܘܒܝܘܡܝܐ ܡܥܡܪܢܐ
ܕܦܠܣܛܝܢܐ ܐܠܗܘܬܐ ܡܬܕܒܪ ܗܘܐ. ܢܩܦ ܗܘܐ ܗܫܠ ܡܢ
ܒܬܘ ܡܕܝܢܬܐ ܗܝ ܕܒܗ ܒܡܠܟܘܬܗ ܘܡܕܒܪܢܘܬܗ ܐܚܝܕܐ
ܡܬܪܒܐ ܗܘܐ. ܘܡܛܠ ܕܒܗܘܢ ܘܐܚܝܢ ܠܐܚܐ ܡܫܠܡܢܐ
ܢܦܩ ܗܘܐ. ܚܝ ܡܢ ܢܡܘܣܐ ܐܢܫܝܐ ܘܠܡܠܬܐ ܐܠܗܝܬܐ ܐܝܟ
ܗܘܐ. ܘܐܫܟܚܐ ܚܟܝܡܐ ܕܢܒ̈ܝܐ ܢܦܩ ܗܘܐ ܘܡܕܒܪܢܘܬܐ
ܐܬܡܠܠ ○ ○ ○

ܘܕܬܪܝܢ ܒܬܪܗ ܠܝܘܚܢܢ ܐܬܡܢܝ. ܘܠܗ ܗܘ ܕܒܡܫܒܘܬܐ
ܥܡܠܬܐ ܡܫܡܫ ܗܘܐ. ܒܝܘܡܘܗܝ ܓܝܪ ܗܕܐ ܗܘܐ ܕܒܢܝܐ
ܗܘܕܝܐ ܘܠܐ ܗܘܐ ܒܠܚܘܕ ܗܝܟܠܐ ܡܫܡܫ ܗܘܐ. ܐܠܐ ܐܦ
ܫܘܒܚܐ ܗܘܐ ܕܟ̈ܗܢܐ ܠܘ̈ܐܝܐ ܗܘܝܐ ܓܝܪ ܒܗܝܟܠܐ ܒܡܘܕܝܐ
ܕܟܗ̈ܢܐ ܡܠܐ ܗܘܐ. ܐܝܟܢܐ ܕܠܗܘܢ ܠܟ̈ܗܢܐ ܕܐܠܗܐ ܡܢ
ܒܡܫܒܚܐ ܬܠܐ ܗܘܐ ܠܗܘܢ. ܘܐܝܟ ܗܘ ܕܒܡܫܒܚܝܢ ܒܥܠܡܘܢ
ܟ̈ܗܢܐ ܗܢܝܢ ܗܘܘ. ܘܡܫܒܚܝܢܐ ܕܒܝܬܐ ܕܐܠܗܐ ܐܝܬܘܗܝ،
ܗܘܐ ○ ○ ○

ܘܕܬ̈ܠܬܐ ܡܬܩܪܝܢܐ ܡܬܩܪܐ ܗܘܐ ܒܫܡܗ ܫܠܘܡ. ܒܪ ܐܡܘܨ
ܕܒܪܘܚܐ ܕܐܠܗܐ ܢܒܝܐ ܗܘܐ. ܐܝܬܘܗܝ، ܗܘܐ ܕܝܢ ܡܢ ܡܠܟܐ
ܡܠܟܘܬܐ ܗܘܐ ܗܢܐ ܐܦ ܢܒܝ ܡܕܒܪܢܘܬܗ ܒܡܬܒܪܢܘܬܐ

ܘܡ̈ܠܠܐ ܘܡܕ̈ܪܫܐ ܘܡܫ̈ܪܝܬܐ ܘܡܬܢ̈ܝܬܐ ܐܚܪ̈ܢܐ
ܘܫܘ̈ܒܚܐ ܘܡܬܥ̈ܢܝܢܐ ܒܗ̇ ܡܬܬ̈ܢܝܢܐ ܟܠܗܘܢ ܐܝܟ ܕܗܘ ܚܕ
ܫܡܥܝܢ ܒܟܠ ܡܠܬܐ ܫܘܕܥܐ ܕܐܠܗܐ. ܡܬܒܩܐ ܐܬܘܬ ܐܠܗܘܬܐ.
ܘܡܬܦܪܦܪܐ ܕܫܠܡܐ ܕܒܗܘܢ܆ ܚܕ ܚܕ ܡܢܗܘܢ ܒܡܫܡܫܢܘܬܐ
ܕܥܒ̈ܕܐ ܗܘ. ܘܠܫܘܠܡܐ ܕܡܫܡܠܝܘܬܐ ܥܡܠܬܐ ܒܗ̇ ܕܠܝܐ
ܦܬܚ. ܦܠܐ ܕܝܢ ܕܢܬܕܡܪ ܐܦ ܒܡܢܝܢܗܘܢ ܕܐܢܫܐ ܕܒܕܡܘܬܐ
ܕܢܩܠܐ ܘܕܫ̈ܠܝܚܐ ܐܬܝܗܘܢ ܗܘܘ ܬܪܥܣܪ. ܦܠܐ ܙܕܩ ܕܢܬܗܐ
ܐܦ ܠܐ ܚܠܝܘܬܗܘܢ ܡܫܡܪܬ ܒܠ ܕܚܕ ܚܕ ܡܢܗܘܢ ܒܡܢܝܢܗ.
ܘܬܡܗܐ ܕܒܠ ܒܢ̈ܝܗܘܢ ܘܡܫܡ̈ܫܬܗܘܢ. ܕܠܐ ܡܬܬܐܡܝܢ ܘܫ̈ܦܝܪܗܘܢ
ܕܒܟܠ ܐܢܫܝܢ ܘܡܫܬܠܚܬܐ ܐܠܝܢ ܗܘܘ ܠܗܘ̈ܕܐ ܕܢܟܦܘܢ
ܗܘ ܡܕܡ ܕܟܠܗܘܢ ܡܠܟ ܗܘܐ. ܘܡܢܐ ܡܬܬܟܒܐ ܕܢܐܡܪ
ܒܬ ܩܠܗܘܢ ܐܠܗ̈ܘܬܐ. ܦܘܫ ܕܐܝܟ ܠܐ ܡܕܡ ܫܒܝܚ ܗܘܘ
ܠܗܘܢ ܢܓܕ̈ܐ ܕܡܫܪ̈ܝܘܬܐ ܦܪܘܫܐ ܕܙܘܙ ܗܘܐ. ܥܣ̈ܠܘܗܝ ܕܕܢܚܐ
ܡܥܠܝܢ ܗܘܘ. ܘܒܗܘܢ ܒܢ̈ܝܐ ܚܠܝܨܘܬ ܡܬܚܫܒܝܢ ܗܘܘ. ܘܟܕ
ܬܘܒ ܥܕܠ ܐܢܘܢ ܕܡܢ ܐܡܬܟܐ ܐܬܝܗܘܢ܆ ܥܒܕܘ ܕܢܐܡܪܘܢ
ܒܠ ܡܕܝܢܬܗܘܢ ܕܒܐܪܥܐ. ܘܟܠ ܗܿܝ ܡܕܝܢܬܗܘܢ ܐܢܫܐ
ܕܒܦܪ̈ܣܐ ܐܬܝܗ ܡܬܕܡܝܢ ܗܘܘ ܘܕܐܡܝܢ ܗܿܝ ܐܘܪܫܠܡ ܒܠܝܬܐ
ܕܒܡܟܢܐ ܐܬܝܗܘܢ ܐܡܝܪܝܢ ܗܘܘ. ܘܕܠܗ̇ ܬܘܒ ܡܬܩܪܝܢ
ܗܘܘ ܕܒܐܪܥܐ ܡܬܕܡܝܢ ܗܘܘ. ܘܡܛܠ ܗܠܝܢ ܡܢܐ ܐܬ ܐܬܝܬܐ
ܟܠܗܘܢ ܕܢܚܐ ܘܐܬܓܠܝܬ ܟܠܗܘܢ ܒܢܝ̈ܢܐ ܡܫ̈ܝܚܐ. ܐܝܟ
ܕܢܚܡܪ ܒܗܘܢ ܢܒܝܗ. ܘܟܕ ܡܢ ܗܝܡܢܘ ܢܓܠ ܠܗ ܠܫܢܬܐ ܒܠ
ܚܕ ܡܢܗܘܢ ܕܢܣܒ ܒܠܒܠܐ ܕܒܡܘܬܐ ܦܡܗ. ܘܐܦ ܐܘܩܕܐ ܒܢ
ܕܡܩ̈ܕܫܘܬܗܘܢ ܒܟܠ ܒܗܘ ܐܬܝܗܘܢ ܗܘܘ. ܬܪܝܢ ܒܢ ܡܢܗܘܢ
ܥܡܘܢܐ ܐܬܝܗܘܢ ܗܘܘ. ܘܒܡܒܡܕܒܪܢܘܬܐ ܕܟܕ ܢܘܪܐ ܒܠܫܘܢ
ܒܡܩ̈ܕܫܘܬܗܘܢ ܒܓܒܪܐ. ܘܐܚ̈ܪܢܐ ܡܢܗܘܢ ܠܝܠܝܐ ܕܦܪܘܩ
ܐܬܠܩܘ. ܘܗܘ ܥܒܕܐ ܕܒܬܪܗ ܐܬܬ ܡܫܒܚ ܒܠ. ܘܒܬܪܗ ܕܡܫܝܠܘܬܐ
ܡܢ ܕܗܠܝܢ ܢܘܒ ܥܩܒܠܘ ܒܝ ܐܢܫܐ ܕܒܦܪܣܐ ܝܘܡ ܐܠܗܐ.

ܒܪܚܡܐ ܕܐܠܗܘܬܗ ܐܬܪ̈ܝ، ܗܘܐ. ܘܕܪܫܐ ܡܢ ܗܠܝܢ ܩ̈ܛܝܢܐ
ܫܡܥܬܐ ܘܐܝܟ ܕܒܬܐ ܕܚܝܠܐ ܐܝܬ ܗܘܐ ܠܗ. ܐܦ ܕܝܢ ܒܡܡܘܡܬܐ
ܕܐܠܗܐ ܡܠܝܐ ܗܘܐ. ܐܬܬܘܗ، ܗܘܐ ܕܝܢ ܦܩܘܕܘܗܝ ܒܢܫܗ
ܡܢ ܐܢܫܐ ܪ̈ܘܡܝܐ ܘܒܕܘܟܬܐ ܕܐܬܬܪܗ ܐܝܟ ܕܪ̈ܘܡܝܐ ܐܬܬܕܪ ܐܦ
ܗܠܘܢ ܒܥܘܠܝܐ ܕܦܠܚܘܬܐ ܐܬܬܘܗ، ܗܘܐ. ܘܡܛܠܗܢ
ܒܡܘܡܬܐ ܡܢ ܟܠܐ ܕܟܠܗ ܐܬܬܘܗܝ ܗܘܘ. ܐܦ ܒܒܝܬܗ ܬܘܒ
ܫܝ ܕܡܟܪܡܘܬܐ ܠܗܕܐ ܕܥܘܬܐ ܒܒܝܬܗ ܐܬܬܪܝ، ܗܘܐ.
ܘܕܪܫܪܗ ܗܘ ܕܒܝܬܗ ܕܦܠܚܘܗܝ ܡܬܬܪܝ ܗܘܐ. ܒܝܘܡܐ
ܕܝܢ ܕܐܠܗܐ ܘܡܡܘܕܝܬܗ ܬܘܡܡܬܐ ܐܝܣܝܗ، ܐܬܬܘܗ، ܗܘܐ
ܘܬܬܪܐܝܬ ܐܝܟ ܒܪܐ ܫܡܝܐ ܠܦܠܚܘܗܝ ܒܒܝܬ ܗܘܐ.
ܘܟܠܡܕܡ ܠܡܪܟܒܗ ܕܡܟܐ ܗܘܐ ܘܐܡܢܐ ܐܝܟ ܢܐܡܪ ܒܠ
ܒܢܝܐ ܕܥܠܡܐ ܐܠܐ ܕܕܡܘܬܐ ܡܠܐܟܐ. ܕܒܢܝܐ ܕܒܬܐ
ܐܬܬܘܗ ܗܘܘ. ܘܠܐ ܗܘܐ ܠܒܪ ܡܢ ܥܪ̈ܬܐ ܐܚܪ̈ܢܐ ܐܝܟܐ.
ܒܡܢܝܬܐ ܒܪ ܡܕܢܪ ܗܘܐ ܒܢܘܗܝ ܦܠܚܘܗܝ ܘܠܒܘܫܐ
ܕܡܡܢܝܢܘܬܐ ܘܠܗ ܐܬܬܘܗ، ܗܘܐ. ܘܠܒܘܫܐ ܕܪ̈ܘܡܝܐ ܐܝܬ
ܗܘܐ ܡܢܝܗܘܢ ܐܝܟ̈ܢܐ ܘܒܡܡܘܕܝܬܐ ܘܒܡܡܘܡܪܝܬܐ
ܕܡܫܝܢܘܬܐ ܫܦܝܪܬܐ ܐܦ ܡܢ ܡܕܡ ܥܘܠܡܐ ܕܡܡܘܕܝܬܗ
ܗܠܘܢ ܐܬܬܝܗ ܘܕܢܫܬܪܐ ܡܢ ܥܘܠܝܐ ܕܦܠܚܘܬܐ ܫܠܝܡܐܝܬ
ܦܠܚ. ܘܢܝܫܐ ܕܐܝܣܪܐ ܟܠܗ ܗܠܝܢ ܥܡܘܕܐ ܘܢܘܩܒܐ
ܐܬܬܘܗ ܗܘܘ ܘܡܟܝܠ ܕܡܘܬܐ ܕܟܠܝܠܐ ܐܝܟ ܪܘܚܐ ܕܒܝܬܐ
ܥܠܝܬ ܐܢܫܘܬܐ ܢܦܫܗ. ܘܡܟܝܠ ܗܘܐ ܒܝܬܐ ܬܡܢܝܬܐ
ܕܡܘܕܐ ܗܠܝܢ ܡܠܘܗܝ ܘܐܝܟ ܗܠܝܢ ܦܘܡ ܒܗ ܗܘܐ ܠܗ ܗܘܐ
ܦܬܓܡܐ ܗܘܘ ܒܡܢܝܢܐ. ܒܬܪ ܕܝܢ ܕܒܬܪܗ ܒܢܝܐ ܦܠ ܡܕ̈ܢܝܐ ܕܡܢ
ܡܕ̈ܢܝܐ ܕܠܐ ܕܡܢ ܠܚܕܕܐ ܐܬܩܝܡ. ܩܠܝܬܐ ܘܡܥ̈ܬܐ ܘܕܪ̈ܫܬܐ
ܘܡܬܦ̈ܢܝܬܐ ܘܡܟܢܫܬܐ ܕܫܒܪ ܐܬܪܒܝ ܠܗܘܢ ܒܐܘܡܢܘܬܐ
ܕܡܡܘܪܘܬܐ ܐܬܬܘܗ، ܘܗܘܐ ܗܘܐ ܕܡܘܬܐ ܐܦ ܒܡܘܡܬܐ ܐܝܬ
ܗܘܐ ܫܠܝܡܐ ܐܡܝܢܐ ܘܡܘܬܐ ܘܡܬܐ̈ܪܐ ܒܢ ܒܢ̈ܝ ܫܘܪܐ

ܕܒܗܘܢ ܐܫܬܡܠܝܘ ܒܣܗܕܘܬܐ ܐܢܫܐ ܐܬܩܛܠܘ ܘܫܡܠܝܘܬܐ
ܕܬܟܬܘܫܐ ܗܟܢܐ، ܒܐܘܡܢܘܬܗܘܢ ܫܠܡ ܗܟܕܬܐ ܕܐܠܗܐ
ܗܘܘ. ܗܟܢܐ ܓܝܪ ܐܦ ܗܘ ܕܒܗܘܢ ܪ̈ܘܕܦܐ ܕܐܬܒܚܪ ܐܚܝܢ
ܐܬܚܙܝܘ. ܐܠܐ ܠܐ ܒܟܠ ܐܝܟ ܗܠܝܢ ܕܒܟܠܗܘܢ ܟܠܗܘܢ
ܡܫܬܒܚܝܢ ܐܚܝܢ. ܒܝܘܡ ܕܒܗܘܢ ܡܠܟܘܬ ܒܗܠ ܕܒܗܘܢ ܕܡܬܩܛܠܐ
ܕܦܓ̈ܪܐ ܘܕܡܘܟܐ ܕܢܦܫ̈ܬܐ ܘܬܪܥܝܬܐ ܘܕܚ̈ܡܬܐ ܕܥ̈ܒܕܐ
ܡܬܩܛܠܐ ܕܒܟܘ̈ܪܐ ܡܫܬܠܛܢܘܬܐ ܕܡܕܒܪܢܘܬܐ ܡܫܬܟܠܢܘܬܐ
ܐܪ̈ܟܢܐ. ܡܬܚܙܝܢ ܗܘܘ ܓܝܪ ܟܠܗܘܢ ܟܠܝܠܐ ܘܬ̈ܠܝܠܐ ܡܢ ܗܘܢ
ܐܪ̈ܩܬܐ ܕܒܗܘܢ ܘܐܝܟ ܓܒ̈ܪܐ ܕܐܦ ܦܓܪܗܘܢ ܒܗܘܢ
ܗܘܐ. ܘܦܓܪܗܘܢ ܕܒ̈ܝܫܘܬܗܘܢ ܘܡܟܪ̈ܗܘܢ ܫܠܝܚܝܢ ܗܘܘ.
ܗܘܢ ܕܒܗ ܗܘ ܥܡܐ ܕܢܚܝܒ ܟܠ. ܦܩܕܝܠܘ ܘܦܠܘܬܘ ܕܡܢ
ܡܕܝܢܬܐ ܘܦܠܘܛܘܣ ܘܦܠܘܣܘ ܕܬܪܥܘܬܗ ܡܢ ܐܪܥܐ ܕܦܠܣܛܝܢܐ
ܐܬܘ. ܐܝܬ ܗܘܐ ܒܗܘܢ ܐܦ ܗܘܫܐ ܥܕܡܐ ܕܒܡܕܝܢܬܐ
ܒܡܕܝܢܬܐ ܡܚܝܢ ܗܘܘ. ܘܠܘ ܡܫܡܫܢܐ ܕܒܕܘܟܐ ܕܐܘܪܫܠܡ.
ܘܗܘ ܐܚܪܢܐ ܐܝܟܢܐ ܕܠܫܡܗ ܥܠܝܗ ܗܘܐ. ܬܐܕܘܠܘܣ ܐܝܟ ܗܘܢܐ
ܘܡܠܐ ܐܬܐܗ ܗܘܬ ܐܦ ܡܬܬܒܬܐ ܕܡܬܬܒܗܘܢ. ܘܒܕܘܟܐ
ܬܘܒ ܕܢܦܫܗܘܢ ܡܫܠܡܝܢ ܗܘܘ. ܡܢܗܘܢ ܓܝܪ ܪܚܝܩܐ ܩܪܝܒܐ
ܘܫܟܝܚܐ ܐܝܬ ܗܘܐ ܠܗܘܢ ܒܕܘܟܬ ܬ̈ܠܝܠܐ. ܘܡܢܗܘܢ ܪ̈ܚܝܩܐ
ܒܡܕ̈ܝܢܬܐ ܘܒܩܘ̈ܪܝܐ ܫܠܝܛܐ ܗܢܝܢ ܗܘܘ. ܐܝܬ ܗܘܐ ܒܗܘܢ ܕܝܢ
ܕܐܦ ܒܗܝܡܢܘܬܐ ܐܠܗܝܐ ܥܕܪ ܡܫܟܚܝܢ ܗܘܘ. ܫܠܝܚܘܬܐ ܕܝܢ
ܥܒܝܕܬܐ ܕܟܠܗܘܢ ܡܫܘܕܥܬ ܐܝܬܝܗ ܗܘܬ. ܘܟܕ ܕܡܘܬ
ܥܡܟܐ ܡܢܗܪܢܐ ܕܐܝܡܡܐ ܒܝܘܡ ܒܡܘܬܒܐ ܦܐܘܬܗ ܕܡܪܝ،
ܦܩܕܝܠܘ ܒܡܪܚܘܬܐ ܕܟܠܗܘܢ ܕܢܦܫܐ ܗܘܬ. ܠܐ ܓܝܪ ܡܕܡ
ܐܚܪܝܢ ܗܘܐ ܠܝ ܕܐܫܬܒܩܘܗܝ، ܠܗܘ ܐܠܗܐ ܘܦܠܚܢܐ ܦܩܕܝܠܘ
ܐܠܐ ܐܢ ܕܐܡܪܘܗܝ، ܡܪܝ، ܗܘ ܕܠܡܬܕܘܬܐ ܗ، ܕܒܗ ܢܦܫܐ
ܡܬܕܡܪܝܢ ܒܗ. ܠܐ ܒܪܢܫܐ ܦܪܫ ܗܘܐ. ܘܡܬܬܟܝܢܘܬܐ ܕܡܢ
ܪܘܚܐ ܕܐܠܗܐ ܘܬܒܥܬܐ ܕܢܦܫܐ ܐܠܗܐ ܠܗ ܗܘܐ ܐܝܟ

ܘܕܝܫܘܥ ܥܠ ܨܠܝܒܘܬܗ ܘܥܠ ܩܝܡܬܗ ܡܬܢܒܝܢ ܗܘܘ ܠܗ. ܟ̈ܠ ܢܒܝܘܬܐ ܗ̇ܝ ܕܟܬܒ̈ܐ ܡܟܪܙܝܢ ܗܘܘ ܠܗ. ܘܡܢܗܘܢ ܡܢ ܢܘܪܐ ܗܕܐ ܕܡܬܚܙܝܐ ܡܪܡܙܝܢ ܗܘܘ ܠܗ. ܡܢܗܘܢ ܡܢ ܗܘ ܕܢܚܐ ܡܫܘܬܐ ܡܪܡܙܝܢ ܗܘܘ ܠܗ. ܘܡܢܗܘܢ ܥܠ ܗ̇ܘ ܕܢܚܐ ܕܥܠܡܘܢ ܕ̈ܢܚܐ ܡܟܪܙܝܢ ܗܘܘ ܠܗ. ܡܢܗܘܢ ܒܫ̈ܢܝܐ ܒܒܘܪܐ ܡܣܢܝܢ ܗܘܘ ܠܗ. ܘܡܢܗܘܢ ܕܝܗܘܕ ܒܦܠܚܘܬܐ ܕܐܡܢܐ ܡܦܩܝܢ ܗܘܘ ܠܗ. ܐܝܠܝܢ ܕܟ̈ܠ ܡܚܝܠܐ ܐܝܬܝܗܘܢ ܗܘܘ ܠܘܬܗܘܢ ܕܢܦܩܐ ܦܪܝܩ ܗܘܘ ܠܗ. ܘܐܝܠܝܢ ܕܟ̈ܠ ܗܝܟܠܐ ܐܝܬܝܗܘܢ ܗܘܘ. ܕܐܬ̈ܪܒܝܬܐ ܢܚܘܪ ܡܦܩܝܢ ܗܘܘ ܠܗ. ܗܘ ܕܝܢ ܥܠܝܡܐ ܒܩܘܡܬܗ ܥܒܝܕ ܗܘܐ ܘܡܠܝܐ ܒܚܟܡܬܐ ܘܫܘܦܪܐ ܘܫܠܝܛܐ ܒܦܪܨܘܦܗ. ܘܗܢܐ ܕܗܘܢܐ ܐܝܬܘܗܝ, ܗܘܐ ܒܕܡܘܬ ܕܗܒܠܐ ܟܕ ܚܘܪܐ ܘܢܘܪܐ ܕܩܘܫܬܗ ܢܗܘ, ܗܘܐ ܘܠܒܫ ܡܢ ܫ̈ܢܝܐ ܕܐܒܗܬܐ ܚܒܘܪܐ ܡܘܕܝܢܘܬܗ ܕܟܦܪܘܩ ܐܝܟ ܗܘܐ. ܟܕ ܕܝܢ ܒܝܕܐ ܢܘܪܐ ܐܬܒܪܝ ܗܘܐ ܒܓܘܗ ܚܕ ܐܢܫܐ ܕܡܢ ܫܪܒܬܐ ܕܡܪܝܡ ܐܬܬܘܗܝ, ܗܘܐ. ܘܐܬܦܘܩܕ ܢܦܫܗ ܦܪܝܐ ܗܘܐ. ܘܐܝܟ ܕܒܫܠܡܐ ܕܐܝܬܘܗܝ ܢܦܫܗ ܠܗܕܐ ܡܢܟ ܗܘܐ. ܐܠܐ ܠܐ ܠܝ ܗܘܐ ܒܝܕܥܬܐ ܫܪܝܪܬܐ. ܟܕ ܗܘܐ ܗܘܕܐ ܕܐܠܗܐ ܒܗܘܪܐ ܐܡܪ ܗܘܐ. ܗܢܐ ܕܝܢ ܫܘܕܐ ܡܢܫܐ ܕܐܡܪܢ ܠܒܘܗܝ ܐܬܬܘܗܝ ܗܘܐ ܡܢ ܐܢܐ ܡܢܬܐ ܕܐܬܚܡܬܐ ܕܒܬ ܠܒܪܝܬ ܘܒܗܢܐ ܫܘܠܡܐ ܕܐܡܪܢ ܒܐܠܗܘܬܐ ܕܝܕܘܥܬܐ ܫܒܝܚܬܐ ܕܗܘܕܐ ܕܡܫܝܚܐ ܐܬܬܠܒܫ ܘܐܬܟܠܠ . . . .

ܡܘܕܝܢܘܬܐ ܕܐܣܛܦܢܘܣ ܘܕܦܘܠܘܣ. ܘܕܝܘܚܢܢ ܘܕܦܘܠܘܣ.
ܘܕܦܛܪܘܣ ܘܕܬܐܘܡܐ ܘܕܡܬܝ. ܘܕܐܢܕܪܐܘܣ ܚܕ ܕܗܘܐ
ܒܡܫܝܚܐ ܬܠܡܝܕܐ ܒܫܢܬ ܫܒܥ ܕܕܪܘܡܝܐ ܕܒܝܫܬܐ.

ܟܬܪ ܗܠܝܢ ܡܫܠ ܚܕܢܐ ܦܢܐ ܠ ܕܢܬܐ ܢܟܬܐ ܕܐܬܟܪܬܐ ܢܬܒܐ ܕܡܘܕܝܢܘܬܐ ܗܕܐ ܦܪܫ ܒܡܠ. ܘܦܪܫܘܢ ܐܝܠܝܢ

ܘܪܙܐ ܕܡܫܠܡܢܘܬܐ ܠܡܕܒܪܢܘܬܐ ܘܡܫܪܝܬܐ ܕܢܘܟܠܘܢ ܘܡܛܠ ܐܢܘܢ
ܡܬܬܘ ܡܢ ܐܬܪܗܘܢ ܐܘܪܚܐ ܘܡܘܡ ܕܢܐ ܐܝܟ ܕܠܟܒܪ، ܒܟܬܒܐ
ܦܪܘܫܐ ܐܢܘܢ ܡܕܡܘܬ، ܢܦܩ، ܠܦܬܟܐ ܕܝܢ ܕܡܬܕܒܪܢܘܬܐ ܐܢܫܐ
ܟܪܟܐ ܐܬܚܙܝܘܢ ܗܘܘ. ܕܠܗܠܝܢ ܗܕܪܐ ܠܟܢܫ ܗܘܘ. ܘܡܕܡ
ܦܘܠܚܢܗ ܡܬܚܙܐ ܐܟܠܘ ܐܢܘܢ: ܘܡܛܠ ܕܡܕܒܠ ܥܠ ܟܢܫܐ
ܕܠܦܠܓܘܬܐ ܐܬܚܙܝ، ܗܘܐ. ܘܡܕܡ ܟܪܝܐ ܡܟܐ ܗܘܝܐ ܒܠܝܢܘܢ:
ܘܥܠ ܡܟܝܢܘܢ ܗܘܝܐ ܕܟܢܫܢܘܢ ܘܦܠܚܝܢܘܢ ܟܢܘܫܐ ܘܦܪܫܐ
ܠܬܒܥܠܘܢ: ܘܡܟܝܢܘܢ ܠܡܗܘܬܐ ܕܗܘܫܐ ܢܬܦܠܚܘܢ: ܚܕ
ܡܟܝܢܘܢ ܕܝܢ ܗܘ ܕܐܪܗ ܥܒܕ ܗܘܐ. ܟܢܘܫܐ ܚܪܝܬܐ
ܡܗܝܡܢܘܬܗ ܐܬܦܬܠܬ. ܘܦܪܫܡܗ ܘܡܠܟܐ ܟܡܘܫܐ ܪܒܘܢ
ܐܬܦܫܘܡ. . . .

ܡܗܝܡܢܘܬܐ ܕܦܠܪܘܣ ܗܘ ܕܡܬܩܪܐ ܗܘܐ ܒܥܠܡܐ. ܟܕ ܥܫܝܢ
ܥܣܪ ܕܪܘܡܝܐ ܕܟܢܘܫܝܬܐ ܕܡܫܘܪܝܐ ܡܗܝܡܢܬܐ . . .

ܟܘܡܪܐ ܟܘܪܬܐ ܟܢܝܫ ܒܝܘܡ ܐܝܟ، ܦܠܪܘܣ ܗܘ ܕܡܬܩܪܐ
ܗܘܐ ܒܥܠܡܐ ܡܗܝܡܢܐ ܕܝܢܐ ܕܡܠܟܘܬܗ ܕܐܠܗܐ ܐܬܚܙܝ،
ܗܘܐ. ܘܡܟܝܢܐ ܐܦ ܒܬܚܬܝܗ ܕܢܠܗ ܦܠܓܘܬܐ ܕܐܠܗܐ
ܐܬܦܟܪ. ܘܡܟܝܢܐ ܐܬܚܙܝ ܒܐܦܘܝܐ ܕܡܗܝܡܢܘܬܗ. ܐܝܟܢܐ
ܕܐܦ ܠܗ ܠܕܝܢܐ ܒܬܘܪܐ ܢܡܟܝܢܘܗ، ܘܠܦܘܢ ܕܥܠ ܦܟܗ
ܦܩܚ ܗܘܐ ܙܘܟܝܬܗ ܐܬܡܟܗ ܗܘܐ. ܘܦܠܓ ܕܝܢ ܐܬܒܟܡܘ ܠܗ
ܕܥܠ ܢܟܡܗ ܢܟܡܗ. ܘܟܟܕ ܚܘܝܐ ܥܠ ܦܘܡܟܗ. ܘܡܢ ܒܢܬܐ
ܕܥܠܘܗ، ܦܩܚ ܗܘ، ܢܬܦܘܪܟ. ܘܥܠ ܥܠܝܢ ܬܟܠܝܢܘܢ ܪܟܝܢܗ
ܡܗܝܡܢܐ ܗܘܐ. ܘܦܝܘܢ ܕܠܗ ܚܕܝܢ ܗܘܘ. ܠܐ ܥܠܝܡܕ ܚܘܡܗ،.
ܐܠܐ ܐܦ ܐܠܝܢ ܕܠܐ ܚܕܝܢ ܗܘܘ ܠܗ ܡܦܝܣ ܗܘܘ ܥܠܘܗ،. ܘܚܕ
ܚܕ ܡܟܝܢܘܢ ܐܝܟ ܕܠܫܢܐ ܕܢܦܫܗܘܢ ܡܟܢܗ ܟܟܝܢ ܗܘܘ. ܘܠܗ
ܠܦܘܡܢܐ ܡܬܟܦܝܢ ܗܘܘ. ܘܡܟܝܢܘܢ ܠܝܟܢܗ ܗܘ ܦܠܟܐ ܡܟܫܠܝܢ
ܗܘܘ. ܘܡܟܝܢܘܢ ܪܗܘܬܐ ܒܬܟܠܝܢܘܢ ܥܠܘܗ، ܡܟܠܝܢ ܗܘܘ.

ܐܝܠܝܢ ܕܒܡܫܡܫܢܘܬܗܘܢ ܢܨܚܝܢ ܗܘܘ ܠܗ ܟܠ ܗܠܝܢ. ܕܚܫ̈ܝܡܘܗܝ ܒܢܝ ܗܘܘ. ܚܡܬܐ ܘܡܪܝܪܘܬܐ ܪܟܝܟܘܬܐ ܡܚܠܬ ܐܢܘܢ. ܘܢܟܦܐ ܗܘܬ ܠܒܪ ܡܢ ܬܪܥܝܬܗ ܕܡܫܝܚܝܘܬܐ ܫܝܢܬܐ ܕܫܠܝܘܬܐ ܦܓ̈ܪܐ ܕܟ̈ܢܫܐ ܐܢܫܐ ܟܕ ܡܬܐܟܠܝܢ ܡܢ ܚܣܡܐ. ܟܕ ܕܝܢ ܢܩܦܬܐ ܦ̈ܠܓܘܬܐ ܒܗܘܢܐ ܐܣܟܡܐ ܗܠܝܢ ܗܘܝܢ ܗܘܘ. ܬܕܡܘܪܬܐ ܐܚܪܬܐ ܕܠܐ ܡܬܡܫܡܠܢܐ ܥܠܗ ܡܫܝܚܝܘܬܐ ܒܟܠܗ. ܢܣܒܐ ܗܘܬ ܓܝܪ ܡܪܬܐ ܦܪܝܫ ܗܘܬ. ܘܡܢ ܥܠܝܐ ܘܦܓܥܘܗܝ ܕܐܦܣܩܘ̈ܦܐ ܕܡܫܝܚܝܘܬܐ ܟܐܘܣܛܡܘܢܐ ܕܕܝܘܢܐ ܐܝܟ ܢܘܦܬܐ ܚܫܝܟ ܗܘܘ. ܘܥܘܡܩܐ ܘܩܠܝܠܘܬܐ ܐܝܟ ܕܥܡ̈ܡܐ ܐܙܕܠܝܒܘ ܘܐܬܦܠܓܘ ܟܕ ܐܦ ܠܐ ܚܕܐ ܢܘܦܬܐ ܡܢ ܥܡܡܐ ܢܛܪܬ ܗܘܬ ܘܫܘܡܠܝܐ ܕܟܠ ܐܢܫ ܗܕܐ ܡܬܡܠܠܐ ܗܘܬ. ܕܟܘ̈ܡܪܐ ܕܗܟܢ ܘܐܦܪܝܐ ܟܦܬ. ܟܘ̈ܡܪܐ ܠܒܪ ܕܠܐ ܢ̈ܡܘܣܐ ܘܡܪܟܐ ܕܠܐ ܫܒܐ ܚܕܒܐ ܠܬܐܘܡܐ ܘܡܪܝܪܬܐ ܠܐ ܗܘܝܪܬ. ܘܕܟܐ ܗܘ ܕܡܢ ܟܘ̈ܡܪܐ ܕܒܐ ܗܘܬ ܘܡܪܟܐ ܕܠܐ ܡܛܪܐ ܡܢ ܟܘܫܟܫ ܒܕܒܘܬ ܕܥܕ̈ܬܐ ܚܣܝܐ ܗܘܬ. ܘܠܟܠܗܘܢ ܗ̇ܢܘܢ ܕܕܠܐ ܐܠܗܐ ܠܗܘܢ ܡܚܫܒܐ ܗܘܬ. ܘܟܕ ܡܬܚܫܒܐ ܠܗ̇ܢܘܢ ܕܠܐ ܗܘܐ ܟܚܢ̈ܫܘܢ ܒܢܘ ܗܠܝܢ ܕܟܬܒ. ܕܗܟܢ ܕܗܠܝܢ ܕܐܬܟܬܒ ܕܫܒܚܬܐ ܗ̇ܝ ܕܢܘܗܪܐ ܠܐܪ̈ܥܐ ܗ̇ܘ. ܐܠܐ ܠܗ̇ܢܘܢ ܐܝܠܝܢ ܕܒܗ ܒܪܟܬܐ ܡܢܚܝܢ ܗܘܘ ܫܪܪܗ ܕܗܘܠܐ ܡܛܠ ܕܐܬܟܬܒ ܐܬܒܢܝ. ܕܚܠܘܢ ܡܢܚܝܢ ܐܢܘܢ ܐܦ ܒܕܡܐ ܠܗܘܡܢܐ. ܗܘܐ ܗܘܟܠ ܫܘܠܛܢܐ ܗܘܐ ܒܦܘ̈ܩܕܐ ܡܕܢ̈ܚܐ ܕܐܠܗܐ ܐܝܠܝܢ ܕܐܬܦܢܝܘܢ ܘܬܬܘ̈ܫܡܫܘܢ ܕܠܗܘܟܠ ܦܠܚܘܬܐ ܡܢ ܟܢܝܫܢ ܐܬܗܕܪܘ. . . .

ܡܕܒܪܢܘܬܐ ܕܐܢܘܫ ܘܕܣܡܝܘܗܝ ܘܕܐܠܗܐ. ܒܫܢܬ ܬ̈ܫ ܕܕܘܟܣܐ ܕܫܢ̈ܘܬܗ ܟܐܫܠܡܘ.

ܒܬܪ ܗܢܘ ܡܕܡ ܟܐܪܩܘܬܐ ܟܕ ܡܬܠ ܒܝܘܡܐ ܗܘܐ ܡܪܩܐ ܕܐܠܗܐ ܐܬܦܠܓܐ ܡܢ ܬܪ̈ܥܝܬܐ ܕܡܫܝܚܝܘܬܐ ܐܫܠܡܘ ܐܬܠܒܫܘ. ܘܡܠܠ ܕܐܫܬܠܡ ܕܡܢ ܐܢܘܢ ܘܡܕܝܢܬ ܕܩܘܣܛܢܛܝܢܐ

ܡܪܢ̇ܐ. ܓܠܝܬܐ ܕܡܫܚܬܐ ܘܫܠܝܚܘܬܐ ܕܡܢ ܟܠܡ ܡܕܒܪܢܘܬܐ ܐܬܐܬ
ܗܘܬ. ܠܐ ܗܘܐ ܕܝܢ ܗܘܒܪ̈ܝܣܘܗܝ ܕܦܐܘ ܕܒܥܡܗܘܢ ܐܘܕܝܬ
ܗܪܢܬ. ܡܛܠ ܕܣܦܠܝܪܐ ܡܢ ܟܠܡ ܐܬܘܬܦ ܘܓܒܪܐ ܘܩܪ̈ܒܐ
ܡܠܟܐ ܗܦܟܬ. ܡܢ ܕܢܟܐ ܡܕܡ ܕܐܬܬܣܝܒ. ܫܕ ܕܝܢ ܡܢ ܦܘܠܘܣ
ܕܡܫܡܫ ܗܘܐ. ܥܠ ܚܘܒܐ ܕܡܕܒܪܢܘܬܐ ܐܬܘܗܝ ܗܘܐ ܡܦܪܢܣܐ
ܕܡܫܬܐ ܘܚܝܠܗ ܗܘܐ ܡܟܣܘܣ ܘܕܟܝܢ ܗܘ ܡܢ ܚܝܠܗ ܠܘܬ ܟܠ
ܐܢܫ ܡܫܕܪ ܗܘܐ. ܘܠܐ ܠܗ ܓܘܢܚܝܬܐ ܐܫܟܚ ܗܘܐ. ܘܡܢ
ܡܫܩܠܗ ܘܠܬܘܬ ܟܠܝܗ ܡܚܣܝܐ ܗܘܬ. ܐܝܟ ܕܟܢܫܪܐ
ܕܗܘܪܡܙ ܟܢܝܫܗܘܢ ܢܦܫ̈ܬܐ ܢܬܚܘܐ ܘܟܠܠܗ ܡܕܒܪܢܘܬܐ ܟܕ
ܟܪ̈ܝܗܐ ܡܓܒ̈ܪܐ ܗܘܬ ܡܫܪܝܐ ܗܘܐ ܠܗ. ܗܘܝܢ ܠܟܫ ܕܗܓܡܘܢܐ
ܦܪܣܐ. ܘܬܡܢ ܟܪ̈ܣܘܣܐ ܣܡ ܡܫܟܢܘܬܗ ܕܒܪܘܓܝܘܬܐ ܗܘ̇.
ܐܘܕܝܬ. ܘܫܠܝܚܘܬܗ ܘܡܫܡܫܢܘܬܗ ܠܘܩܒܠ ܟܠ ܕܢܩܘܦ ܕܒܢ̈ܝܐ
ܬܡܢ ܢܘܝܬ ܘܕܡܘܝܐ ܬܐܡܪ ܡܢ ܗܓܡܘܢܐ ܐܫܬܠܛܬ. ܗܘ ܕܝܢ
ܗܢܐ ܕܢܟܐ ܟܠ ܡܐܡ ܟܘܡܪ ܟܠ ܡܫܘܬܗ ܡܚܘܒܐ ܗܘܐ. ܘܠܐ
ܡܪܫܡܢܘܬܗ ܘܡܟܪܙܢܘܬܗ ܡܚܘܝܐ ܗܘܐ. ܘܠܒܪ ܡܢ ܢܟܣ̈ܘܗܝ
ܕܟܢܫܐ ܡܬܕܒܪ ܗܘܐ ܗܢܝܐ ܕܐܝܟ ܟܠ ܩܠܝܠܐ ܕܠܐ ܢܟܫܐ
ܕܩܘܦܠܝܐ ܢܫܡ ܗܘܐ ܘܡܬܠܒܫ. ܐܝܟ ܕܠܐ ܢܬܡܪܩ̈ ܘܕܠܗ
ܬܘܒ ܕܗܕܐ ܓܠܝܬܐ ܕܐܬܬܟܬܒܬ ܕܦܘܠܘܣ ܕܟܗ ܟܢܘܫܝܐ
ܟܡܕܢܘܬܐ ܐܫܬܘܕܝܘ ܓܙ̈ܝܪܘܗܝ ܡܫܬܐ ܕܢܬܐܡܠܘܢ ܡܢ
ܫܘܬܐ ܐܬܩܢܪ ܘܕܢܬܦܠܪܘܢ ܟܦܠܐܢܬ ܟܠܠܐ ܘܟܐܢܫܝܢܐ
ܐܝܟ ܕܡܢ ܦܠܢܐ ܢܬܐܟܠܘܢ ܢܦܘܪܐ ܕܝܢ ܡܢ ܪܘܫܡܐ ܠܗܘܢܐ
ܗܘܕܝܐ ܒܪܒܢܐ ܡܥܠܡܝܢ ܗܘܘ. ܘܕܠܐ ܢܬܓܠܒܘܢ ܡܢܝܢ
ܦܓ̈ܪܝܗܘܢ ܕܡܘܕܝܢܐ ܡܪܕܦܝܢ ܗܘܘ. ܫܘܬܐ ܗܟܝܠ ܕܒܢ̈ܐ
ܘܩܠܝܠܐ ܐܦ ܦܘܫܬܐ ܕܥܡܟܐ ܒܗܘܪܐ ܕܒ̈ܢܝ ܐܢܫܐ ܠܟܐ ܘܠܗܠ
ܡܬܢܚܡ ܗܘܘ. ܐܡܝܢܐ ܕܐܦ ܦܓܡܗ ܕܡܕܒܪܢܘܬܐ ܓܒ̈ܪܐ ܦܓ̈ܫܐ
ܕܒ̈ܢܝ ܐܢܫܐ ܐܫܬܡܥܘ. ܘܟܠ ܐܢܫ ܟܠ ܗܠܝܢ ܐܟܠܐ ܠܟܫ
ܗܘܐ. ܕܠܐ ܡܢ ܡܟܣܬ ܐܝܟ ܗܠܝܢ ܟܢܘܫܬܐ ܐܬܦܪܢܣ ܗܘ̇. ܐܦ

ܐܬܝܗܘܢ ܗܘܘ. ܘܕܘܒܪܗ ܗܘ ܕܝܢ ܫܠܝܐ ܕܐܘܪ̈ܫܠܡܝܐ ܐܬܘܗܝ،
ܗܘܐ. ܘܟܠ ܗܠܝܢ ܕܝܗܒ ܠܠܩܘܪܝܛܐ ܕܡܕܝܢܬܐ ܘܠܐܘܪܬܘܪܘܣ
ܘܠܐܟܣܢܝ̈ܐ ܡܫܡܫܝܢ ܗܘܘ. ܐܝܟܢܐ ܕܫܠܝܡܬ ܗܝ ܡܕܡ
ܕܡܢ ܟܢܫ ܫܬܪܐ ܢܦܠ ܢܝܚܘܢ. ܘܟܠܗܘܢ ܩܕ̈ܝܫܐ ܕܡܢ ܩܢܘܡܗܘܢ
ܘܩܢ̈ܝܢܗܘܢ ܘܚܪ̈ܝܫܘܬܗܘܢ ܐܦ ܟܠܗܐ ܕܥܠ ܦܬ̈ܘܪܐ ܢܬܩܢܘܢ ܘܢܫܡܫܘܢ
ܠܬܘܒܐ ܘܕܐܟܠܝܗܘܢ ܐܝܟ ܕܐܦ ܡܫܡܫܢ ܕܩܕ̈ܝܫܐ ܢܐܟܠܘܢ.
ܘܟܠ ܡܕܡ ܕܡܬܝܗܒ ܒܡܘܗܒܐ ܐܬܩܢ ܕܢܬܦܠܓ ܡܢ ܢܦܫܗ. ܘܡܢ
ܗܘ ܕܝܗܒ ܕܩܕ̈ܝܫܐ. ܐܦ ܗܠܝܢ ܗܟܢ ܗܘܢܐ ܡܬܬܕܒܪܝܢ ܗܘܘ ܐܦ
ܠܐ ܚܣܝܪܐ ܗܘܐ ܕܠܐ ܗܡܝܡܢܘܬܐ ܐܬܝܗܘܢ ܗܘܘ. ܗܘܘ ܕܝܢ
ܕܐܝܠܝܢ ܕܗܘ ܗܘ ܐܬܚܙܝܘ ܘܘܘ

ܡܫܬܘܕܥܐ ܗܟܝܠ ܕܗܘܐ ܘܕܠܘܬܐ ܕܐܢܫܘܬܗ ܐܝܠܐ ܡܫܬܡܠܝܐ
ܗܘܐ. ܘܟܠܗܘܢ ܗܠܝܢ ܕܡܢ ܟܠ ܕܘܟܐ ܐܝܟ ܗܘܐ. ܘܢܦ̈ܫܬܐ
ܕܟܠ ܐܢܫ ܒܐܘܠܨܢܐ ܘܫܘܬܦܐ ܦܝܫܝܢ ܗܘܘ. ܐܠܐ ܫܠܝܐ
ܐܠܗܐ ܡܛܠ ܗܠܝܢ ܕܝܗܒ ܗܘ. ܠܡܣܟܢܘܬܐ ܠܦܘܩܢ ܕܐܠܗܐ
ܐܬܝܗܘܢ ܗܘܘ ܢܦܩ ܗܘܐ. ܐܝܟ ܕܢܘܦܩܘܢ ܠܡܣܟ̈ܢܝܗܘܢ
ܕܕܝܢܐ ܘܠܐܟܣܢܝ̈ܗܘܢ ܢܬܦܪܢܘܢ. ܘܘܘ

ܐܝܟܐ ܕܝܢ ܩܠܝܠܐ ܡܢ ܚܝܠܐ ܕܡܫܝܚܐ. ܕܡܫܬܘܕܥܐ ܕܫܪܝܪܐ
ܠܡܣܟܢ ܗܘܘ. ܐܦ ܡܫܪܪܬܐ ܕܐܠܗܐ ܢܦܫܗܘܢ ܡܚܝܠܐ ܗܘܬ.
ܘܦܝܫܘܢ ܠܢܦܫܗܘܢ ܐܝܟܘ. ܘܟܕ ܡܬܦܪܣܐ ܠܬܠܡܝܕ̈ܐ ܒܡܫܡܫܬܗ
ܕܡܬܕܒܪܬܐ ܡܫܡܫܐ ܗܘܐ. ܡܢ ܥܠܡܐ ܥܒܪܘ ܟܠܗܘܢ ܘܕܚܝܠܐ ܡܢ
ܦܓܪܐ ܡܢܗ ܟܠܗܘܢ. ܠܝܬ ܠܡ ܓܒܪ ܐܢܫܐ ܠܒܪ ܡܢ ܚܕ ܐܠܗܐ
ܒܒܪܐ ܘܒܪܘܚܐ ܕܩܘܕܫ. ܘܟܕ ܐܫܬܐܠܘ ܕܡܢ ܐܝܟܢ ܐܘܕܥܘ
ܕܡܫܝܚܐ ܐܬܝܗܘܢ. ܘܡܚܕܐ ܕܡܬܠܡܕܝܢ ܓܒܪ ܕܢܨܐ ܕܡܫܬܐ
ܡܛܠ ܗܘܘ. ܘܕܠܝܠܝܐ ܕܠܐ ܒܩܕܡ ܠܗܘܢ ܗܘ ܕܐܘܕܥܘ ܒܗ
ܐܪܙܐ. ܘܡܫܡܫܝܢ ܓܒܪ ܥܡܗܘܢ ܗܘܐ ܐܝܟܢܫܘܬܐ ܒܚܝܪܝܬܐ
ܡܬܦܪܥܐ ܗܘܐ ܒܚܝܠܐ. ܘܥܡܗܘܢ ܕܝܢ ܕܠܬܐ ܓܒܪܢܘܬܗܘܢ
ܘܬܠܬܡܢܝܢ ܕܝܢܐ ܬܪܝܢ ܐܚܪܢ، ܗܠܝܢ ܐܬܚܙܝ ܗܘ. ܘܘܘܘ
ܗܘܬ ܠܗܘܢ ܕܝܢ ܒܪܬ ܠܡܫܬܐ ܒܗ ܒܡܫܬܐ ܫܬܐ ܒܬܠܬ

ܕܠܐ ܡܕܒܪܬܐ ܐܬܬܣܝܡܘܢ ܗܘܘ. ܐܝܟ ܕܢܬܚܫܒܘܢ ܠܡܕܒܪܬܐ ܕܥܒܪܐ ܡܝܠܐ ܗܘܬ. ܐܦ ܡܢ ܗܢܘܢ ܕܥܕܡܐ ܗܘܘ ܠܗ ܠܐ ܐܡܪܢ. ܐܦ ܒܠܒܗܘܢ ܝܠܝ. ܐܘ ܠܡܣܬܟܠܘܬܐ ܕܠܐ ܡܬܡܠܠܐ. ܕܐܦ ܫܠܛ ܗܘ ܕܗܢܐ ܕܡܬܚܙܐ ܒܪ ܒܠܒܗ. ܘܫܠܛ ܒܠܒܗܘܢ ܡܕܒܪܢܘܬܐ ܕܟܠ ܕܘܟܐ ܡܝܠܐ ܗܘܬ. ܘܠܐ ܒܠܒܗ ܫܠܛ ܗܘܐ ܐܠܐ ܐܦ ܫܠܛ ܗܘ ܡܡܠܠܘܬܐ ܕܪܘܚ ܩܘܕܫܐ ܡܢܗ. ܘܟܕ ܡܢ ܐܠܗܐ ܟܠܗ ܗܘܬ. ܡܡܠܠܘܬܐ ܒܐܪ̈ܚܬܗܘܢ ܕܫܡܥܢ ܗܘܘ. ܟܕ ܒܠܒܗܘܢ ܡܝܠܐ ܗܘܬ. ܘܕܠܐ ܫܚܩܐ ܠܗܘܢ ܐܠܗܐ ܡܕܡ ܕܒܥܘ ܒܗ ܡܬܟܫܦܝܢ ܗܘܘ. ܘܟܕ ܫܠܛ ܥܠ ܐܝܟ ܒܥܕܢ ܟܠܐ ܫܠܝܛܐ ܡܝܠܐ ܗܘܬ ܠܟܠܗ ܒܢܝܢܐ ܕܥܘܠܐ ܕܣܥܪ̈ܘܗܝ. ܦܐܝܐ ܗܘܬ ܠܣܥܘܪܬܐ ܘܠܕܒܪܢܐ ܐܝܟ ܗܘܬ. ܘܡܕܡ ܗܘ ܒܝܬܘܗ ܡܫܬܡܫ ܐܝܟ ܘܡܠܟ ܥܡܠ ܕܡܢ ܚܝܠܐ ܢܦܫܗ. ܘܡܫܡܫܢܐ ܘܥܕܪܝܢ ܒܟܠܗܘܢ ܢܕܒܐ ܬܫܡܫܬܗ ܕܗܘܐ ܘܟܠܐ ܐܝܟ ܕܐܬܟܠܢ.

ܡܕܒܪܢܘܬܐ ܕܐܦܝܣܩܘܦܘܬܗ ܘܕܘܒܪܗ ܘܕܘ̈ܒܪܘܗܝ ܘܕܡܫܝܚܘܬܗ.
ܕܒܝܬ ܡ̈ܪܝ ܪܒܘܠܐ ܕܫܠܝܚܘܬܗ ܒܡܫܝܚܐ.

ܘܟܕ ܕܝܢ ܐܬܟܢܫ ܐܦܝܣܩܘܦܐ ܒܟܕ ܗܘܐ ܡܢ ܒܬܪ ܗܠܝܢ ܕܐܬܡܛܝ ܬܘܒ ܡܢ ܐܝܟܢܐ ܕܐܬܟܬܒܘ ܗܕܐ ܐܘܪܚܐ ܕܬܪܝܢ ܕܗܕ̈ܪܐ ܕܐܠܗܐ ܕܐܬܬܣܝܡܘ ܗܘܘ ܡܟܐ ܘܬܠܬܝܢ ܒܡܫܝܚܐ ܠܐܬܪ̈ܢ ܐܬܕܪܘ ܘܬܘܒ ܐܦ ܗܠܝܢ ܒܠܒܗܘܢ ܦܝܘܢ ܚܫ̈ܐ ܕܗܕ̈ܪܐ ܕܡܬܡܢܘܢ ܒܒܢܝܢܗܘܢ ܘܒܬܠܝܢܗܘܢ ܗܒܪܘ ܘܗܕܝܢ ܡܢܗܘܢ ܠܡܠܠܘܢ ܕܒܠܗܦܝܢܐ ܐܬܕܪܘ ܘܡܢܗܘܢ ܠܦܘܝܢ ܕܬܝܒܐ ܕܒܠܒܗܘܢ ܐܝܟ ܕܢܬܕܪܘܢ ܒܫܘܒܚܐ ܕܟܫܝܪܘܬܐ ܘܡܬܒܪܐ ܐܬܬܠܒܘ ܗܘܘ. ܒܗܠܝܢ ܕܝܢ ܡܢ ܥܠܠ ܒܥܠܬܗ ܕܪܘܒܘܠܐ ܘܡܢ ܕܒܬܐ ܕܗܕ̈ܪܐ ܡ̈ܕܥܐ ܗܘܘ ܗܢܐ ܘܫܥܬܐ ܒܟܢܘܫܬܐ ܘܥܠܬܐ ܠܪܘܒܘܠܐ ܕܒܢ̈ܝܡܘܬ ܝܗܒ ܗܘܬ ܘܐܬܚܫܒܬ ܡܫܘܚܬܐ ܕܐܠܗܐ ܒܠ ܡܬܟܫܦܝܢܘ ܦܪܘܫܐ ܒܟܠܗ ܐܬܕܪܬ ܕܒܠܗܘܢ ܒܢ̈ܝܐ ܕܡܕܒܪܢܘܬܐ ܡܫܝܢܐ ܘܡܫܬܟܚܢܐ ܫܪܝܪܐ ܘܡܬܟܪ̈ܝܢܐ ܕܐܬܬܪ̈ܘܬܐ

ܫܠܝܚܘܬܐ ܕܪܒܢܢ ܝܫܘܥ ܘܡܟܝܟܘܬܗ ܠܟܠܬܐ ܕܢܟܠܗ ܘܐܘܡܘܬܒܟ ܘܠܘܩܒܠ ܕܟܠ ܡܢܗ ܕܠܡܐ ܗܘܬ ܒܕܘܟܬ. ܗܘ ܕܝܢ ܡܫܡܫܢܐ ܡܛܠ ܗܠܝܢ ܒܥܠܕܒܒܝܢ ܕܟܒܫܬ ܕܠܐ ܕܫܠܝܐ. ܫܡܥܬܗ ܐܝܟ ܕܫܡܥܬ ܥܢܐ ܐܪܕܡܥܬ. ܘܟܡܘ̈ܪܐ ܕܢܬܢܝܚܘܢ ܒܗ ܕܠܐ ܕ̈ܫܡܥܝܢ ܩܕܡ ܗܘܐ ܐܡܢܐ ܕܡܟܬܒܢܘܬ ܚܕ ܡܢ ܒ̈ܢܝ ܐܢܫܐ ܠܐ ܐܫܬܘܕܝ ܗܟܢܐ. ܘܗܟܢ ܐܢܐ ܕܐܠܘ ܡܟܬܒܢܐ ܗܘܝܬ ܕܬܗܘܐ ܡܢ ܒܗܘܢ ܕܛܠܝܘܬܐ ܐܟܠ ܗܘܐ. ܘܟܕ ܥܢܘܬܗ ܒܫܘܬܐ ܕܕܡܥܐ ܗܘܟܢܬ. ܘܟܒܕܐ ܘܒܡܠܬܐ ܝܠܦ ܕܐܡܪ ܗܘ ܒܝܠܐ ܐܠܗܐ ܗܘ ܕܠܐ ܡܬܕܟܐ. ܗܘ ܕܐܦ ܠܛܠܝܘܬܐ ܕܟܘܪ̈ܗܬܐ ܒܫܠܝܘܬܐ ܕܡܬܒܪܘܬܐ ܡܚܝܢ ܘܡܫܠ ܗܕܝܢ ܠܬܐܘܕܘܣܝܣ ܛܠܝܘܬܐ ܠܫܘܬܐ ܘܠܐܦܝܣܩܘܦܐ ܫܘܐܫܬ ܒܝܢ ܘܡܗܘܬܐ ܕܟܢܫ ܢܘܪܐ ܒܠܫܢ ܦܫܡ. ܥܡܗ ܕܝܢ ܕܡܬܡܚܝܬܐ ܐܝܬܘܗܝ ܗܘܐ ܫܘܬܐ. ܘܟܕ ܐܟܡܐ ܒܐܪܟܐ ܙܒܢܐ ܐܝܬܘܗܝ ܗܘܐ. ܘܗܘ ܐܫܬܪܝ ܡܢ ܡܫܪܝܐ ܡܟܪܣܬ ܐܝܟܐ ܕܐܦ ܠܡܠܟ̈ܘܬܐ ܐܚܪ̈ܢܐ ܘܥܡܗ ܘܠܐܦܝܣܩܘܦܐ ܘ.ܘ.ܘ.ܘ.

ܡܢ ܒܬܪ ܗܠܝܢ ܕܝܢ ܒܫܘܠܡܗ ܡܘܕܝܢܐ ܠܐܦܝܣܩܘܦܐ ܐܬܦܢܝ. ܘܫܠܝܛܘܬ ܐܦ ܗܢܐ ܐܬܟܬܫ. ܘܟܕ ܥܒܕܬܐ ܡܢ ܕܢܚܐ ܒܥܠܡܐ ܐܬܝܩܪ. ܕܢܬܓܠܠ ܡܓܙܪ ܕܒܢܐ ܕܗܘܦܐ ܕܥܒܠ ܙܥܝܐ ܡܓܠ. ܘܟܕ ܕܝܢ ܠܕܘܟܬܐ ܗܝ ܕܒܗܘܢܐ ܕܦܠܟܢܐ ܬܟܡ ܡܟܦܐ ܗܘܐ. ܡܢ ܡܦܠܚܢܐ ܗܘ ܕܢܨܗ ܥܒܠ ܗܘܐ. ܟܕ ܗܘܐ ܕܒܢܐ ܗܠܝܢ ܙܘܥܐ ܝܗܒ ܠܗ. ܘܟܕ ܝܕܥܐ ܗܘܐ ܡܦܠܚܢܐ ܒܟܕ ܠܗ. ܒܡܠܬܗ ܒܡܫܟܢܐ ܘܥܒܝܕܬܐ ܦܩܕ ܥܠ ܡܒܩܪ ܬܕܒܝܪܬܐ ܘܡܨܒܬܐ ܬܫܒܘܚܬܐ ܘܝܩܝܪܘܬܐ ܠܐܠܗܐ ܗܘ ܕܠܗܕܐ ܒܗܘܬܐ ܐܡܥܗ. ܡܟܡ ܗܘܐ. ܘܗܕܝܢ ܫܠܚ ܩܢ̈ܐ ܒܟܢ ܥܢܐ ܘܥܠܡܟܐ ܒܠܫܘܢ ܟܕ ܗܘܐ ܘܕܟܝܠ ܢܛܠ ܠܗܘܢ ܐܠܗܐ ܒܦܪܢܐ ܡܬܝܒܝܢ ܗܘܐ. ܘܒܬܪ ܗܠܝܢ ܫܠܚ ܡܘ̈ܪܐ ܒܟܠܕ̈ܝܐ ܡܝܠܐ ܗܘܐ. ܡܠ̈ܟܐ ܓܒܪ ܡܟܡܘܢ ܒܗܘ ܒܕܢܐ ܗܦܝܟ ܗܘܘ ܠܗ. ܘܟܕ ܢܦܩ ܬܘܒ ܒܡܠܬܗ ܐܦ ܒܠ ܥܒܕ̈ܢܐ ܝܠ ܘܒܠ ܐܢܫܝܢ ܕܡܢ ܒܡܫ̈ܡܫܢܐ

ܗܘܬ ܒܓܢܝܘܬܐ ܐܢܬܬ ܗܘܬ. ܘܡܡܟܪܗ ܗܘܬ ܒܬܘܠܬܐ
ܗܘܬ ܘܠܡܣܒܐ ܕܢܣܘܒܬܐ ܕܟܝ̈ܢܗ ܡܨܒܝܐ ܗܘܬ ܠܐ ܡܫܟܚܬ.
ܘܟܕ ܥܒܕܗ ܗ̈ܠܝܢ ܡܬܪ̈ܐ ܥܠ ܗܠܝܢ ܓܒܪܐ ܐܡܪܬ ܗܘܬ.
ܥܠ ܕܫܠܝܛܢܐ ܠܢܫܐ ܓܒܪܐ ܘܢܫܐ ܡܢ ܗܘܐ. ܡܛܠ ܗܢܐ
ܗܘܠ ܠܘܩܕܡ ܒܡܣܘܬܐ ܠܗܘܠܗ ܦܓܪܗ ܣܓܝ ܗܘܐ ܘܗܕܝܢ
ܐܬܬܠܝܬ ܦܬܟܪ̈ܐ ܐܬܬܪܘܡ. ܠܐ ܗܘܐ ܣܓܝ ܐܦ ܐܠܐ ܐܬܬܪ̈ܝܡ
ܘܬܠܬ ܙܒ̈ܢܝܢ ܒܫܢܐ ܥܒܕܐ. ܘܦܓܪܐ ܦܓܪܐ ܡܐܦ ܙܒ̈ܢܬܐ
ܦܬܟܪ̈ܬܐ ܒܚܒܟܐ ܕܟܘܬܗ̇ ܕܬܪܝܢ ܗܘܘ ܠܗ ܠܐܘ ܘܐܬܟܢܫܘ.
ܘܐܬܬܠܝܟܘ ܒܠܒܗ ܐܬܪ̈ܐ ܘܡܢ ܦܘܩܕܢܗ ܕܦܓܪܘܢܐ ܦܓܪܐ
ܡܢܐܝܬ ܐܬܬܢܝܚܘ ܒܗ. ܒܪܟܬܐ ܗܘܘ ܒܬܪ ܗܘܢ ܕ̈ܝܢܐ
ܒܐܘܣ̈ܟܡܘܗܝ ܘܒܡܠܟ̈ܬܐ ܒܪ̈ܝܫܘܗܝ ܘܟܕ ܫܠܝܛ ܗܘܐ
ܠܦܠܚܬܐ ܒܬܫܥܝܬܗܘܢ، ܦܘ ܗܢܐ ܕܢܐ ܫܟܬܐ. ܦܓܥ ܘܦܠܚܬܐ
ܐܢܬܬܐ ܐܚܪܬܐ ܕܦܓܪܗ ܒܝܬܐ ܗܘܬ ܘܒܢܝܗ̇ ܫܠܝܛܐ ܗܘܘ.
ܐܢܫܐ ܕܡ ܙܟܐ ܐܢܫܐ ܕܠܒܝܪܘܬܐ ܕܦܓܪܗ ܘܫܒܩ ܗܘܐ ܐܝܬ
ܗܘܐ ܠܗ. ܘܒܫܡܘܬܐ ܘܠܐ ܡܪܫܒܘܬܐ ܕܗܠܝܢ ܕܒܫܘܬܗ
ܒܗܘܬܦܐ ܗܘ، ܠܐ ܡܫܟܚܬ. ܘܡܢ ܡܓܕܠ ܦܫ ܐܢܫܐ ܦܓܪܐ
ܕܡܢ ܦܓܪܘܢܐ ܡܢܓܝܢ ܗܘܘ ܡܟܬ ܒܗ ܡܓܒܝܢܐ ܘܐܡܪܐ.
ܕܒܗܘܢ ܠܐܘܟܬ، ܠܝܬ، ܗܟܢܐ ܡܫܟܚܬ ܕܠܐ ܕܢܣܒܝܢ ܗܘܐ ܐܝܬ.
ܘܟܕ ܗܠܝܢ ܕܦܓܠܘܢ ܙܒܢܐ ܥܒܕ ܗܘܐ. ܡܪܝܐܝܬ ܡܬܒܝܢ
ܗܘܐ. ܘܕܝܢܘܬܗ ܡܢܗܘܢ، ܠܦܠܚܬܐ ܗܘ، ܕܦܓܪܗ ܐܢܐ ܕܘܠܝܛܢܐ
ܥܒܕ ܗܘܐ. ܦܫܛ ܗܘܐ ܕܟܕ ܡܬܬܠܝܢ ܒܗ ܠܡܓܪܬܗ
ܕܢܦܘܩܝܢ ܐܢܬܘܬܗ، ܕܡܢ ܒܝܬܗ ܕܢܦܘܩ ܦܓܪܐ ܡܬܦܓܪܘܬܐ
ܗܘܬ. ܘܦܓܪܘܢܐ ܦܠܚܬܐ ܒܡܫܬܗ ܕܐܬܟܢ ܦܫ ܗܘܐ ܠܗ.
ܦ، ܕܡ ܦܠܚܬܐ ܘܠܫܠܝܛܢܐ ܐܦ ܠܒܪܬ ܡܠܘ ܕܡܫܡܫܐ ܒܗܪܬ.
ܘܦܫ ܠܗܘܢ ܕܦܓܪܗ ܡܬܡܬܝܢ ܗܘܘ. ܕܦܠܓܪܐ ܫܬܠܝܢ ܒܗ
ܦܠܚܬܐ. ܘܥܠ ܦܓܥ ܒܠܚܘܕܝܗ ܫܬܘܩ. ܐܡܫܢܐ ܕܬܬܒܥ
ܒܘܫܡܗ. ܗܘܝܢ ܦܠܚܬܐ ܢܓܝܫܬܐ ܒܚܝܠܐ ܗܘ ܕܐܪܗܘܡܝܘܬܐ

ܚܒܫ ܠܗܘܢ ܐܟܣܢܝܘܬܗܘܢ ܕܢܦܫܗܘܢ ܠܚܝܠܗܘܢ ܒܦܘܩܕܢܐ ܕܢܒܝ̈ܐ ܦܓܪܐ ܘܢܦܫܐ ܠܗܘܢ ܗܘ ܡܦܪܢܣܢܗܘܢ ܠܡܦܩܢܗܘܢ. ܘܒܗܘܢ ܘܒܡܦܩܢܗܘܢ ܘܒܡܥܠܢܗܘܢ ܘܒܡܕܒܪܢܘܬܗܘܢ ܬܬܐܪܟ ܡܗܝ̈ܡܢܐ ܬܗܘܐ ܗܘܘ. ܘܒܪܚܡܘܬܗܘܢ ܘܒܡܦܪܢܣܘܬܗܘܢ ܡܬܒܣܡܝܢ ܗܘܘ. ܘܡܢܐ ܡܣܬܟܠ ܐܢܐ. ܕܠܐ ܗܘܐ ܟܠܒ ܡܢ ܐܝܟܢܐ ܕܐܠܗܐ ܐܬܒܚܪ ܗܠܝܢ. ܒܬܪ ܕܝܢ ܡܢ ܟܬܒܐ ܒܘܚܪܢܐ ܗܘܢܐ ܒܒܩ̈ܐ ܕܢܘܪܐ ܕܥܠ ܡܦܩ̈ܢܗܘܢ ܐܬܬܗܝܒܘ ܡܢ ܬܠܡܝ̈ܕܘܗܝ ܕܡܫܝܚܐ ܚܠܦ ܐܝܢܐ. ܘܬܘܒ ܒܚܝ̈ܠܘܗܝ ܕܡܫܝܚܐ ܒܗܘܢܐ ܒܗܝܢ ܗܘܐ ܠܗܘܢ. ܘܗܕܝܢ ܒܬܪܬܐ ܒܢܘܪܐ ܡܬܦܫܠ ܗܘܐ. ܘܗܠܝܢ ܗܟܢܘ ܠܐ ܗܘܐ ܒܠܚܘܕ ܒܬܪܐ ܐܠܐ ܐܦ ܒܟܠܗ ܒܥܘܪܐ ܘܗܝܡܢܘܬܐ ܡܢ ܢܦܫܐ ܘܒܬܪ ܗܠܝܢ ܠܡܬܠܠܘ ܕܢܦܫܐ ܐܝܟ ܕܢܦܘܩ ܒܫܘܬܐ ܐܫܬܠܡܘ. ܢܦܫ ܕܝܢ ܕܕܡܢ ܠܗܠܝܢ. ܒܬܪ ܩܠܝܠ ܙܒܢܐ ܐܦ ܗܠܬܐ ܚܕ̈ܝܢ ܡܢ ܩܠܘܦܛܝܢܐ. ܗܢܘܢ ܕܡܢ ܩܕܡ ܩܠܝܠ ܐܡܪܢ ܒܠܚܘܕܘܗܝ ܦܢܘܢ ܕܠܡܬܒܥ ܕܠܗܘܢ ܐܬܬܗܝܒܘ ܗܘܘ. ܡܛܠ ܕܠܐ ܗܘܬܪܬܐ ܡܢ ܠܦܘܢ ܢܦܠܘ ܗܘܘ. ܘܐܦܠܐ ܠܢܦܫܐ ܘܠܩܠܝܦܛܝܢܐ ܕܡܬܒܥܐ ܗܘܐ ܠܠܗܕܪܘܬܐ ܡܫܟܐ ܢܦܫܗܘܢ. ܘܒܫܘܬܐ ܗܦܝ̈ܟܬܐ ܐܝܠܝܢ ܕܠܐ ܗܦܟܝܢ ܐܢܫܝܢ ܕܢܬܒܥ ܐܢܝܢ ܗܡܢܘ. ܒܫܢܬܐ ܕܝܢ ܕܟܠܗܘܢ ܐܘܠܝ̈ܢܗܘܢ ܗܘܢܐ ܡܫܟܚ ܒܪܝܐ ܡܢܘ ܗܘܘ. ܐܢܫܝܢ ܕܝܢ ܟܢܫܐ ܡܕܢܚܐ. ܒܙ ܟܝ ܠܗܬܐ ܒܢܦܫ ܗܘܘ. ܘܒܡܕܢܚܐ ܕܡܬܒܥܐ ܐܠܗܐ ܐܫܟܚܢ ܗܘܘ. ܐܬܠܒܒܘ ܘܐܒܗܬܗܘܢ ܕܢܦܘ ܢܦܫܐ ܕܡܕܝܢܬܗܘܢ ܒܬܠܡܝ̈ܕܘܗܝ ܘܒܡܫܝܚܘܗܝ ܗܒܪܘ ܐܘܠܝܢܐ ܐܫܬܝܢ ܕܝܢ ܘܐܦ ܒܐܬܪܘܬܐ ܕܙܘܪܬܐ ܡܢ ܗܠܝܢ ܡܦܘ. ܘܒܙ ܒܬܠܡܝ̈ܕܘܗܝ ܘܒܚܝ̈ܠܘܗܝ ܢܦܫ ܐܦ ܒܗܘܪܡܐ ܡܫܚܐ ܒܟܬܒܘܗܝ ܐܬܬܪܘܪܘ. ܘܬܘܒ ܐܫܬܝܢܐ ܬܘܪ ܡܢ ܗܠܝܢ ܠܗ ܠܡܪܐ ܡܫܬܪܝܬܐ ܪܘܚܐ ܐܬܘ ܘܒܬܪ ܒܠܗܝܢ ܐܦ ܒܡ ܡܫܬܐ ܐܬܬܩܒܠܘ ○ ○ ○

ܘܬܘܒ ܒܙ ܡܢ ܗܠܝܢ ܥܕ ܗܫܐ. ܐܝܬܐ ܠܗ ܠܡܦܩ ܠܝܬܐ ܐܝܕܐ ܕܐܦ ܒܦܘܫܩܗܘܢ ܐܫܟܚܢܐ ܗܘܬ. ܐܠܐ ܒܪܚܡܐ ܫܠܝܚܐ ܕܡܫܝܚܐ

ܐܬܢܣܒ ܗܘܐ. ܐܝܟ ܕܡܢ ܡܕܒܪܢܘܬܐ ܣܓܝܐܐ ܪܒܬܐ. ܡܫܝܚܐܝܬ
ܒܡܫܘܬܐ ܒܐܘܪܚܐ ܕܠܘܩܒܠܢܐ ܘܡܠܘܗܝ ܒܥܡܘܕܝܗ ܢܫܡܬܐ
ܗܘܘ. ܘܡܬܬܪܝܐ ܒܠܝܐ ܐܪܡܝܐ ܠܘܬ ܘܫܘܐܝܬ ܡܬܬܪܝܐ
ܕܡܣܬܪܐ ܘܠܗ ܠܡܕܒܪܢܘܬܐ ܗܝ ܕܐܬܠܒܫܘ ܡܫܡܫܢܐ ܐܝܠ.
ܘܡܢܝܐ ܒܩܠܗ ܕܫܘܒܚ ܡܕܒܪܢܐ ܡܢܐ ܐܝܬ ܠܗܘܢ. ܣܓܝܐܬ
ܗܘܬ ܒܪ ܪܒܬܐ ܗܝ ܗܕܐ. ܐܝܕܐ ܕܫܡܝܐ ܗܘܬ ܕܒܡܘܕܝܐ
ܒܬܪܒܐ ܢܣܒܐ ܠܗ. ܡܘܕܝܐ ܗܘܘ ܕܡܢ ܣܕܪܐ ܕܗܘܝܐ ܐܫܟܚܢܐ
ܬܡܢܐ ܘܡܢ ܥܠ ܟܠܗܘܢ ܠܒܢܬ ܕܗܝܐ ܒܪܝܟܝܢ ܗܘܘ. ܘܠܡܫܡܠܝܘܬܗܘܢ
ܗܠܝܢ ܒܢܝܢܗܘܢ ܣܓܝ ܗܘܘ. ܗܕ ܗܘܐ ܕܠܗܘܢ ܡܕܒܪܢܐ
ܒܬܘܒܠܢܐ ܡܫܝܐܐ ܘܠܒܘܫܬܐ ܕܠܐ ܡܬܚܫܒܐ ܒܡܥܡܘܕܝܬܐ
ܕܐܠܗܐ ܡܘܕܝܢ ܗܘܘ. ܘܡܘܕܝܐ ܗܢܘܢ ܕܠܗܘ ܡܫܝܚܐ ܕܐܬܦܪܩ
ܐܬܓܠܝ ܠܗܘܢ ܡܢ ܢܦܫܐ ܘܫܒܩ ܠܗܘܢ ܐܒܪܗܡ. ܗܕ ܐܝܬܐ
ܠܐ ܡܩܠܗܘܢ. ܐܫܬܡܠܝܐ ܕܝܢ ܗܢܘܢ ܕܡܢ ܡܪܝܡ ܒܒܠܕܒܪܐ
ܕܐܠܗܐ ܐܬܝܗܒܘܢ ܗܘܘ. ܗܢܘܢ ܗܠܝܢ ܒܐܠܗܐ ܡܪܝܐ ܕܟܠ
ܘܒܕܝܢܐ ܕܡܪܝܐ ܒܣܘܬܪܗܘܢ ܒܡ ܐܘܠܨܢܗܘܢ ܡܘܕܝܢ ܗܘܘ.
ܘܐܫܬܡܠܝܐ ܕܡܢ ܐܒܪܗܡ ܕܢܫܪܘܢ ܠܫܬܪܐ ܒܠܗܘܢ ܢܠܘܫ
ܗܘܘ ܕܠܐ ܢܫܪܘܢ ܠܫܬܪܐ ܒܗܘ ܪܒܐ ܒܡܘܪܝܐ ܕܒܢܝܗܘܢ
ܡܬܬܥܝܪ ܗܘܘ. ܘܡܘܕܝܐ ܗܢܘܢ ܕܡܢ ܢܦܫܐ ܒܠܗܘܢ ܡܪܝܗܘܢ
ܒܫܪܪܬܐ ܕܫܬܪܐ ܡܬܬܓܠܝܢ ܗܘܘ. ܣܓܝܐܝܢ ܗܘܘ ܘܡܫܒܚܝܢ ܘܣܓܝܢ
ܘܡܫܒܚܝܢ. ܗܕ ܒܫܡܝܢ ܐܫܬܡܠܝܐ ܒܐܠܗܐ ܕܐܒܪܗܡ ܘܡܘܕܝܢ
ܒܗܘ ܐܠܗܐ ܕܐܝܟ ܦܘܡܗ ܡܘܕܝܢ ܒܗ. ܘܡܫܡܫܝܢ ܣܠܩ ܗܘ
ܐܝܟܢܐ ܕܐܬܚܙܝܬ ܡܫܝܚܐܝܬ ܒܦܪܘ ܒܗ. ܦܓܥܝܢ ܗܘܘ ܕܡܢ ܬܪܐܝܬ
ܘܢܦܩܘܗܘܢ ܡܢܝܢܝܢ ܗܘܘ. ܗܕ ܫܡܥܝܢ ܠܒܪܘܢܐ ܕܡܫܡܫܢܐ
ܕܦܫܝܢ ܘܡܫܬܡܠܝܐ ܒܒܬܪܗ ܠܡܫܬܡܠܝܢܐ ܦܪܝܢ ܗܘܘ. ܘܒܡܘܢܐ
ܕܢܦܫܐ ܠܗܘܢ ܡܫܬܦܝܢ ܗܘܘ. ܦܘܪܢܐ ܒܪ ܗܕ ܦܠܓܐ ܗܘܐ
ܠܗܘܢ ܦܪܐ ܗܘܐ ܘܐܬܦܪ. ܐܝܠܝܢ ܐܫܟܚܢܐ ܐܪܡܝܐ ܕܢܫܐܠ
ܘܐܣܝܪܐ ܕܒܐܘܪܫܠܡ ܠܗܘܢ ܕܝܢ ܗܘܘ. ܕܡܢ ܒܢܬ ܒܒܪܝܐ

ܐܝܟ ܕܡܠܝܠ ܢ.ܒ. ܕܠܡܟܬܒܬܐ ܗܘܬ ܕܐܬܟܬܒܬܐ ܕܐܠܗܐ ܗܝ، ܕܠܗ ܢܠܒܪܐ ܠܝܬܘܬܐ. ܡܛܠ ܗܝ، ܕܠܗ ܒܫܘܬܗ ܘܠܐ ܡܬܦܫܩܢܘܬܗ ܕܠܘܬ ܟܬܒܘܗܝ ܕܐܠܗܐ ° ° °

ܡܩܘܡܐܝܬ ܕܝܢ ܐܣܬܟܝܢ ܗܠܝܢ ܐܝܟ ܕܠܡܗܝܡܢܘܬܐ ܐܠܗܝܢ ܕܐܦ ܡܫܝܚܘ̈ܗܝ ܗܘܝܢ ܒܕܡܐ ܠܢܒܝ ܒܝ ܡܗܡܢܝܢ ܐܢܫܝܢ ܡܢ ܕܢܬܒܥܐ ܒܠܐܘܪܚܐ ܦܓܪܢܝܐ ܕܐܒܗܬܐ ܒܠܘܗܝ. ܕܒܫܘܠܡܐ ܘܒܬܡܗܘܪܬܐ ܐܝܟ ܕܠܡܬܕܒܪܢܘܬܐ ܢܦܫܬ ܐܢܫ ܠܥܠܡ ܐܠܘܐ ܕܐܡܪܝܢ ܒܬܪ. ܢܦܫܐ ܕܝܢ ܦܓܪܐ ܕܢܦܫܗܘܢ ܘܡܫܠܡܘܬܗܘܢ ܕܐܢܫܐ ܣܓܝܐܐ ܗܢܘܢ ܕܠܗܘܢ ܒܗܘܢ ܐܝܬܝܗܘܢ. ܕܒܫܘܠܡܗܘܢ ܢܬܒܥܐ °.

ܡܫܪܝܘܬܐ ܕܩܠܗܘ ܘܕܠܡܠܟܘܬܐ ܘܫܬܐ. ܒܫܢܬ ܬܫܥ ܕܐܪܘܦܣܐ ܕܒܝܘܡܬ̈ܐ ܒܩܘܪܐ.

ܒܕܡܐ ܠܫܢܬ ܫܬ ܕܐܪܘܦܣܐ ܕܒܝܘܡܬ ܘܡܫܝܚܝܐ ܕܠܡܟܠ ܘܫܦ ܗܘܐ ܢܬܒ ܗܘܐ ܘܩܪܝܐ ܒܢܝܐ ܕܡܕܝܢܬܐ ܒܡܪܘܬܐ ܐܬܟܢܫܘ ܗܘܘ ܗܢܘܢ ܕܐܬܩܪܝ ܗܘܘ ܦܪܦܝܪܘ ܒܐܪܥܐ ܕܬܒܐ ܗܝ، ܕܐܬܩܦܬ ܥܠ ܚܢܢ ܐܝܟܢܐ. ܘܡܛܠ ܫܢܝܐ ܕܐܩܪܐ ܕܐܬܩܦܘ، ܒܐܪܥܐ ܗܝ، ܐܬܬܥܝܪ ܫܢܬܐ ܐܦ ܠܥܠܡ ܕܡܠܝܢ ܠܗ ܕܢܬܦܪܘ. ܦܪܦܝܪܘ ܗܘܐ ܗܘܐ ܫܢܬܐ ܡܛܠܐ ܠܗܘܢ ܒܢܝܐ ܩܪܝܐ ܕܡܕܝܢܬܐ ܕܐܬܩܝܡܘ ܒܠܚܘܕ ܐܪܥܐ ܕܐܝܟܢܐ ܕܝܢ ܚܢܢ ܐܬܩܦܘ ܗܘܘ ܡܟܐ ܩܕܡ ܬܠܬܐ ܫܒܥܝܢ ܘܐܬܩܪܝܘ ܚܪܬܐ ܒܢ ܢܒܝܐ ܩܠܝܠܐ ܡܕܝܢܬܐ ܠܩܘܡܝܐ ܕܐܝܬ ܗܘܐ ܒܩܘܣܛܢܛܝܢܐ ܕܐܬܩܪܝܘ، ܗܘܐ ܫܢܬܐ ܦܪܡܠܝܘܢ. ܗܘ ܕܒܗ ܒܝܘܡܐ ܠܐܪܥܝܘܗܝ ܡܬܟܘܝܢ ܡܢ ܫܘܠܛܢܐ ܐܚܪܢ ܗܘܐ. ܐܬܩܪܝܘ، ܗܘܐ ܚܢܢ ܒܪܝܐ ܐܢܫܐ ܕܡܢ ܫܡܝܐ ܪܘܚ ܗܘܐ. ܒܪܘ ܗܘܐ ܚܢܢ ܒܡܦܪܢܘܬܗ ܠܗܘ ܕܡܢ ܩܕܡܘܗܝ، ܡܛܠ ܕܡܢ ܐܪܥܢܝܐ ܕܡܬܒܪܐ ܐܬܩܪܝܘ، ܗܘܐ. ܘܡܬܒܪܘܬܐ ܕܕܡܐ

ܡܕܡ ܒܟܠ ܘܡܛܝܒܬ ܒܟܠ ܫܘܦ̈ܪܝܢ ܒܡܐܠܘܦܢܐ ܕܡܕܒܪܢܘܬܗ ܐܬܟܫܪ. ܘܡܢ ܟܠܗܘܢ̈ ܗܘ̈ܕܐ ܕܒܝܬܗ ܥܒܝܕ ܗܘܐ. ܡܛܠ ܒܡܕܒܪܘ ܕܟܘܠܘܦܘܬܐ ܘܡܕܒܪܢܘܬܗ ܕܒܢܝ̈ܐ ܐܠܗܝ̈ܬܐ ܘܐܢܫ̈ܝܬܐ ܡܫܡܠ ܗܘܐ. ܘܕܠܗ ܕܗܘܐ ܡܛܝܒܬ ܒܟܠ ܡܕܡ. ܠܗܕܡ ܢܗܘܐ ܕܢܬܒܛܠ ܒܝܕ ܥܠܐܟܐ ܘܗܘܢ ܦܬܟܪܐ ܗܘ ܐܘܪܫܠܡ ܢܗܒ ܗܘܐ. ܘܠܢܬܬܐ ܕܢܦܫ ܠܬܝܠܡܐ ܡܬܥܠܝܐ ܐܝܟ ܗܘ ܗܘܐ ܒܠܘܫܒܐ. ܘܡܢ ܢܗܘܗ ܕܡܬܠܐ ܠܐ ܡܬܦܠܚ ܗܘܐ. ܘܢܫܐ ܕܠܩܘܒܠܐ ܠܐ ܫܒܝܩܝܢ ܠܗ ܒܝܬܝܢܐ ܡܩܝܡܐ ܠܗܘܬ ܐܬܦܫܝܢ ܘܡܫܐܠܬ ܒܝܕܥܬܗ ܫܪܝܐ ܗܘܐ. ܘܠܐ ܐܫܟܚ ܕܢܬܦܛܪ ܐܝܟ ܕܦܩܕ ܗܘܐ ܘܪܫܐ ܒܬܪܟܢܘܬܗ ܕܢܫܐ ܒܟܠܐ ܕܗܘܕܐ ܢܫܝܒܘܗܝ ܠܗܘܕܐ ܕܗܠܐ. ܗܢ ܒܡ ܩܘܠ̈ ܡܗܘܕ̈ܢܐ ܕܒܒܝܬ ܐܗܘܪܐ ܕܡܢ ܠܟܠ ܒܬܝܢܝ ܢܫܟܚ ܠܗܘܢܐ ܗܝ ܕܗܘܐ ܡܪܘܪܐ ܕܒܗܠܝܢ ܟܠܗܘܢ ܝܬܒܬܐ ܒܝܬܗ ܠܗܘܟܠ ܡܩܕܫܐ ܕܐܠܗܐ ܐܬܢܝܚ. ܐܡܪܐ ܗܝ ܦܘܪܩܢܐ ܘܡܫܘܡ ܒܪܢܫܐ ܢܗܘܐ ܠܗ. ܦܫܝܩܐ ܗܝ ܕܝܢ ܕܗܢܐ ܡܢ ܗܠܝܢ ܕܐܬܡܢ ܐܫܟܚ ◦ ◦ ◦

ܘܠܐܠܐܬ ܒܪ ܘܡܪܡܘܬܗ ܘܠܐ ܗܘܐ ܠܗܦܟܐ ܦܬܟܪܐ ܡܛܠ ܗܠܝܢ ܕܐܡܪܢ ܠܡܗܘܐ ܕܗܢܐ ܒܐܢܫܐ ܕܐܠܗܐ ܐܫܪܝܗ ܗܘܐ. ܘܡܫܐܠܬ ܘܡܪܢܐܬ ܒܗ ܡܬܚܫܒ ܗܘܐ. ܘܗܘ ܕܒܠ ܒܝܡ ܒܪܘܡܐ ܒܪܡܘܬܗ ܕܡܢ ܗܘܐ. ܘܦܠܚܘܬܐ ܕܡܕܡܘܗܝ ܦܐܡ ܗܘܐ. ܡܬܬܦܪܫ ܗܘܐ ܘܒܠ ܒܠܗ ܒܡܬܐ ܕܠܘܬܝܢܐ ܡܫܬܘܠ ܗܘܐ ܒܝܕ ܠܠܝܐ ܡܢ ܒܘܠܦ ܒܡܐܘܬܗ ܐܫܠܝܗ. ܘܡܢ ܟܠܗܘܢ̈ ܐܝܬܘܗܝ ܐܝܟ ܡܫܬܘܕܝܐ ܐܘܫܒܚܐ. ܘܒܗ ܒܡܘܪܐ ܡܫܒܚܬ̈ ܗܝ ܕܒܗ ܗܠܝܢ ܒܠܗܘܢ ܒܝܫܬܐ ܕܡܢ ܠܟܠ ܒܬܝܢ ܗܦܪ ܗܘܐ. ܓܒܪ ܕܗܢܐ ܕܡܬܡܫܚܢܘܗ ܝܫܘܥ ܕܐܬܒܪܘܬܗ ܠܡܘܬܐ ܒܝܘܡܐ ܐܫܬܠܡ ܗܘܐ. ܘܥܒܕܐ ܠܗܘܕܡ ܘܡܫܡܫܢܐ ܕܫܝܫ ܡܢ ܟܠ ܡܩܘܬܡ ܐܬܦܪܩ ܒܗ. ܐܡܬܝ ܕܟܠܗ ܩܠܐ ܕܫܡܝܐ ܕܒܝܫܐ ܘܐܘܫܠܬܐ ܘܝܫܘܬܐ ܒܐܕܝܘܗܝ. ܡܢܗ ܡܬܗܘܬܐ ܡܢ ܟܠ ܦܩܝܕܢ ܐܬܝܬܘܢ ܗܘܘ.

ܢܕܒ ܗܘܐ. ܠܡܕܒܪܐ ܗܘܐ ܠܗ ܕܡܘܟܟܘܬܗ ܪܒܐ ܗܘܐ ܘܦܐܝܐ. ܘܡܫܬܡܥܢܘܬܐ ܕܠܡܕܒܪܢܘܬܗ ܘܟܢܫܗ ܕܐܚܝܐ ܘܡܟܟܘܬܐ ܫܦܝܪ ܗܘܐ. ܕܘܡܚܣܢܘܗܝ ܕܝܢ ܫܦܝܪ ܗܘܐ. ܘܠܘܬ ܟܠܗܘܢ ܒ̈ܢܝ ܐܢܫܐ ܕܟܝܢ ܡ̈ܙܟܐ ܗܘܐ ܕܢܬܩ̈ܪܐ. ܘܗܘ ܗܘܐ ܡܛܠ ܕܢܬܡܠܐ ܒܡܘܕܝܢܘܬܗ ܒܡܠ̈ܠܘܗܝ ܕܢܦܫܐ ܐܫܬܝܢܘ ܒܗ. ܘܡܛܠ ܕܡܢ ܡܕܒܪܢܘܬܗ ܕܠܘܬ ܡܕܝܢܘܬܗ ܠܟܠܗ ܟܢܫܐ ܕܕܝܪܐ ܫܦܪ. ∘ ∘ ∘

ܘܟܕ ܡܢ ܗܢܐ ܗܘܕܐ ܥܒܕ ܗܘܐ. ܗܘ ܗܢܐ ܕܐܢܐ ܚܟܝܡ ܒܫܘܬܗ ܠܗ ܠܒܪ ܙܘܢ ܕܢܬܦܪ̈ܘܢ ܫܒܝ̈ܚܐ: ܥܠܘ̈ܗܝ ܕܒܡܕܝܢܬܐ ܕܒܫܘܬܗܘܢ ܡܬܦܪܣܝܢ ܘܟܕܐ ܘܥܠܬܐ ܟ̈ܠܝܠܝܢ ܕܡܫ̈ܡܫܢܬܐ ܕܥ̈ܒܕܝܗܘܢ ܦܬܝܢ ܗܘܘ ܘܡܫܒ̈ܚܝܢ ܘܒܫܘܒܚܗܘܢ ܒܫܠܝܘܬܐ ܕܥ̈ܕܬܐ ܕܐܠܗܐ ܫܒܝܚܝܢ ܗܘܘ. ܘܐܝܟ ܕܒܗܘܢ ܡܬܦܪܣܘ ܠܠܒܘ̈ ܐܫܬܕܪܘ. ܘܬܘܒ ܟܕ ܡܢ ܗܠܝܢ ܘܠܗܠܐ ܥܡܝܢܐ ܘܐܠܗܐ ܡܫܡܠܝܬܐ ܠܫܘܢܬܐ ܡܢܗ ܗܘܐ. ܘܬܘܒ ܡܢ ܗܠܝܢ ܗܟܢܐ ܗܘ ܥܒܝܕܐ ܥܒܕ ܗܘܐ. ܘܥܠ ܐܘܪ̈ܚܐ ܐܚܪ̈ܬܐ ܗܘܐ. ܘܕܟܫܘ̈ ܒܪܘܬܗܘܢ ܡܢ ܗܘܐ. ܘܠܐܘܟܡܐ ܕܡܗܝ̈ܡܢܐ ܥܠܦ ܐܢܘ̈. ܘܦܩܕ ܬܘܒ ܐܦ ܡܢ ܗܠܝܢ. ܘܥܠ ܥܠܘ̈ܗܝ ܕܟܢܬ ܘܠܢܘܗ ܐܚܪ̈ܬܐ ܗܘܐ. ܥܠ ܕܐܦ ܗܘ ܠܒܪ. ܕܡܢ ܒܬܪ ܙܢ ܗܘܐ ܗܘܕܐ ܕܐܠܗܐ ܦܠܚܘ̈ܬܗ ܕܗܢܘ ܚܕ ܐܢܘ̈. ܘܬܘܒ ܡܢ ܥܠܘ̈ ܥܒܕ ܗܘܐ. ܘܥܠ ܐܘܪ̈ܚܐ ܐܚܪ̈ܬܐ ܗܘܐ. ܘܡܛܪ̈ܕܐ ܠܗܘ̈ ܠܒܪ ܗܘܐ. ܘܠܐ ܐܬܬܚܝܬ ܡܢܗ ܕܒܫܘܬܗ ܡܕܒܪܐ ܐܠܐ ܐܦ ܒܝܘܡܐ ܕܢܦܩܬܐ ܠܡܫܬܪܝܘ ܡܬܠܝܨ ܗܘܐ. ܘܬܠܬ ܫ̈ܢܝܢ ܬܠܬܐ ܠܒܪܢܫܐ ܕܦ̈ܓܪܐ ܠܒ̈ܢܝܐ ܐܬܠܡ ܗܘܐ. ܘܠܐܘܪ̈ܚܐ ܬܘܒ ܟܠܗ ܐܘܪ̈ܚܐ ܐܫܠܡ ܗܘܐ. ܗܘ ܕܝܢ ܕܗܢܐ ܫܘܢܝܐ ܗܠܝܢ ܟܠܗܝܢ ܕܟܬܒ ܒܫܢܬܐ ܫܬܐ ܗܘܝ ∘ ∘ ∘

ܘܡܢ ܒܬܪ ܫܘܠܡܗܘܢ ܕܗܠܝܢ ܕܟܬܝܒܢ ܐܦ ܗܘ ܥܡܟܐ ܕܐܒܝܕ ܒܠ ܒܡܫܠܡܘ ܗܘܕܐ ܕܐܠܗܐ ܥܡܟܐ. ܗܘ ܕܐܝܬܘܗܝ ܗܘܐ

ܫܢܐ ܕܦܩܕ ܠܗ ܠܡܫܝܚܐ ܦܓܪܐ ܕܡܫܪܝܘܬܗ ܠܟܠܐܢܫ ܡܕܡ
ܠܟܠܗܘܢ ܕܡܕܡܘܗܝ، ܦܫܛܝܢ ܗܘܘ ܐܫܬܒܩ ܠܐ ܬܘܒ ܐܫܟܚ
ܕܟܢܘܫܐ ܬܪܥܢܐ ܐܝܟ ܡܕܡܥܐ ܠܘܬ ܡܠܟܘܬܐ ܢܦܩ. ܘܠܡܫܡܫܘ
ܕܡܠܐ ܕܐܬܠ ܒܦܪܗܣܝܐ ܣܓܝܐ ܗܘܐ. ∘ ∘ ∘

ܘܟܕ ܡܢ ܕܝܢ ܕܗܕܐ ܡܠܟܘܬܐ ܕܟܣܝܬܐ ܥܠ ܗܘܐ. ܐܬܬ ܠܗ ܠܟܠ
ܐܪܥܐ ܕܡܥܡܪܢܐ ܗܘܬ ܕܒܟܠܗܘܢ ܡܠܟܘܬܐ ܡܫܝܚܝܬܐ ܠܗܕܐ
ܡܫܡܫܢܘܬܐ ܐܬܦܪܣܬ. ܘܠܟܠܗܘܢ ܥܡܡܐ ܗܘܬ ܠܟܠܗܘܢ ܕܢܫܡܐ
ܕܐܝܬ ܒܡܫܝܚܐ ܐܬܠܒܫܬ ܗܘܘ. ܟܕ ܡܕܡ ܠܐ ܐܡܪ ܠܗܘܢ
ܐܦ ܠܐ ܐܘܠܨܢܐ ܕܬܟܝܒܐ ܐܝܬ ܒܟܠܗܘܢ. ܗܝ ܕܝܢ ܒܫܡܫܬܐ
ܡܕܥܬܐ ܠܟܠܗܘܢ ܗܝ ܡܣܬܒܪܢܐ ܠܫܡܥܝܢܐ ܒܡܪܝܘܬܗ
ܕܠܗܘܢ ܠܦܠܚ ܡܕܡܟ. ܘܠܐܘܠܨܢܐ ܘܠܬܟܝܒܐ ܕܠܗܘܢ ܘܡܫܝܚ
ܗܘܘ ܒܦܓܪܗ ܒܟܬܒܬ ܗܢܐ ܡܠܟܐ. ܘܠܟܠܕܟܒܐ ܗܘ
ܕܠܡܫܠܡܘܢ ܦܠܓ ܗܘܐ ܒܫܘܡܠܝ ܝܪܚܗ. ܘܠܕܝܢܐ ܦܪܥܐ
ܘܡܢܐ ܒܫܠܛܢܘܬܗ ܘܒܝܓܪܬܗ ܙܘܥܐ ܕܢܦܫ ܡܟܟܬ. ܘܠܘܬ
ܡܕܝܢܬܐ ܐܚܪܢܐ ܐܝܟ ܕܫܠܝܚܐ ܒܥܕܬܗ ܠܗܘ ܦܓܪܘܢܐ
ܒܫܢܐ. ܘܡܟܐ ܕܝܢ ܐܬܚܘܝ ܗܘܐ ܚܕ ܒܟܬܒܐ. ܗܘ ܕܒܗ ܡܕܝܢܬܐ
ܐܬܕܝܫ ܗܘܐ ܒܫܡܪܝܐ. ܘܒܝܬܐ ܗܘܐ ܕܡܢ ܟܠ ܐܬܪܘܬܐ.
ܘܟܝܬܐ ܕܡܢ ܐܬܪܟܢܬ. ܗܢܐ ܗܘܕܝܢܐ ܐܘܬܒܪ ∘.

ܡܬܚܘܝܬܐ ܕܥܘܡܪܢܘܬܗ. ܒܫܬ ܫܢܝܢ ܕܐܪܡܝܐ ܕܩܫܘܫܬܗ.
ܒܡܕܝܢܬܐ ܡܕܒܪܬܐ.

ܐܪܟܠܐܘܣ ܗܘܐ ܗܓܡܘܢܐ ܒܝܗܘܕܝܐ. ܘܗܘܝܐ ܚܕ ܒܬܪ،
ܐܚܪ ܐܬܝܗܘܢ ܗܘܐ. ܘܗܘܝܐ ܗܘܐ ܗܘ ܡܢ ܒܢܝܗܘܢ ܡܬܚܘܝܬ
ܗܘܐ. ܘܫܪܒܬܗ ܕܠܡܫܠ ܒܟܠ ܫܢܝܢ ܡܬܦܠܓ ܗܘܐ ܘܒܗܢܐ
ܐܘܠܨܢܐ ܗܘ ܒܢܝܐ ܚܕ ܗܘܡܐ ܕܐܡܪܢ ܢܬܡܟܢ. ∘ ∘ ∘
ܒܗ ܗܟܠ ܒܗܘܢܐ ܗܘܡܐ ܕܐܡܪܢ ܒܠܗܘܢ ܒܪ ܐܢܫܐ ܚܕ
ܕܒܠܗ ܒܗܡܝܪܗ ܡܬܠܬ ܗܘܐ. ܘܗܠܝܢܐ ܕܐܘܗܬܐ ܡܬܐܪܐܬ

ܐܬܪܒܝܬ ܘܡܠܦܢܘܬܗܘܢ ܫܡܠܝܐ ܗܘܬ. ܘܕܝܪܝܘܬܗ ܒ̈ܢܝ ܠܘܬܗܘܢ
ܡܢܗܘܢ ܕܒܢܐ ܗܘܬ. ܘܡܛܠ ܗܠܝܢ ܟ̈ܠܗܝܢ ܕܡܢܗܘܢ ܡܚܠܠܐ
ܗܘܬ. ܐܬܚܫܒܬܘ ܒ̈ܢܝܐ ܐܝܟ ܗ̇ܘ ܕܡܡܟ ܕܠܐ ܒܪܘܚܐ ܘܕܠܐ
ܒܦܠܚܘܬܐ ܒܒܪܬ ܗܘܬ. ܘܫܦܝܪܘܬܐ ܕܡܫܠܡܢܘܬܐ ܘܡܪܥܝܬܗ
ܠܡܪ̈ܥܝܬܗ ܡܫܡܫܢܐ ܦܪܘܫ. ܕܒܟܠ ܓܝܪ ܥܘܠܡܢܐ
ܕܡܠܘܦܢܐ ܠܚܘܕ ܗܘܐ. ܘܠܐ ܕܒܢܝܐ ܡܢܝܐ ܠܒܫ ܐܝܟ ܗ̇ܘ
ܕܡܠܟܐ ܡܢܗ ܕܝܠܝܕܐ ܐܬܚܙܝ. ܘܡܪܥܝܬܗ ܫܡܥܬܐ ܘܫܡܥܬܐ
ܠܡܗ ܐܬܟܠ ܘܡܛܐ ܠܗ ܠܝܠܝܕܘܬܐ ܕܐܬܒܚܝ. ܘܡܛܠ ܕܐܫܬܡܫ
ܒܗ ܝܠܝܕܘܬܐ ܗܝ ܐܝܟ ܒܪܢܫܘܬܐ ܠܘܩܒܠ ܫܘܡܠܝܐ ܕܡܫܠܡܘܬܐ
ܡܢܟܐ ܗܘܬ. ܡܬܪܐܝܬ ܕܝܢ ܡܫܡܫܢܐ ܦܪ̈ܝܐ ܫܡܪ̈ܝܐ ܡ̈ܢܝܐ
ܟ̈ܠܗܘܢ ܘܬܘܕܝܬܗ ܡܬܦܫ ܗܘܐ. ܕܒܟܐ ܕܐܬܚܫܘ ܡܟܠܝ ܓܘܗ
ܡܢ ܟ̈ܠܗܘܢ ܐܬܬܪܝܬ. ܘܡܛܠ ܕܗܝ ܝܠܝܕܘܬܐ ܗܘܐ ܡܡܫ ܒܪܢܫܐ
ܬܡܡܢܐ ܘܫܪ̈ܝܐ ܒܙ ܥܠܡܐ ܘܒܪܬ. ܘܒܕܡܠ ܒܢܝܐ ܗܘܬ.
ܘܡܛܐ ܠܗ ܕܐܬܒܚܝ. ܗܝ ܕܝܢ ܦ̈ܘܩܕܢܘܗܝ ܐܪܥܢܬ ܘܡ̈ܠܘܗܝ ܦܬܚܬ.
ܘܦܬܓ̈ܡܐ ܚܙܝܐ ܒܗܘ ܒܕܝܢܐ ܕܐܘܠܨܢܗ ܚܙܝܐ ܗܘܬ. ܠܐܝܟܢܐ
ܗܘܬ ܕܝܢ ܒܡܦܬܓܡܗ ܘܡܚܘܝܬܐ ܕܡܘܡܬܗ ܘܡܠܠܐ ܙܒܢܐ
ܠܡܫܡܫܢܐ ܐܬܒܪܝܐ ܗܘܬ. ܡܢܐ ܠܡܢܐ ܐܝܬܝܗ ܘܪܒ ܐܢܫܐ. ܘܠܐ
ܕܝܢ ܐܝܬ ܗ̇ܘ ܡܢܘܡ ܕܡܠܝܠܐ ܗܘܬ ܕܐܬܚܫܒ ܒܐܡܪܝܟ ܐܬܚܫܒܬܗ.
ܡܬܪܐܝܬ ܕܝܢ ܫܪ̈ܝܐ ܐܢܫܐ ܠܡܫܬܡܫܬܐ ܕܐܘܠܨ̈ܢܝܗܘܢ ܕܡܘܕܐ
ܕܐܠܗܐ ܫܘܒܚ ܕܐܬܚܫܒ. ܠܠܘܬܗ ܓܝܪ ܟܠ ܗܘܐ ܦܢܝܐ ܗܘܬ.
ܘܒܗܘܢ ܡܡܠܠܐ ܗܘܬ. ܕܒܢܝܐ ܡܢ ܦܘܩܕܢ ܠܐܘܠܨ̈ܢܝܗܘܢ
ܢܬܦܫܘܢ. ܐܝܟܢܐ ܕܬܬܦܠܓ ܠ ܒܟܡܐ ܡܫܠܘܬܐ ܐܦ
ܒܦܠܚܘܬܐ ܕܒܢܝܐ. ܠܐ ܓܝܪ ܡܬܡܫܢܐ ܗܘܬ ܒܙ ܙܒܢܐ ܐܢܫܐ
ܡܢ ܫܟܝܢܘܗܝ ܕܐܬܚܫܒܬ ܒܫܝܢܘܗܝ. ܘܫܝ ܡܫܐ ܕܡܛܠ
ܦܘܪܫܢܐ ܕܒܬܪ ܒܫܘܬܪܐ ܙܒܢܐ ܗܘܐ ܡܕܡܝܟ ܦܢܝܐ ܐܢܫܐ.
ܕܐܬܚܫܒ ܕܐܡܪܡ ܠܗܘܬ ܐܠܗ ܐܦ ܠܟܝܢܗ ܙ̈ܕܝܩܐ ܕܠܗܘܢ
ܦܠܛܘܣܐ ܡܪܡ ܩܠܝܠ ܒܒܢܐ ܗܘܬ. ܗܘ ܕܝܢ ܕܢܟܐ ܙܒܢܐ. ܒܙ

ܣܢܐܘܗܝ ܢܘܦܠܘܢ. ܘܟܠ ܚܝܠ ܢܣܒܪܘܢ ܐܝܟ ܕܠܦܠܚܘܬܐ ܢܚܒܢܘܢ. ܠܚܣܘܬܐ ܢܣܦܘܢ. ܘܠܗܘ ܚܝܐ ܕܡܚܝܢܐ ܢܬܒܪܢܘܢ. ܘܡܢ ܡܣܡܡ ܒܢܫܐ ܕܥܒܕܬܐ ܠܗ ܢܬܚܠܘܢ. ܐܠܐ ܡܢ ܐܠܦܩܐ ܕܢܘܪܐ ܥܒܘܢ ܕܠܚܠܡ ܠܗ ܕܚܕܡ ܢܬܚܠܘܢ. . . .

ܘܟܕ ܗܠܝܢ ܗܘ ܡܘܫܐ ܕܐܠܗܐ ܒܡܠܐ ܙܡܪܐ ܒܗ ܦܘܡܐ ܐܡܪ ܗܘܐ. ܘܡܟܝܢܬܗ ܕܐܘܦܝܪ ܐܝܟ ܬܡܠܟܐ ܕܠܐ ܡܦܠܐ ܦܐܡ ܗܘܐ ܚܙܬܐ ܘܪܦܝܗ ܦܪܘܫܐ ܚܢܐ ܐܬܦܩܠ ܗܘܐ. ܘܦܩܕ ܕܣܘܬܐ ܢܚܡܘܢ ܚܠܘܗܝ. ܗܘ ܕܝܢ ܠܚܢܢܐ ܘܡܚܝܢ ܚܠ ܡܘܬܐ ܠܚܢܢܐ ܘܠܘܡܠܐ ܠܐ ܐܦܩ ܗܘܐ. ܘܡܠܠܘܬܐ ܕܪ̈ܓܠܘܗܝ ܘܠܒܢܘܬܐ ܕܪ̈ܚܡܘܗܝ ܠܘܡܠܘ ܕܣܘܬܐ ܒܝܬܐ ܐܙܠ ܗܘܐ. ܘܕܒܐ ܚܢܬܐ ܐܪ̈ܒܥܗ ܗܘܬ. ܘܡ̈ܢܝܢ ܠܗ ܡܒܣܡܢܐ ܗܘܬ. ܘܟܕ ܒܕܝܠ ܢܫܐ ܐܢܬ ܗܘܬ ܒܗ. ܬܘܒ ܠܚܢܬ ܐܘܪ̈ܚܐ ܐܫܬܠܡ. ܘܡܘܡܐ ܚܕ ܬܡܢ ܚܝܐ. ܘܡܢ ܒܬܪܗ ܦ̈ܠܚܐ ܐܬܬܠܡ ܒܗ. ܦܘܠܚܢܗ ܒܢܒܐ ܐܫܬܕ. ܢܫܡܗ ܕܝܢ ܕܦܠܚܢܐ ܐܦܝܡܗ ܒܐܪ ܗܢܐ ܗܘܬ ܘܠܦܠܚܘܬܐ ܕܒܢܒܐ ܕܠܬܡܢ ܡܥܪܘܒܐ ܗܘܬ ܐܙܠܬ. ܘܒܡ ܬ̈ܠܐܒܐ ܘܒܚ̈ܢܝܐ ܕܣܘ̈ܕܐ ܡ̈ܪܥܐ ܐܬܦܫܠܬ. ܘܒܕܡܐ ܠܡܪܐ ܡܚܝܠ ܬܠܬܘܗܝ ܘܪܟܝܒܘܬܗ ܕܐܦ̈ܝܗܘ ܐܒܐ ܗܘܐ. . . .

ܡܘܕܝܢܘܬܐ ܬܘܕܝܬܐ ܕܐܘܪܚܐ ܒܬܠܬܐ ܕܐܠܗܐ. ܒܥܬ ܣܦ̈ܪܐ ܕܢܘܚܐ ܕܒܣ̈ܦܪܬ. . .

ܒܕܡܐ ܠܥܢܬ ܣܡܚܢ ܙܘܗܪܐ ܒܣ̈ܦܪܬ ܐܬܡܚܝܢ ܗܘܐ. ܘܢܗܪܐ ܐܬܝܗ̇ܘܢ ܗܘܐ ܚܝܢ ܘܡܘܡܐ ܬܪ̈ܝܢ ܒܗ ܒܢܘܪܐ. ܘܦܠܠܬܐ ܚܕܐ ܐܠܗܘܬܐ ܘܡܫܒܚ ܒܟܠ. ܡܢ ܗܠܝܢ ܬ̈ܠܬܐ ܕܒܪܗ ܕܐܠܗܐ ܕܟܝܢܪ ܡܫܒܚܬܐ. ܗ̇ ܕܐܬܐܠܗ ܒܪܬ ܡܫܒܚܘܪܐ ܬ̈ܪܝܢ ܐܬܝܬ ܗܘܬ ܘܒܣܘܡܐ ܕܒܢܐ ܕܠܗܬ ܐܠܝܢ ܕܡܦܠܓܠ ܡܘܕܝܢܘܬܐ ܕܐܠܗܐ ܡܫܡ ܒܢܬ ܕܒܢܐ ܕܡܦܪܫܢܐ ܢܬܒܡ ܗܘܘ.

ܒܢܝܢ ܗܘܘ ܠܗ ܗܟܝܠ ܘܡܫܕܪܝܢ ܒܡܕܝܢܬܗ ܕܐܘܪܫܠܡ
ܒܡܕܢܚܐ ܠܗ ܠܦܠܣܛܝܢܐ ܐܟܘܬܗ. ܘܗܕܐ ܕܝܢ ܒܬܘܒ ܐܝܬ ܗܘܐ
ܡܕܡܗܘܝ. ܠܐ ܗܘܐ ܡܕܡ ܐܚܪܢ ܕܢܦܩܐ ܗܘܐ ܠܒܪܝܐ ܐܠܐ
ܒܠܚܘܕ ܕܦܪܘܛܝܢܐ ܐܝܬܘܗܝ، ܡܬܚܙܐ ܗܘܐ. ܘܒܕܒܪܐ ܕܝܢ ܚܕ
ܡܠܠܐ ܕܠܡܕܝܢܬܗ ܡܠܠ ܗܘܐ. ܒܥܕܢܐ ܒܗ ܗܘܕܐ ܕܐܠܗܐ ܟܠ
ܗܘܐ. ܘܬܪܝܗܘܢ ܦܣܩܐܝܬ ܚܕ ܡܢܗܘܢ ܒܪܝܐ ܡܟܠܘ. ܗܟܢ ܕܝܢ
ܕܡܢܐ ܗܘܐ ܚܙܐ ܗܘܐ ܠܚܫܐ ܕܦܪܘܩ. ܚܕ ܓܒܪ ܚܠܦ ܐܠܗܐ
ܕܥܠ ܡܗܡܢ ܗܘܐ. ܘܡܚܫܢܐ ܡܛܠ ܡܠܬܐ ܕܦܪܘܩ ܡܟܬ ܗܘܐ.
ܘܫ ܓܒܪܢܐ ܕܡܠܐ ܠܦܘܪܫܢܗܘܢ ܒܘܣܡܝܬ ܢܦܫ. ܗܘ ܕܝܢ ܗܢܐ
ܕܢܝܐ ܐܝܬܘܗܝ ܗܘܐ ܐܘܪܚܢܘܗܝ ܕܟܒܪܘܬܐ ܡܛܠ ܕܒܥܠ
ܕܟܒܪܘܬܐ ܒܦܠܣܛܝܢܐ ܐܝܬܘܗܝ ܗܘܐ. ܘܟܕ ܐܬܐ ܕܝܢ
ܡܗܡܢܘܗܝ ܠܗܕܐ ܚܙܬܐ ܕܡܢ ܠܒܠ ܐܬܬܥܝܩ. ܐܝܟ ܕܡܛܠ
ܫܠܝܚܘܬܗ ܕܐܘܪܫܠܡ ܥܘܠܝܢܐ ܕܒܥܬܐ ܐܘܕܥ ܠܗ. ܘܠܦܘ
ܡܛܠܠܐ ܕܡܛܠ ܡܕܝܢܬܗ ܡܢ ܡܕܝܢܬܐ ܐܚܪܬܐ. ܘܒܠ ܡܢ ܟܠ ܥܒܕܝܢ
ܒܥܕܢܗ. ܘܠܦܘ ܗܘܕܐ ܕܐܠܗܐ ܒܗ ܒܡܕܝܢܬܗ، ܚܙܐ ܗܘܐ. ܠܗ ܕܡܢ
ܚܘܬ ܥܝܢܐ ܡܬܐܡܪ ܚܙܐ ܗܘܐ. ܡܢ ܒܬܪ ܗܢܝܢ ܕܐܬܦܪܣܘܗܝ
ܒܐܘܪܫܠܡ. ܡܕܡܟܬ ܐܫܬܐܠ ܗܘܐ ܗܘܕܐ ܐܦܢܘܗ ܕܐܢܐ ܒܓܪ
ܒܐܠܗܘ. ܗܘ ܕܝܢ ܒܡܠܐ ܙܩܦܐ ܠܒܠܘ ܒܢܫܐ ܐܡܪ ܗܘܐ. ܐܘ
ܐܢܫܐ ܫܪܝܐ ܕܐܦܢܘܢܐ ܗܢܐ ܕܐܢܐ ܒܗ. ܠܐ ܗܘܐ ܡܛܠ
ܚܠܬܐ ܒܒܥܬܐ ܠܗܢܐ ܐܦܢܘܢܐ ܐܬܬܫ. ܗܘܕܐ ܐܢܐ ܓܒܪ
ܕܘܠܗܢܐ ܥܒܪܐ ܕܐܠܗܐ ܘܠܒܠܗ ܡܗܡܢ ܐܢܐ ܕܐܬܒܗ ܠܡܫ
ܐܠܗܐ ܒܠܚܘܕܘܗܝ، ܘܠܝܫܘܥ ܕܒܬܪܗ ܘܠܗܘ ܒܪܗ ܕܡܫܝܚܐ
ܘܕܐܪܒܥܐ ܬܪܬܝܢ ܘܬܫܬܡܥܢ. ܘܟܠ ܕܐܬܐ ܒܠ ܡܛܠ ܗܢܐ
ܥܡܟܐ. ܒܫܘܬܦܐ ܕܪܘܚܐ ܡܡܠܠ ܐܢܐ. ܠܐ ܗܘܐ ܓܒܪ ܒܡܠܬܐ
ܐܝܬܘܗܝ ܠܗܘܢܐ. ܐܠܐ ܐܢ ܓܒܪ ܒܪ ܫܘܪܝܐ. ܗܘ ܕܒܗ ܒܪܡܫܐ
ܠܡܕܝܢܬܐ ܡܢܗ ܐܢܐ. ܘܒܠ ܐܦ ܗܡܢܘܬ، ܡܬܬܟܪܢܐ. ܕܐܬܠ
ܠܗܘܢܐ ܠܐܠܗܝ ܕܝܠܝ ܡܢܗ ܕܥܠ ܡܕܝܢܬܐ ܒܫܘܒܚ. ܘܒܬܪ

ܗܘܐ. ܗܕܐ ܕܝܢ ܐܝܬܝܐ ܕܒܠܘܓܝܐ ܒܬܪ ܐܘܣܝܘ ܐܓܒܘ
ܠܐܓܒܝܐ ܕܗܘܕܘܬܐ ܐܬܚܪܝ. ܘ. ܘ. ܘ.

ܡܫܡܠܝܘܬܐ ܕܐܓܒܘ ܒܝܬ ܐܪ̈ܡܝܐ ܕܕܘܩܐ ܕܒܢܘܗܕܪ̈ܐ. ܘ.

ܒܝܬ ܐܪ̈ܡܝܐ ܕܕܘܩܐ ܕܒܢܘܗܕܪ̈ܐ. ܘܫܡܗܐ ܒܪܘܒܬܐ ܐܝܬܘܗܝ ܗܘܐ ܒܒܗܘܢ ܒܥܒܪ ܐܫܪ. ܘܒܗ ܒܗܝܐ ܢܘܡܐ ܡܒܗܘܡܝܢܘܗ ܢܟܐ ܕܐܬܘܪܝܐ ܠܡܒܝܢܘܬܐ ܩܣܪܝܐ ܐܝܬܐ ܗܘܐ. ܘܡܫܬܡܗܪ ܗܘܐ ܕܡܕܝܢ ܫܒܬ ܢܘܗܐ ܠܐܠܗܘ̈ ܫܪܝܐ ܕܡܬܠܬܝܗ ܡܬܚܒܫܝܢ. ܘܒܗ ܓܢܪ ܒܗܝܐ ܢܘܡܐ ܒܐܕܪܐ ܕܒܝܬ ܠܐܒܗ ܒܒܪ ܗܘܐ. ܘܡܬܒܒܐ ܗܘܐ ܕܒܡܒܐܬܬܗ ܕܐܬܘܪܝܐ ܡܕܝܢ ܕܡܫܬܪ ܡܢ ܐܠܝܢ ܕܒܫܘܪܐ ܡܬܒܒܪ̈ ܗܘ. ܢܫܘܐ ܗܘܐ. ܘܡܒܢܐ ܗܘܬ ܒ ܗ̄ ܫܢ̈ܝܐ ܫܪܝܐ. ܐܠܐ ܕܗܘܕܐ ܕܐܠܗܘܬܐ ܠܡܒܠܬܐ ܕܢܘܬܐ ܐܫܟܪ، ܗܘܐ ܒܕ ܡܢ ܡܕܝܢ ܗܘܢܐ ܢܒܗܘܗܐ ܐܢܬ ܗܘܐ ܕܒܡܒܐܬܬܐ ܕܡ̈ܠܟܐ ܠܢܘܬܐ ܕܐܘܒܗܘܪܐ ܕܦܪܝܡ ܒܐܘܩܛܘܗܝܡ ܘܡܥܢܠܩ ܡܢ ܫ̈ܕܐ ܡܕܝܢ ܫܕܪܐ ܢܒܕ ܗܘܐ ܒܒܢܐ ܕܡ̈ܠܟܐ. ܘܒܫܒܒܐ ܕܘܒ̈ܪܐ ܫܕ̈ܬܐ ܘܢܘܒ̈ܪܐ. ܘܬܘܒ ܐܦ ܒܫܕܬܐ ܕܒܠ ܓܢܘ. ܕܢܘܬܐ ܘܒܫܠܝܘܬܐ ܕܓܒ̈ܪܐ ܐܬܠܝ̈ܛܐ ܘܡܘܓܒܐ ܘܢܫܐ ܗܓܒܐܐ ܢܘܗܐ ܠܫܪܝܐ ܘ ܘ ܘ

ܡܬܒܒܐ ܗܘܐ ܗܒܠ ܕܐܦ ܒܗܝܐ ܒܐܕܪܐ ܕܒܝܬ ܠܐܒܗ ܕܡ̈ܠܟܐ ܕܡܕܝܢ ܢܟܐ ܘܡܬܒܪܐ ܢܒܕ ܒܗ ܒܒܐܕܪܐ. ܘܒܠܗܘܢ ܡܦ̈ܫܬܐ ܕܢܘܗ ܠܗܘܢ ܡܕܝܢ ܫܒܬ ܠܐ ܒܒܪ ܗܘܐ. ܒܡܕܝܢܐ ܕܡܕܝܢ ܕܢܫܡ ܗܘܐ ܒܠܗܘ، ܘܡܒܠ ܗܘܐ ܒܠ ܦܪ̈ܘܢܐ ܢܟܐ. ܐܝܬܐ ܠܡܓܒܬܐ ܗܘܕܐ ܕܐܠܗܘܬܐ ܕܒܥܠܘܗܝ ܘܫܡܘܬܐ ܡܓܒܬ ܗܘܐ. ܘܒܥܒܕܘܬܐ ܕܒܡܒܪܗ ܗܐܐ ܗܘܐ. ܘܕܝܬܐܠ ܡܢ ܫܒܬܐ ܒܬܦܪ̈ܘ ܢܦܠ ܗܘܐ. ܥܒܗ ܕܝܢ ܐܝܬܘܗܝ، ܗܘܐ ܐܓܒܘ. ܗ̄ܘ ܕܒܠܗܘ، ܘܒܠ ܬܒܠܐ ܐܬܗܩܕ ܕܡܢ ܫܒܬܐ ܬܐܒܠܝ. ܘܡܢܒܐ ܐܝܬܝܐ ܥܒܗ ܥܣܪܐ ܕܬܒܠܐ ܐܬܕܒܪܬ.

ܕܐܘܪ̈ܗܝܐ ܕܐܝܟܢܐ ܦܝܣܐ ܠܘܬ ܠܡܦܠܠܗ̇ ܕܫܠܡܐ ܗܕܐ
ܕܐܝܬ ܒܡܠܟܘܬܐ ܐܬܪ̈ܐ ܐܫܬܠܡ ܗܘܐ. ܘܡܢ ܒܬܪ ܕܒܪ
ܚܠܦܘܗܝ ܛܥܢ ܒܫ̈ܢܐ ܦܪ̈ܣܝܬܐ ܘܐܫܬܪ. ܐܝܠ ܠܐܠܗܘܬܐ
ܡܕܝܢܬܐ ܘܡܥܪܒܐ ܗܘ ܕܐܝܬ ܗܘܐ ܠܗ ܫܘܠܛܢܐ ܕܗܪܒܘܬܐ
ܒܥܠܡ ܐܪܥܐ ܕܐܦܛܠܘܣ ܦܛܪ. ܘܫܒܩܗ ܒܗ ܕܐܢ ܡܫܐܝܬ
ܠܪ̈ܘܡܝܐ ܘܠܒܪ ܡܢ ܢܟܣ̈ܝܗ ܕܐܘܪܚܝܢ ܗܘܘ. ܒܗܕܐ ܕܐܠܗܐ
ܡܒܝܢ ܗܘܐ. ܘܫ̈ܠܝܬܐ ܦܪܫܬܐ ܕܐܠܗܐ ܠܢܘܗܪܐ ܘܠܚܘܒܬܐ
ܘܠܝܬܪܐ ܕܦܓܪܐ ܡܫܠܡ ܗܘܐ. ܘܟܕ ܗܠܝܢ ܡܢ ܒܢ̈ܘܗܝ
ܕܐܬܠܝܠܐ ܠܚܒܪܐ ܡܣܬܟܪ ܗܘ. ܠܗܘ ܫܘܪܝܐ ܕܡܚܝܢ ܗܘܐ
ܠܐܚܘܗܝ ܢܦܫ ܗܘܐ ܗܘܐ ܘܦܠܓܐ ܕܐܠܗܐ ܐܝܟ ܢܘܪܐ ܠܗ
ܡܟܘܠ ܗܘܐ. ܘܫܒܚܬܗ ܒܫܪ̈ܒܘܗܝ ܐܝܟ ܕܒܫܒܚܬܐ ܒܥܘܬܐ
ܡܫܬܪܪܐ ܗܘܬ. ܘܒܪܚܡܘܬܐ ܠܘܬ ܪ̈ܫܝܘܗܝ ܡܫܪܐ ܒܗܠܐ
ܐܬܦܢܝ. ܘܟܬ̈ܒܐ ܢܚܘܬܐ ܘܡܟܬ̈ܒܐ ܕܒܐܝܢܘܬܐ ܠܗ ܡܢܚܡܬ
ܗܘܐ. ܘܒܐܪ̈ܥܘܗܝ ܦܬܓܡܝܢ ܒܠ ܐܦܝܗܘܢ ܡܢܝܢ ܗܘܐ. ܘܒܠ
ܫܡܗ ܒܠ ܐܪܒܥܐ ܐܪ̈ܟܝܗ ܗܘܐ. ܘܟܕ ܡܬܕܪܝܢ ܗܘܘ ܠܗ
ܦܬ̈ܓܡܘܗܝ. ܕܒܚܪ̈ܘܫܘܗܝ ܡܫܘܬܐ ܡܛܠ ܠܗ. ܟܕ ܐܡܪ
ܗܘܐ ܠܗ. ܕܠܐ ܠܒܪ ܡܢ ܒܝܬܐ ܒܠ ܒܚܪ̈ܘܗܝ ܕܐܠܗܐ ܦܬܓܡܐ
ܠܡܦܩܘ. ܘܡܛܠ ܕܡܢ ܡܪܕܘܬܐ ܦܪܝܫܬܐ ܐܬܚܘܝ ܗܘܐ. ܡܢ
ܢܚܘܬܐ ܐܦܝܗܘܢ. ܗܘܐ ܕܠܒܪ ܡܢ ܢܚܘܬܐ ܡܬܕܒܪ ܗܘܐ ○ ○ ○

ܘܡܛܠ ܗܠܝܢ ܟܠܗܝܢ ܕܒܟܕ ܗܘܐ ܐܠܗܐ ܡܫܬܪܪܬ
ܒܡܫܒܪܢܘܬܐ ܦܪܝܫܬܐ ܥܡܪܐ ܕܟܦܪܢܗ ܐܬܟܒܪܘ ܗܘܘ ܘܗܢܘܢ
ܗܘܐ ܘܐܝܟ ܕܠܐܚܘܗܝ ܒܢܝܬܗ ܘܒܪܒܪ̈ܘܗܝ ܘܦܠܓܘܗ
ܘܡܒܪܢܘܬܗ ܕܒܟܐ ܗܘܐ. ܗܟܢܐ ܐܦ ܡܗܝܡܢ ܒܪ̈ܚܡܘܗܝ
ܠܫ̈ܪܪܐ ܕܝܗܒ ܗܘܘ. ܘܡܫܬܠܛܢܐ ܕܒܥܘܢܝܗܘܢ ܡܟܐ ܕܫܠܟܐ
ܠܬ̈ܪܥܘܗܝ ܡܢ ܐܘܪܚܐ ܕܪܘܚܐ ܡܛܠ ܗܘܐ ○ ○ ○

ܗܢܐ ܗܟܝܠ ܒܟܕܘ ܕܫܡܥ ܒܐܠܗܘܬܐ ܡܕܝܢܬܐ ܬܫܒܘܚܬܐ
ܕܫܠܡ ܫܪܪܗ ܬܘܒ ܗܘ ܗܘܐ. ܘܡܠܠܐ ܕܒܗܬܐ ܬܘܒ ܐܦܠܓܬ

ܒܡܘܪ̈ܕܗ̇ ܕܡܕܝܢܬܐ ܗܘܐ ܡܕܡ ܕܗܘܐ ܐܬܩܕܡ ܗܘܐ. ܘܒܪܘܡܠܐ ܐܚܝܕܐ ܗܘܬ ܒܝܕ̈ܝܐ ܡܬܬܠܝܢ ܗܘܘ ܕܝܠܗ ܪ̈ܗܘܡܝ ܗܘܘ. ܘܓ̈ܠܠܐ ܦܓܪ̈ܐ ܘܩ̈ܛܠܐ ܐܚܝܕܐ ܘܚܠܩܝܢ ܡܘܫܒ̈ܬܐ ܕܢܩ̈ܫܬܐ ܒܕܡܐ ܕܐܦ ܩ̈ܛܠܬܐ ܢܩ̈ܫܬܐ ܕܡܬܦܠܘܢܐ ܡܬܦܠܓ̈ܢ ܗܘ. ܠܚܝܬܐ ܗܕܐ ܢܩܦ. ܘܟܠܗ̇ ܡܕܝܢܬܐ ܥܡ ܬ̈ܠܕܝܗ̇ ܫܘܐܝܬ ܬܫܒܘܚܬܐ ܠܐܠܗܐ ܕܒ̈ܢܝܢܫܐ ܒܠܫܢܗܘܢ، ܡܫܒܚܝܢ ܗܘܘ. ܘܟܠܐ ܙܒܢܐ ܒܥܒܕܗ ܕܡܥܝܢܐ ܡܘܕܝܢ ܗܘܘ ܕܫܡܥ ܚܝܠܐ ܒܫ̈ܢܘܗܝ، ܕܗܘܝܐ ܕܢܡܒܪ ܐܩ̈ܠܝܢܐ ܘܡܫܘܬܗ ܗܘ، ܦܪ̈ܫܬܐ ܠܟܠܗܘܢ ܫ̈ܪܝܐ ܐܝܟ ܗܘܝܐ ܡܚܠ ܥܘܠܒܐ ܠܬܫܒܘܚܬܐ ܕܐܦܣܩܘܗ ܗܘܐ ܒܬ̈ܪܝܢ ܟܢܫ̈ܐ ܘܕܡܒܪܢܗ ܒܡܢܝܢܐ ܢܘܚܐ ܗܘܐ ܡܬܒܥܕ. . . .

ܡܕܝܢܬܐ ܕܐܠܩܘܫ

ܐܟܘܬܗܘܢ ܕܝܢ ܕܗܠܝܢ ܕܩܘ، ܒܐܦܣܘܣ ܗܘܕܐ. ܡܢ ܒܬܪ ܕܡ ܡܠܠ ܐܚܘܗ، ܒܪ ܐܒܘܗ، ܘܒܪ ܐܡܗ ܕܝܠܗ ܕܐܦܣܘܣ ܡܕܝܢܐ ܗܘܬ. ܕܥܡܗ ܗܘܐ ܐܠܩܘܫ ܗܕ ܒܩ̈ܠܐ ܕܐܠܗܐ ܠܡܫܠܡܘ ܡܫܪܒ ܗܘܐ. ܘܐܦ ܒܡܫܡܫܢܘܬܐ ܕܫܪܪܗ ܐܝܟ ܕܒܢܝܐ ܡܬܝܒܫ ܗܘܐ. ܐܦ ܩܘܡ ܠܡܫܠܡܘ ܒܩ̈ܝܘܬܐ ܘܒܬ̈ܓܪܐ ܒܟܡܗ ܡܬܬܦܫܝܢ ܗܘܘ. ܘܐܝܟ ܗܕܪܐ ܕܡܪܟܐ ܚܕ ܠܡܫܠ ܚܕ ܡܢܟܝܢ ܗܘܘ. ܘܕܐܢܝܢܐ ܡܢ ܓܒ̈ܝܐ ܢܗܒ ܘܟܘܬܐ ܡܬܬܒܥܝܢ ܗܘܘ. ܗܢܐ ܕܝܢ ܬܫܒܘܚܬܐ ܐܠܩܘܫ ܡܢ ܡܕܡ ܕܐܚܘܗ، ܢܛܠ ܢܦܫܗ ܠܐܠܗܐ. ܪ̈ܚܡܘ ܠܚܠܘܨܘܬܐ ܐܫܬܠܡ ܗܘܐ. ܘܟܠ ܒܦܘܩ̈ܕܢܝ ܕܡ̈ܠܟܐ ܕܪ̈ܚܡܐ ܪܘܪܒܐ ܡܫܡܫ ܗܘܐ. ܘܠܐ ܗܘܐ ܒܠܚܘܕ ܒܡܪܕܘܬܐ ܕܡ̈ܠܝܐ ܪܒܐ ܗܘܐ ܐܠܐ ܐܦ ܒܫܡܫܘܬܐ ܕܪ̈ܘܡܝܐ ܡܦܝܣ ܗܘܐ. ܘܒܚܝܠܐ ܕܡܫܝܚܘ ܗܘܕܐ ܕܒܢܐ ܦܓܥܐ ܐܬܘܗܝ، ܗ̇ܘܐ. ܘܒܫܘܠܛܢܐ ܐܠܗܝܐ ܡܢ ܠܥܠ ܐܝܟ ܕܒܐܪܥܢܘܬܐ ܕܚܝܫ ܠܦܠܚܘܬܐ ܐܬܓܠܝ ܗܘܐ. ܘܩܘ ܗܢܐ ܐܠܩܘܫ ܒܬܪ ܗܕܡܘܗܝ ܬܫܡܫܬܐ ܕܡܕܡ ܚܢܢ ܐܫܬܡܠܝܬ ܘܡܫܡܪܢܘܬܗ ܕܒܝܬܐ

ܘܕܐܠܗܐ ܐܒܘܗܝ، ܒܠܚܘܕ ܝܕܥ ܗܘܐ ܐܝܬܘܗܝ. ܘܟܕ ܠܐܝܘ ܠܗܘܢ ܗܒܠ ܘܐܙܕܕܒܘ ܘܒܝܬܘ ܦܘܝܢ ܕܫܡܥܘ ܡܬܬܥܝܢ ܗܘܘ. ܬܘܒ ܠܒܝܬ ܐܘܪ̈ܚܐ ܐܘܟܠܘܗܝ، ܘܠܫܡܥܐ ܕܒܬܪܗ ܡܕܡܘܗܝ، ܬܘܒ ܕܗܘ ܙܢܝܐ ܡܙܢ̈ܝܐ ܟܠܝ ܡܢ ܙ̈ܢܥܐ ܡܙܥܘܗܝ، ܗܘܘ. ܘܟܢ ܬܘܒ ܒܗܕܘܬܗ ܡܕܡܟܬܐ ܦܘ، ܗܘܐ. ܘܟܕ ܡܬܒܥܘܢܐ ܘܩ̈ܠܝܘܗܝ، ܘܟܠܘ ܠܒܥܘܐ ܕܟܫܟܫ ܗܘܐ ܠܢ̈ܟܝܢܘ ܝܟܘ. ܒܝܪܬܐ ܦܓܪ ܟܠܗܘܢ، ܕܟܘܡܟܡܗ ܕܡܟܐ ܢܟܕܘܢܝܗ، ◦ ◦ ◦

ܬܕܡܘܪܬܐ ܕܝܢ ܐܝܕܐ ܕܡܢ ܟܠܗ ܗܘܐ ܗܘܟܪܢܐ ܗܘܬ. ܝܕܥ ܐܢܐ ܕܠܐ ܡܬܡܡܟܢܐ ܠܦܘܢ ܕܠܐ ܗܘܐ ܒܝܪܬܐ ܕܟܝ̈ܢܘܗܝ ܐܟܘܬ، ܝܘܦܢ ܠܬܕܡܘܪܬܐ ܡܟܕܝܢ ܐܢܘܢ ܟܢ ܩ̈ܠ ܐܢܫܐ ܕܠܐ ܢܡܟܝܘܢ ܠܥܡܟܐ ܕܐܕܢܐ ܐܝܟ ܕܠܝܪܬܐ ܕܟܝܢܐ ܟܢܙ ܕܝܢ ܠܐ ܕܕܡ ܠܝ ܕܐܝܟ ܠܒܢܐ ܘܗܘܝ̈، ܗܡܟܢܘܬܐ ܢܟܗܐ ܐܦ ܐܢܫܝܢ ܬܕܡܘܪܬܐ ܐܢܐ ܕܟܡܘܢܝܢ ܕܗܘܕܐ ܕܐܠܗܐ ܐܘܬܒܪܬ ܘܗܘ̈ܕܐ ܕܗܠܝܢ ܕܐܬܦܬܚ ܠܟܘܢ ܠܟܠܗܘܢ ܟܡܘܪ̈ܗ ܕܗܘܪܐ ܡܕܝܬܐ ܡܢ ܐܢܫܝܢ. ܡܛܠ ܕܐܦܠܐ ܚܕ ܡܢ ܟܡܘܪܗ ܕܡܕܝܬܐ ܡܢ ܗܕܐ ܚܙܬܐ ܕܝܠܬܐ ܙܢܩ ܗܘܐ. ܟܕ ܓܝܪ ܟܡܘܡܟܘܗܝ، ܕܡܟܐ ܕܢܠܐ. ܟܙ ܐܢܫܐ ܕܐܠܗܐ ܐܬܒܪ، ܗܘܐ. ܘܟܐܩ̈ܐ ܟܬ̈ܠܘܗܝ، ܐܘܪ̈ܚ ܗܘ، ܟܙܒܬܗ ܫܘܒܥܐ ܙܟܐ ܘܪܘܟܐ ܦܬ̈ܝܐ ܘܟܠܠܐ ܬܫܒ̈ܚܐ ܠܥܡܟܐ ܙܟܐ ܕܠܝܢ ܗܘܘ. ܘܪܘܟܐ ܡܟܐ ܐܦ ܠܗ ܠܡܕܝܢܬ ܡܙܟܠ ܗܘܘ. ܘܟܠ ܐܢܫ ܟܪܘܟܬܐ ܘܟܕܝܠܬܐ ܐܕܘܗܝ، ܠܥܡܟܐ ܦܢܝܠ ܗܘ،. ܡܛܠ ܕܗܟܙܘ ܕܐܬܬܐ ܟܘܠܗ ܟܡ ܟܡܘ̈ܙܘܗܝ، ܟܗ ܟܢܘܡܟܐ ܦܘ ܡܬܦܝܓܠ ܗܘܐ. ܘܟܢ ܟܕܢܐ ܗܘ ܦܪ̈ܐ ܡܫܟܐ ܕܗܘܕܐ ܕܐܠܗܐ ܐܝܟ ܦܘ ܕܐܦܠܐ ܕܢܩܦܙܘܗܝ، ܡܟܐ ܐܥܒܕ ܗܘܐ. ܦܓܡܘܗܝ، ܘܟܕ ܬܠ̈ܠܐ ܡܕܡܬܪܟܐ ܕܡܕܝܬܐ ܗܡܢ ܗܘܐ. ܘܟܢ ܟܕܢܐ ܗܘ ܐܘܠܝܢܐ ܘܪܘܟܐ ܬܦܟ ܗܘܐ. ܘܡܬܕܡܟܐ ܗܘܐ ܠܐܝܠܕܐ ܕܡܢ ܐܠܗܐ ܐܬܝܠܕ ܗܘܐ. ܘܟܙܝ̈ܙܐ ܦܓܘܥܐ ܟܠ ܟܘܠ ܐܢܫ ܡܬܠܝܫ ܗܘܐ. ܘܠܟܠܗܘܢ

ܥܡܠ ܗܘܐ. ܘܬܠܡܝܕܘܗܝ، ܓܘܪܐ ܓܒܪܐ ܒܢܘܪܐ ܡܫܬܠܡܐ ܡܫܝܚ ܗܘ، ܐܝܟܢܐ ܕܒܕܡܘܬ ܡܐܪܘܬܐ ܒܗܘܪܐ ܕܬܠܡܝܕܘܗܝ ܢܦܫ ܒܗܘܟܠܗ ܘܒܗܘܢ ܒܬ̈ܪܡܗܘܢ، ܐܝܟ ܕܩ̈ܫܝܐ ܡܬ̈ܪܥܐ ܢܘܪܐ ܡܕܐ ܗܘܬ ܘܒܫܕܐ ܡܢ ܗܠܝܢ ܕܥܠܘܗܝ ܒܒܢ̈ܝ ܗܘ، ܒܕ ܒܣܝܥܐ ܓܠܝܢܐ ܐܢܬܘܗܝ ܗܘܐ. ܐܝܟ ܗܘ ܕܕܠܐ ܚܫܐ ܒܡܣܝܒܪܢܘܬܗ ܥܒܕ ܗܘܐ. ܡܢ ܠܓܘ ܕܝܢ ܐܝܬ ܗܘܐ ܠܗ ܡܕܒܪܢܐ ܗܘ ܐܠܗܐ ܕܒܗ ܥܡܪ ܗܘܐ. ܘܓܠܝܐܝܬ ܠܟܠ ܐܢܫ ܒܕܡܘܬ ܥܢܘܝܐ ܡܬܚܙܝܐ ܗܘܐ. ܘܡܛܠ ܗܕܐ ܠܒܝܬܗ ܓܠܝܐܝܬ ܕܗܘ ܫܘܪܗ ܕܡܫܝܚܐ ܐܦ ܒܬ̈ܪܘܦܠܝܢܐ ܓ̈ܠܝܢܐ ܐܬܒܢܝܘ ܠܫܝܬܗ. ܘܒܦܪܗܣܝܐ ܓܠܝܐܝܬ ܡܣܒܪܝܢ ܗܘܘ. ܘܒܩܠܐ ܪܡܐ ܘܒܡܠܬܐ ܓܠܝܬܐ ܒܗܘܕܘܬܗ ܕܐܠܗܐ ܡܘܕܐ ܗܘܐ. ܘܡܘܕܐ ܫܠܝܛܘܬܗ ܥܠ ܫܠܡ ܒܗܘܐ ܕܫܘܒܚ ܡܟܪܙ ܗܘܐ. ܕܡܪܝܐ ܗܘ ܒܟܠܝܢ ܠܐܝܠܝܢ ܕܠܘܬܗ ܐܦ ܗܢܘܢ ܡܬܦܢܝܢ

° °   ° °   ° °

ܘܗܕܐ ܒܠܚܘܕ ܫܪܝܬܐ ܬܫܒܘܚܬܐ ܐܦܝܣܩܘܦܗ ܢܝܫܐ. ܐܝܟ ܕܬܐܪܘܦ ܢܘܗܝ ܗܘܐ. ܗܢܘܢ ܒܢܝ ܐܠܦܘ̈ܗܝ ܕܡܕܢܚܐ ܒܕܡܘܬ ܕ̈ܝܘܐ ܡܫ̈ܬܠܛܢܐ ܥܒܕܝܢ ܗܘܘ ܘܒܦܘܩܕܢܗܘܢ ܒܐܒܐ ܪܒܐ ܡܣܬܒܪܝܢ ܗܘܘ. ܘܐܝܟ ܗܘ ܕܡܢ ܕܡܛܠ ܡܣܝܒܪܢܘܬܗ ܕܠܘܬ ܡܠܟܐ ܕܡܪܘܗ ܐܝܟ ܗܘ ܕܗܢܘܢ ܗܘ ܡܢܘܣܬܗܘܢ ܡܬܢܟܪܝܢ ܗܘܘ. ܘܡܢ ܒܐܝܕܝܐ ܡܬ̈ܢܪܐ ܡܫܚܡ ܗܘܘ. ܥ̈ܬܝܕܘܢ ܒܠܘܗܝ ܡܫܬܡܢ ܗܘܘ. ܘܒܬ̈ܚܝܬܘܢ ܒܠܘܗܝ ܡܬܓܘܫܝܢ ܗܘܘ. ܘܕܝܐܡܪ ܕܡܢ ܐܡܟܐ ܗܘ ܘܡܢܘ ܐܝܠܝܢ ܗܘܘ ܠܗ ܘܒܪ ܡܢܘ ܘܐܝܟܐ ܒܡܪ ܡܟܐܠܝܢ ܗܘܘ ܠܗ. ܘܕܢܒܚ ܘܢܬܠܦܘ ܠܦܘܠܚܢܐ ܦܓܪܝܢ ܗܘܘ ܠܗ. ܗܘ ܕܝܢ ܒܟܠܗܘܢ ܐܝܟ ܕܒܚ̈ܕܘܬܐ ܒܢ̈ܝܫܐ ܫܦܝܪ ܗܘܐ. ܘܐܝܟ ܕܒ̈ܥܕܬܐ ܡܫ̈ܬܠܛܢܐ ܡܬܟܬܫ ܗܘܐ ܒܗܘܢ. ܘܡܬܟܬܫܐ ܠܢܝ ܡܢܗܘ̈ܢ ܠܐ ܢܦܩ ܗܘܐ. ܘܚܠܝܡܐ ܒܗܕܐ ܒܪܬ ܡܠܐ ܡܬܚܫܒ ܗܘܐ. ܒܕ ܡܘܕܐ ܒܡܫܝܚܐ ܕܐܠܗܐ ܗܘ ܘܒܪܐ ܐܝܬܘܗܝ ܕܐܠܗܐ

ܕܪ̈ܘܡܐ ܥܡ ܩ̈ܠܝܐ ܕܡܟܬܒܢܘܬܐ ܒܪܗܘܡܬ ܒܬ̈ܐ ܒܡܬܒܢܝܢܘܬܗܘܢ
ܠܟܠܗ. ܘܥܠ ܐܩ̈ܘܗܝ ܠܐ ܡܣܝܡ ܗܘܘ. ܘܟܕ ܐܬܡܟܐ ܒܐܪܥܐ
ܒܬ̈ܠܝܗܘܢ ܠܐ ܡܬܒܛܠܝܢ ܗܘܘ. ܘܟܠܡܕܡ ܦܣܩܝܢ ܘܦܩ̈ܕܘܗܝ
ܡܬܥܒܪܝܢ ܗܘܘ. ܘܟܕ ܚܠܦܝܢ ܗܠܝܢ ܫܠܝܐܝܬ ܥܣܪ ܗܘܐ.
ܘܡܕܡܝܬ ܠܟܠ ܐܘܪܚܐ ܫܡܘܥܐ ܐܬܦܠܓ ܕܐܝܟ ܗܘܐ. ܘܠܠܐ
ܘܐܡܪܝܢܐ ܬܘܒ ܒܗܕܐ ܬ̈ܠܝܗܘܢ ܐܬܡܪܨܘ ܗܘ.. ܘܟܕ ܢܗܝܐ
ܐܢܫ̈ܐ ܠܟܠ ܕܐܝܟ ܠܐܦܝܘܗܝ ܡܠܟܐ ܒܪܢܫ ܚܝܠܐ ܐܬܬܘܗܝ
ܘܬܡܢ ܐܪܡܝܘܗܝ ܡܠܟܘܬܐ ܬܘܕܝܬܐ ܕܒܥܘܬܗ ܘܕܪܘܫܬܗ
ܒܠܠܐ ܐܪ̈ܓܐ ܒܬܫ̈ܒܚܐ ܗܘ.. ܘܟܠ ܕܡ̈ܠܝ ܕܬܫܒܚ̈ܬܐ ܒܗ
ܒܗܕܐ ܕܐܠܗܐ ܗܘ ܗܘܐ. ܘܦܓܪ ܕܡܠܟܘܬܗ ܫܘܪܘܫܗ
ܒܒܢܝܐ ܕܒ̈ܢܝܐ ܡܠܟܘܬܗ ܘܫܡܗܘܢ. ܘܡܫܒܚܐ ܥܠ ܐܦ̈ܘܗܝ
ܘܥܠ ܡܕܡ ܥܒܕ ܗܘܐ ܐܢܫܝܢܐ ܕܡܛܠ ܡܫܒܚܬܐ ܡܢ̈ܝܬܐ
ܦܝܠܝܦܘܣ ܐܬܩܛܠ ܗܘܐ. ܐܡܪܝܢ ܕܐܦܠܐ ܣܦܪ̈ܘܗܝ ܕܝܢ ܗܘܘ
ܠܐ ܡܠܘ. ܗܘ ܗܟܠ ܥܒܕܐ ܕܡܫܝܚܐ ܒܪܡܘܬ ܐܠܗܘܬ ܒܢܝܗ
ܘܡܠܟܘܬܗ ܐܬܩܛܠ ܗܘܐ ܘܬܘܪܐܝܬ ܒܬܘܟܠܢܐ ܕܥܠ ܐܠܗܘܬ
ܦܐܪ ܗܘܐ ܘܟܕ ܡܠܟܘܬܐ ܡܫܬܠ ܗܘܐ ܠܗ ܡܠܟܘܬܐ ܗܘ
ܬܘܒ ܡܢ ܗܕܐ ܕܒܝܫܘܬܐ ܐܬܬܘܗܝ، ܗܘܐ ܠܐ ܐܡܝܪ ܗܘܐ
ܘܬܘܒ ܡܫܬܠ ܗܘܐ ܠܗ ܕܒܪ ܡܠܘ. ܘܡܢ ܐܡܬܝܐ ܗܘ ܘܐܡܪܐ
ܒܥܒܪ ܗܘܐ. ܘܗܘ ܠܐ ܡܕܡ ܐܢܫܝܢ ܐܘܕ.. ܐܠܐ ܐܢ̈ܝ ܕܒܕܝܐ
ܗܘ ܕܡܫܝܚܐ. ܗܘ ܕܝܢ ܡܠܟܘܬܐ ܡܛܠ ܗܠܝܢ ܕܬܐܪܬ ܥܠ
ܥܢܘܬܗ ܡܬܗܦܟ ܗܘܐ ܘܬܐܪܬ ܒܥܒܕܘܬܗ ܦܓܥ ܗܘܐ. ܡܛܠ
ܒܪܬ ܥܠܡ ܕܗܘܐ ܕܠܐ ܡܬܕܒܪܐ ܗܘܬ ܘܦܓܥ ܕܬ̈ܠܝܗܘܢ
ܒܬܘܠܐ ܕܡܚܒܒ ܒܡܫܝܚܐ ܢܬܦܪܫ. ܘܢܘܪܐ ܢܕܠܩܘܢ ܒܗܘܢ.
ܘܟܠܗܘܢ ܕܝܢ ܕܕܝܢܐ ܡܕܡ ܕܐܬܦܩܕ ܠܗܘܢ ܥܠܡܐ. ܘܬܠܐ
ܗܘܐ ܗܘ ܫܘܕܐ ܒܪܘܚܐ ܡܫܝܚܐ ܐܝܟ ܕܒܣܝܬܐ ܕܫܠܝܬܐ
ܢܕܠ ܠܟܠܗܘܢ ܚܝ̈ܘܗܝ، ܒܗ ܒܟ̈ܘܗܝ، ܘܪ̈ܦܘܬܗ ܒܗܘ̈ܪܐ ܡܗܘܪܝܢ
ܗܘܘ. ܘܟܠܗ ܥܡܠܝܬ ܡܚܒܒ ܗܘܐ. ܘܕܡܘܬܐ ܐܘܪܚܬܐ ܦܪܘܦܘܗ

ܘܠܒ̈ܢܝܐ ܢܫܘܢ. ܘܥܠܝܗܘܢ ܡܕܒ̈ܪܢܘܬܐ ܒܝ̈ܘܪܐ ܫܠܝܛܐܝܬ ܦܐܫ
ܗܘܘ. ܕܓܒ̈ܪܐ ܡܢ ܢܫ̈ܝܗܘܢ ܘܒ̈ܢܝܗܘܢ ܠܡܬ̈ܠܐ ܕܫܬܦ̈ܪܐ
ܢܬܒܥܘܢ. ܘܠܥܠܝ̈ܡܐ ܘܠܝ̈ܢܘܩܐ ܟܕ ܡܬܦܪܢܝܢ ܒܒ̈ܬܐ
ܘܥܩ̈ܬܐ ܘܡܬܬܟܢܫܘܬܐ ܕܟ̈ܠ ܡܕܝܢܬܐ ܚܙܝܢ ܗܘܘ. ܘܗܝܕܝܢ
ܒܥܡܛ̈ܢܗܘܢ ܠܗܘܢ ܦܐܫ ܗܘܘ. ܘܡܫܬܒܐ ܕܐܬܦܩܕܘ ܗܘܘ
ܕܢܬܒܥܘܢ ܐܠܝܨ ܗܘܐ ܠܗܘܢ. ܘܟܕ ܗܢܐ ܡܫܬܘܠܐ ܕܠܐ ܠܐ ܗܘܐ
ܡܢ ܟܠ ܦ̈ܢܝܢ ܠܟܘܠ ܐܢܫ ܡܬܝܒܠ ܗܘܐ. ܦܘ ܡܕܡ ܟܟܠ ܐܫܦܩܘ
ܗܘܕܐ ܕܫܒ̈ܪܐ ܟܠܒܐ ܕܡܢ ܟܠ ܬܚܠܝܡ ܡܬܦܪ ܗܘܐ ܗܦܟ. ܟܕ ܐܢܫ
ܟܗܢܐ ܘܡܒܪܢܐ ܠܐ ܐܦܪܚ ܗܘܐ. ܐܦ ܡܢ ܕܠܝ ܕܟܗܢܐ ܒܟܝܬܐ
ܦܘܫ ܗܘܘ. ܟܗܝ ܗܘܐ. ܘܠܘܬܗ ܕܡܫܡܫܢܐ ܕܐܬܦܪܐ ܡܢܟ.
ܘܠܒܢܐܝܬ ܡܢ ܡܕܡܗܘܢ. ܘܡܢ ܟܠܗ ܦܠܓܗܐ ܕܠܘܬ ܡܫܡܫܢܐ
ܦܐܡ ܗܘܐ ܐܬܦܩܘ. ܘܠܐ ܗܘܟܐ ܠܟܠܗܘܢ ܟܕ ܠܘܬ ܡܫܡܫܢܐ
ܐܬܦܪܟܘ ܗܘܐ. ܘܟܕ ܗܘ ܐܘܪܟܢܘܗ ܡܟܢܫܐ ܗܘܐ. ܦܪܟ
ܘܐܢܫܗ ܕܡܟܢܐ ܠܟܗܘ ܗܘܐ ܘܡܢ ܢܘܫܐ ܦܠܓܐܐ ܕܫܬܦܪܐ
ܟܠܒܗܝ. ܘܟܐܗܟܟܐ ܡܢܬܪܐ ܘܡܟܝܟܐ ܡܢ ܟܗܝܡܗܘܬܐ
ܐܠܗܘܬܐ ܕܢܬܦܢܐ ܡܢ ܦܠܚܘܬܐ ܡܟܦܫ ܗܘܐ ܠܗ. ܟܕ ܐܡܪ ܠܗ
ܕܠܐ ܠܡ ܝܕܥ ܠܝ ܕܢܗܦܘܟ ܡܢ ܫܕ ܐܠܗܐ ܕܫܪܪܐ ܟܠܢܘܕܗܘܢ.
ܘܠܫܬܦܪܐ ܕܠܐ ܢܫܟܐ ܘܠܒ̈ܢܝܐ ܟܝܒܟܐ ܢܕܒܫ. ܗܘ ܕܝܢ ܕܢܠܬܗ
ܡܢ ܟܠ. ܡܗܝܡܢܘܬܗ ܕܠܘܬ ܬܥܒܕܐ. ܟܕ ܦܠܚܐ ܐܫܦܝܘ ܟܒܕ
ܗܘܐ ܘܡܛܠ ܡܗܝܡܢܘܬܗ ܫܠܡ ܕܢܫܘܒ ܡܢ ܟܠܗ ܐܟܣܢܝܘܬܗ ܕܟܪܗ
ܗܘܐ. ܕܠܟܒܪܐ ܕܦܠܓܐܘܬܐ ܢܗܘܐ ܡܬܟܢܫܐ. ܘܟܠ ܠܗܘܢܟܐ
ܘܟܠ ܟܘܠ ܡܟܬܒ ܐܫܟܚ ܘܡܢ ܦܠܓܗܐ ܠܟܝܒܬܐ ܠܐ ܐܝܬܠܗ.
ܘܟܐܡܕܟܬܐ ܕܟܝܬܐ ܘܟܠܢܟܐ ܕܡܟܠܠ ܬܫܒܘܚܬܐ ܫܕܐܝܬ ܟܠܠ.
ܐܡܟܢܐ ܕܟܟܠ ܐܦ ܠܗܘܢ ܠܬܪܘܫܘܗܝ، ܐܢ ܡܫܡܫܢܐ ܗܘܬ
ܕܢܗܘܐ ܢܟܝܐ ܗܘܐ. ܘܕܢܫܘܢ ܡܢ ܦܠܓܘܬܗܘܢ ܡܟܠܐ ܗܘܐ.
ܘܠܦܪܘܣܐ ܕܓܒܐ ܘܠܗܘ ܡܫܝܚܐ ܕܟܘܠܐ ܘܠܐܠܗܐ ܐܠܗܐ ܢܕܒܘܢ. ܘܟܕ
ܗܠܝܢ ܗܘ ܗܘܕܐ ܦܪܫܐ ܕܐܠܗܐ ܦܩܕ ܗܘܐ. ܗܢܘܢ ܡܫܡܫܢܐ

ܕܩܬܘܠܝܩܐ ܐܬܦܪܫ ܗܘܐ ܘܡܕܒܪܢܘܬܐ ܕܥܕ̈ܬܐ ܐܬܬܘܗܝ،
ܗܘܐ. ܘܒܡܘܡܬܐ ܕܒܥܐ ܘܒܐܘܪ̈ܚܬܐ ܥܡܘܪܐ ܢܩܫ ܢܦܫܗ ܗܘܐ.
ܘܠܐ ܡܢ ܬܪܥܝܬܗ ܕܦܠܚܐ ܐܘܕܥ ܗܘܐ. ܐܦ ܠܐ ܡܢ ܣܒܪܬܐ
ܕܦܠܚܘܬܐ ܐܬܕܟܪ ܗܘܐ. ܘܐܝܟ ܫܬܩܘܬܐ ܕܚܠܝܡ ܦܬ̈ܓܡܐ
ܡܫܬܪܢܘܬܗ ܦܘ ܠܒܣܝܡܘ ܐܦ ܗܘܐ. ܘܠܦܪܨܘܦܘܬܐ ܫܠܝܛܘܬܐ
ܘܠܡܫܘܬܐ ܐܝܟ. ܘܕܒܝܫܬ ܘܐܝܟ ܕܪܕܡ ܗܘܐ. ܠܡܠܟܘܬܐ
ܕܐܠܗܐ ܢܦܫܗ ܐܝܬܝ ܗܘܐ. ܘܟܕ ܡܬܪܕܘܬܐ ܗܘܬ. ܘܡܢ ܒܪܘ
ܫܒ. ܘܠܒܝܬ ܐܒܗ̈ܘܗܝ ܐܙܠ ܗܘܐ. ܠܐ ܡܫܟܚ ܗܘܐ ܕܢܚܙܐ ܒܗ
ܦܨܘܢ ܕܒܢܝܫܐ ܦܘܡ ܗܘܐ ܠܗ. ܡܛܠ ܐܘܦܩܣܘܢ ܦܨܘܢ
ܕܠܒܠܗ ܠܐ ܕܡܢ ܗܘܘ. ܫܒ ܠܗ ܡܢ ܠܘܬܗܘܢ ܘܠܐ ܐܬܟܠܠ
ܠܗ ܐܦܠܐ ܥܠ ܢܦܫܗ ܕܡܫܬܝܐ ܕܫܪ ܢܗܘܐ ܠܡܫܠܡ. ܡܬܕܒܪ
ܗܘܐ ܕܝܢ ܒܐܡܘܢܘܬܗ ܒܪܫܘܬܐ. ܘܚܝܠܐ ܕܐܠܗܐ ܗܘ
ܕܠܗ ܠܗ ܗܘܐ. ܠܗܕܐ ܡܕܝܢܬܐ ܕܠܝ ܐܬܬܐ. ܗ̇ܝ ܕܒܗ ܫܠܝܐ
ܕܡܕܝܢܬܐ ܡܬܬܕ ܗܘܐ. ܘܒܗ ܕܠܝ ܒܒܝܬܐ ܚܒܪ ܗܘܐ.
ܘܒܝܠܦܢܐ ܐܠܗܝܐ ܢܦܫܗ ܡܫܪܪ ܗܘܐ. ܘܟܬܒ̈ܐ ܡܕܢ̈ܚܝܐ ܡܢ
ܦܫܝܠܘܗ ܗܘܕܐ ܒܠܫܢܐ ܐܬܪܝܐ. ܘܦܫܩܐ ܕܪܘܒܐ ܡܫܪܐ
ܡܢ ܠܘܬܗ ܒܥܐ ܗܘܐ. ܕܡܛܠ ܗܢܐ ܥܠ ܡܫܠܡܢܘܬܐ ܕܡܕܝܢܬܗ
ܕܐܦܣܩܘ ܐܬܟܬܒܬ ܕܐܡܬܪ ܠܝ ܗܘܐ ܐܝܟ ܘܕܐܝܟ ܫܘܠܡܐ
ܗܘܐ ܠܗ. ܒܗܠ ܚܝ̈ܠܐ ܕܡܥ̈ܒܕ ܗܘ ܒܗ. ܘܡܟܢ ܕܦܠܓܐ
ܢܦܫܗ ܡܡܟܢܐ. ܘܠܐ ܢܬܒܕܪ ܥܠ ܠܚܡܘܬܗ. ܘܥܠ ܦܪܘܣܐ
ܕܠܗ ܘܥܠ ܡܫܡܫܢܘܬܗ ܘܥܠ ܒܪܬ ܩܠܗ
ܕܠܗ ܡܦܩܘܢܐ ܘܥܠ ܦܘܫ ܦܠܓܘܬܗ ܕܠܗ ܕܒܝܐ. ܘܬܘܒ ܡܢ
ܒܗܠ ܠܡܬܕܒܪܘ ܥܠ ܗ̇ܝ ܕܘܡܘܬܗ ܕܦܠܚ ܗܘܐ ܒܗ ܦܠܚܐ
ܕܐܠܗܘ. ܟܕ ܚܙܐ ܐܪܕܘܩܐ ܕܥܠܡ ܕܬܪ̈ܝܢ ܩܪ̈ܝܢ ܐܬܬܚܙܝ ܗܘܐ.
ܒܥܢܬ ܬܠܬ ܕܠܗ ܕܐܪܕܘܩܐ ܐܣܛܪ̈ܬܐ ܕܡܫܡܫܢܘܬܗ ܦܘܡ
ܡܕ̈ܫܬܐ ܐܝܬ. ܗܠܝܢ ܕܟܗܢ ܗܘܐ ܗܘܐ ܕܥܠ ܐܝܟ ܒܦܠܚܘܬܐ
ܦܘܠܚܢܐ ܘܥܡܠ ܦܠܚܐ ܕܡܦܩ̈ܘܢܐ ܕܡܕܝ̈ܢܬܐ ܢܕܥܘܢ

ܕܦܘܠܝܛܝܐ ܕܡܠܟܘܬܗܘܢ ܥܠܝܗ ܗܘܘ. ܘܠܡܫܐ ܥܡܡܝܐ ܠܒܫ ܗܘܘ. ܘܠܡܕܝܢܬܗܘܢ ܡܠܟܘܬܐ ܝܗܒ ܗܘܘ. ܒܪܒܢܘܬܗ ܡܢ ܢܨܚܢܝܗܘܢ. ܕܠܘܬ ܚܕܐ ܐܬܦܪܢܣܘ ܗܘܘ ܘܦܪܫܐ ܕܠܐ ܥܢܝܢܐ ܠܟܠ ܚܕܐ ܡܢܗܝܢ ܗܘܘ ܡܫܡܫܢܘܬܐ ܠܡܕܒܪܢܐ ܕܡܠܟܘܬܗܘܢ ܠܐ ܐܬܡܨܝܬ ܒܕܡܐ ܕܥܢܝܐ ܕܟܠܗ ܒܡܘܠܗ ܡܠܟܘܬܐ ܕܪܘܡܝܐ ܐܬܦܪܣ. ܡܢ ܒܬܪ ܦܠܓܝܢ ܕܥܡܡܐ ܒܪܡܫܬ ܢܦܪܫ ܕܝܢ. ܘܒܪ ܥܡܗ ܒܪܬܐ ܕܐܠܗܐ ܕܟܠ ܒܗܠ ܘܡܠܟܐ ܐܠܗܐ ܒܟܠܗ ܒܪܝܬܐ ܐܬܦܢܝ..

ܡܕܒܪܢܘܬܐ ܕܐܦܝܦܢܝܘܣ ܒܡܠܬ ܬܠܬ ܕܐܘܪܘܦܐ ܕܒܣܘܦܬܢ. ܒܣܘܪܝܐ ܡܕܒܪܢܘܬܐ..

ܗܘܐ ܡܪܢܝܐ ܘܦܪܢܣܐ ܒܢܝܐ ܘܡܫܢܐ ܕܒܢܝܢ ܕܦܘܠܝܛܝܐ ܕܪܘܡܝܐ ܠܟܝ ܗܘܐ. ܘܡܢ ܫܘܪܝܗ ܐܝܟ ܕܐܡܪ ܐܠܗܐ ܢܦܩ ܗܘܐ ܕܢܬܦܠܓ. ܡܠܟ ܡܢ ܦܘܠܘܣ ܕܗܘܘ ܡܕܒܪܢܝܗ ܐܘܪܘܦܐ ܦܪܘܩܐ ܕܟܠܢ ܦܠܓܐ ܗܘܐ. ܡܫܡܫܢܘܬ ܗܘܐ ܕܝܢ ܗܘܐ ܘܦܘܠܚܢܐ ܕܠܐ ܪܘܚ ܢܦܠ ܠܡܠܟܘܬܐ ܐܝܟ ܕܡܫܒܚܬܐ ܡܢ ܩܕܝܡ ܗܘܘ. ܘܦܘܠܚܢܐ ܠܟܠ ܐܬܪ ܐܬܡܒܪܘ ܗܘܘ. ܘܒܪܢܫܐ ܡܢ ܡܕܡ ܕܒܪܝ ܗܘܐ ܠܗܘܢ ܐܬܦܪܣܘ. ܐܝܟܢܐ ܗܟܠ ܡܠܟܐ ܐܢܬ ܕܦܘܠܚܢܐ ܕܬܫܒܚܬܐ ܐܝܟ ܕܬܫܥܝܬܐ ܥܠ ܢܘܚܡ ܐܠܗܐ ܕܗܘܕܐ ܐܦܝܦܢܝܘܣ ܗܘ ܕܥܒܕܘܗܝ ܐܝܟܢܐ ܠܚܘܪܝ ܩܕܝܡ ܡܠܟܐ ܗܘܐ. ܠܗܘܢ ܕܝܢ ܡܢ ܡܕܢܚܐ ܗܘܐ ܕܠܘܩܒܠ. ܘܡܢ ܡܕܢܚܐ ܦܘܠܘܣ ܕܒܡܠܟܘܬܗ ܕܟܠܡܐ ܗܘܐ ܡܫܡܫܝܢ ܗܘܘ. ܘܡܟܠܠܘܬܐ ܕܐܡܫܝܚܘܬܗ ܠܡܬܦܪܢܣܘ ܒܟܪܘ ܡܕܒܪܢܘܬܐ ܐܬܥܬܪ ܗܘܐ. ܘܒܗܘܬܐ ܕܦܘܠܚܢܐ ܦܪܘܩܐ ܒܥܠ ܗܘܐ. ܐܠܐ ܗܠܝܢ ܠܐ ܡܕܡ ܐܝܬ ܒܗܝܢ. ܕܗܫܐ ܠܗܕܐ ܬܫܒܚܬܐ ܕܒܟܠ ܡܬܬܒܪܬܐ. ܐܝܟ ܕܡ ܦܠܓܐ ܕܡܠܟ ܘܒܪܢܫܐ ܡܠܘܬܐ ܕܗܝ ܢܦܫܐ ܡܢܥܬ ܒܟܠ ܢܦܫ ܘܕܘ ܦܠܓ ܠܡܬܕܒܪܘ ܕܐܝܟ ܒܡܕܒܪܢܘܬܐ ܕܐܝܟ ܗܝ ܡܢ ܒܢܝܢܐ ܘܡܢ ܢܦܫܐ

ܒܝܘܡܐ ܓܝܪ̇ ܕܐܫܬܘܕܝܬܐ ܝܗܒ ܐܢܘܢ ܘܒܝܢܐ ܪܒܐ ܕܠܐ ܡܬܕܟܐ
ܥܬܝܕ ܐܢܘܢ. ܘܕܢܚܫܘܩܘܢ ܠܡܣܬܐ ܒܒܕ ܐܢܘܢ. ܘܒܪܥܝܬܗ
ܠܡ̈ܫܡܫܢܐ ܘܠܡܠܠܘ ܠܟܡܐ ܕܒܡܗ ܡܟܠܠ ܗܕܐ ܠܟܢܫܘܬܗܘܢ
ܒܬܡܗܐ ܐܫܡܥܗܘܢ، ܘܦܩܕ ܟܠܗܘܢ ܡܫܡܫܢܐ ܕܠܟܝܬ
ܫܡܫܐ ܢܬܠܡܕܘܢ ܘܬܡܢ ܐܬܟܬܪܘ ܡܩܒܠܬܐ ܩ̈ܠܝܠܐ. ܘܒܪ
ܩܘܡ ܥܠܝܗ ܐܘܪܚܐ ܐܬܬܣܝܡܘ ܗܘܘ. ܐܝܟܢܐ ܓܝܪ ܡܫܝܚܐ
ܘܦܪܨܐ ܐܢܫܘܗܝ، ܕܚܙ ܡܢ ܦܘܡ̈ܝܢ ܣܩܘܒܠܐ. ܐܬܐ ܡܢ ܓܒܐ ܡܕܢܚܐ
ܘܬܚܒܫܬ ܠܟܝܬ ܐܘܪܚܐ ܕܢܦܩܘܪ ܠܐܢܫܘܗܝ، ܐܙܠ ܗܘܐ.
ܘܡܛܠ ܕܡܢ ܩܕܡ ܕܢܬܠ ܠܟܝܬ ܐܘܪܚܐ. ܒܐܓܘܢܐ ܩܪ̈ܝܒܐ
ܕܡܕܒܪܢܘܬܐ ܐܬܬܩܢܬ ܠܟܝܬ ܫܡܥܢܐ ܬܫܠܡܬ ܟܠ. ܘܐܝܟ
ܓܝܪ ܕܠܗܘܕܝܘܬܐ ܡܟܝܠ ܗܘܐ. ܠܡܫܡܥܢܐ ܐܬܟܢܫ. ܘܗܕܡ
ܠܐܘܪܚܐ ܕܢܦܩ ܢܦܫܐ ܕܐܝܟܢܐ ܕܬܪܝܢ ܐܬܬܠܝܛ ܗܘܐ.
ܘܐܬܒܗܬܘ ܕܗܠܝܢ ܐܦ ܕܢܦܫܗ ܘܒܪ ܘܗܢܐ ܐܝܟܢܐ ܓܒܐ ܡܢ
ܠܟܝܬ ܗܢ̈ܕܝܐ ܕܐܠܗܐ ܐܬܚܙܝ ܠܗ. ܫܠܚ ܐܝܟܢܐ ܕܬܫܡܫܬܐ
ܕܠܬܗܘܢ ܘܐܝܟܢܐ ܕܡܬܚܫܒܢܘܬܗ ܕܕܢܚܘܗ ܕܠܘܬ ܗܢ̈ܕܝܐ
ܒܐܝܟ ܡܫܡܫܢܐ ܡܫܬܐ ܦܩܕ ܟܠܗܘܢ، ܐܬܬܗܘܦ ܗܟܠ
ܐܦ ܗܢܐ ܒܡ ܗܘܘܢ ܡܕ̈ܘܢܐ. ܘܗܘܘ ܟܠܗܘܢ ܬܠܡ̈ܝܕܐ ܒܡܫܝܚܐ.
ܕܐܬܬܗܘܢ ܠܡܫܬܐܘܘ ܘܟܢܫܘܗ ܐܬܬܗܘܢ، ܗܘܐ ܡܢ ܒܥܠܘܗ.
ܘܕܢܩܫܘܗ ܐܬܬܗܘܢ، ܗܘܐ ܡܢ ܓܪܒܐܠܘ ܡܕܝܢܬܐ. ܘܪܘܡܠܘܗ
ܐܬܬܗܘܢ، ܗܘܐ ܦܪܘܩܐ ܕܒܕܬܐ ܘܕܢܩܦܠܘ ܡܕܝܢܬܐ.
ܘܐܟܬܓܠܝܐ ܬܪ̈ܝܢ ܦܢܝܗ ܘܐܠܗܢܕܪܘܗ. ܘܐܫܪܝܐ ܬܘܒ
ܐܠܗܢܕܪܝܐ. ܘܬܪܝܢ ܗܢܘܢ ܕܐܬܘ ܒܠܫܢܗܘܢ ܕܡܫܪܬܐ ܠܟܝܬ
ܐܘܪܚܐ ܐܫܬܠܡܬ ...

ܗܠܝܢ ܟܠܗܘܢ ܫܡܥܬ ܒܗ ܒܡܕܢܚܐ ܐܫܬܠܡܬ ܕܪ̈ܫܝܗܘܢ
ܢܬܒܠܘܢ ܘܡܐܪ̈ܥܬܐ ܘܚܙܘܪ ܒܐܪܙ ܗܢܐ ܫܪܒܐ ܗܘܐ. ܘܒܗ
ܒܝܘܡܐ ܫܘܠܡܐ ܚܕ̈ܡܐ ܕܩ̈ܠܝܠܐ ܗܘܐ. ܕܠܗ ܕܗܘ ܙܒܢܐ
ܘܩܠܝܠܐ ܘܪ̈ܘܡܐ ܕܒܬܪܬܘܬܗ ܒܬܪ ܡܫܢܝ ܗܘܐ. ܘܦܘܢ

ܡܕܝܢܬܐ ܕܐܝܓܦܛܘܣ ܘܕܬܪܝܢ ܐܠܟܣܢܕܪܝܐ ܘܕܬܪܝܢ ܕܡܩܕܘܢܝܐ
ܘܕܦܠܣܛܝܢܘܣ ܘܕܪܘܡܝܘܣ ܘܕܟܠܗܘܢ. ܟܠܗ ܬܪܬܝܢ ܕܐܪܝܘܦܣܐ
ܕܒܩܘܡܬܗܘܢ ܒܡܕܝܢܬܐ ܡܒܕܪܬܐ.

ܟܐܕܐ ܗܘܐ ܕܟܠ ܒܡܥܡܪ ܒܡܕܝܢܬܗܘܢ ܚܝܝܢ ܗܘܘ. ܐܦ
ܗܦ ܒܡܕܝܢܬܐ ܗܘ ܗܘܐ ܟܕܐ ܗܘܐ ܗܘܐ. ܒܡܪܘܬܗ ܒܪ ܪܘܡܝܐ
ܕܪܟܒܐ ܡܬܚܙܝܐ ܗܘܐ. ܘܫܝܢܬܐ ܒܬܐܦܪܘ ܡܬܒܕܒܪܐ ܗܘܬ
ܘܫܪܝܐ ܗܪܝܢܐ ܘܒܚܪܢܝܐ ܒܐܘܦܪܝܡ ܡܒܕܡ ܕܢܫܘܢ. ܘܥܡܟܐ
ܘܦܟܐ ܠܗܬ ܥܠ ܐܢܫ ܪܘܦ ܗܘܐ. ܕܐܝܟܢܐ ܗܘ ܕܥܒܕ ܡܠܟ
ܥܡܗ ܐܬܕܒܪ ܘܬܠܬܐ ܕܒܡܢܗ ܒܝܬ ܥܒܕܐ ܕܫܘܦܪܐ ܐܢܫܝܐ
ܒܐܘܡܢܘܬܐ ܕܗܘܕܝܐ ܠܬܐܦܪܘ ܢܬܕܒܪ. ܕܡܢ ܣܘܓܐܐ ܢܬܐܟܠܘܢ.
ܗܕܐ ܕܝܢ ܡܘܡܢܬܐ ܗܘܐ ܗܘܐ ܐܘܪܚܗ ܡܠܟܘܬܐ ܠܫܢܝܐ.
ܘܥܕ ܕܡ ܦܠܟܐ ܕܗܠܝܢ ܐܬܬܟܡܢ ܕܐܙ ܬܘܟ ܘܚܠܝܫܐ ܐܢܫܝܐ
ܡܥܫܠܝܢ ܒܡܘܫܬܗܘܢ ܘܫܠܬܝܐ ܒܦܓܪܗܘܢ ܒܡܚܫܐ ܥܬܐ
ܐܬܬܗܘܢ ܗܘܘ. ܘܟܕ ܡܦܡܘܢܐ ܠܬܐܦܪܘ ܐܙܠ ܗܘܐ.
ܘܡܬܦܪܩܐ ܕܡܕܝܢܬܐ ܒܪܬ ܗܘܐ. ܒܬܪܐ ܗܠܝܢ ܥܬܐ ܠܒܝܬܐ
ܕܡܕܡܘܢ ܡܢܗ. ܘܐܬܪܐ ܕܒܥܡܘܢ ܦܘܢ ܠܟܘܬܪܗܘܢ ܡܢܪܘ
ܘܡܕܡ ܕܝܢܐ ܐܘܪܚܗܘܢ ܡܪܗ. ܘܫܘ ܡܕܡ ܕܡܢ ܐܢܫܝܐ ܒܬܥ
ܗܘܐ ܕܢܦܩܐ ܠܗܘܢ ܒܕ ܠܡܘܡܗܘܢ ܦܟܪܝܢ ܗܘܘ. ܒܒܒܕܐ
ܫܡܗ. ܘܡܡܒܪܘܬܗܘܢ ܡܬܪܬܐ ܘܕܠܝܠܘܬܐ ܕܝܒܝܫܘܢ
ܕܠܗܬ ܡܕܝܢܬܐ ܫܡܗ. ܡܕܡܝܡ ܗܘܘ ܕܡ ܒܕ ܦܟܝܡ ܗܘܘ.
ܡܐܒܝܪܝܡ ܗܘܘ ܕܒܬܘܦܠܝܢܐ ܐܢܫܝܢ ܘܕܢܬܕܪܘ ܒܬܐܦܪܘ ܬܘܒ
ܠܫܘܬܐ ܒܡ ܦܘܢ ܐܢܫܘܗܝ ܕܟܠܗ ܐܝܟܢܐ ܡܢ ܐܘܪܚܗܘܢ
ܡܟܡܘܢܐ ܒܓܝܡ ܗܘܘ. ܗܕܐ ܕܝܢ ܒܗܠܝܢ ܠܒܡܘܬܐ ܕܥܘܒ
ܡܣܝܡ ܕܒܬܠܝܠܐ ܕܠܗ. ܠܟܠ ܐܢܫ ܡܫܘܐ ܗܘܐ. ܘܠܘܫܡܐ
ܕܦܪܘܢܐ ܒܫܠܝܡܘܬܐ ܕܐܬܠܝܠܘܗܝ ܡܒܘܫܐ ܗܘܐ. ܘܦܠܢܐܝܬ
ܘܕܝܫܢܝܬ ܡܫܘܡܐ ܗܘܐ. ܕܠܐ ܢܘܪܐ ܘܠܐ ܩܪܝܠܐ ܐܦܠܐ
ܫܘܬܐ ܒܪܢܝܬܐ ܠܦܠܝܫܘܗܝ ܕܒܢܐ ܠܐ. ܡܒܥܝܢ ܠܡܒܥܒܕܘ.

ܠܐ ܗܘܐ ܕܝܢ ܡܛܠ ܡܕܡ ܕܢܦܩܐ ܠܕܠܝܐ ܐܬܦܪܫ ܗܘܐ ܡܛܠ
ܕܥܠܘܗܝ ܕܡܪ̈ܘܗܝ. ܘܥܠܘ ܒܡܕܝܪ̈ܗ ܕܠܐ ܒܕܠ ܐܝܬܘܗܝ ܗܘܐ.
ܘܟܕ ܠܢܡܘܣܐ ܕܦܓܪܘܬܐ ܕܐܬܚܪܝܐ ܠܐ ܐܫܬܥܒܕ ܗܘܐ.
ܘܠܬܠܡܝ̈ܕܐ ܡܢܬܐ ܕܠܐ ܢܦܩܐ ܠܗ ܦܓܪ ܗܘܐ. ܡܛܠ ܕܒܪ ܐܢܫܐ
ܗܘܐ ܒܡܕܝܢܬܐ ܒܟܠ ܡܕܡ. ܘܒܢܦܫܗ ܠܐܠܗܐ ܝܗܒ ܗܘܐ.
ܘܡܛܠ ܢܦܫܗ ܘܡܛܠ ܫܪܒܐ ܕܕܘܪܐ ܕܡܬܝܪܬܘܬܗ ܫܢܝܐ ܡ̈ܢܗ
ܐܦ ܡܢ ܡܕܡ ܕܢܫܬܠܛ ܠܡܫܡܫܢܘܬܐ ܡܢ ܒܡܕܝ̈ܢܬܗ ܕܡܕܝܢܬܐ ܘܡܢ
ܗܘܐ ܘܡܢ ܒܪܐ ܦܓܪܢܐ ܘܡܢܗܘܬܐ ܕܒܢ̈ܝܬܐ ܘܡܫܡܫܢܐ ܒܡܕܝ
ܗܘܐ ܕܡܢ. ܐܬܚܙܝܘ ܗܘܘ ܒܪ̈ܝ ܩ̈ܕܝ ܒܪܐ ܡܕܝܢܬܐ ܫܪܟܢ
ܒܡܫܬܘܕܝ ܘܟܕ ܠܒܪ ܕܝܢܐ ܕܡܫܡܫܢܐ ܐܬܦܪܫܘ ܒܥܠܘ̈ܗ
ܡܢܦܪܬܐ ܕܡܫܡܫܢܘܬܐ ܗܢܐ ܐܬܠܚܡܐ ܕܒܝܢܘܬܐ ܪ̈ܒܐ.
ܘܡܫܒܚܐܢܬ ܦܘ ܕܢܐ ܒܬܫܒܚܬܐ ܡܢ̈ܐ ܠܗܬܗ ܐܬܚܫܒ ܘܬ̈ܓܪܐ
ܕܫܠܝܐ ܕܠܐ ܡܢܝܢ ܥܠ ܦܓܪܗ ܐܦܠܐ ܗܘܐ ܘܡܦܪ̈ܩܐ ܕܪܘܒܐ
ܦ̈ܝܘܗܝ ܕܠܐ ܡܫܡܫܐ ܕܢܬܒܬܒܘܢ ܒܓ̈ܒܘܗܝ ܐܫܬܘܝ ܘܡܥܠܝܢ
ܥܠܝܢ ܗܘ ܗܘܕܐ ܫܠܬܢܐ ܕܐܠܗܐ ܐܝܟ ܡܬܒܢܐ ܐܬܬܒܥ.
ܘܡܫܘܬܐ ܕܬܬܒܩܫܘܗ ܐܫܪܝܐ ܒܡܫܡܫܢܘܬܐ ܕܡܫܘܬܐ ܕܟܢܐ
ܢܘܪܐ ܓܙܪܬܐ ܢܘܚ. ܢܘܪܐ ܗܘܬ ܕܝܢ ܙܦܬܐ ܘܓܙܪܬܐ ܗܝ
ܕܒܗ ܢܚܐ ܗܘܐ. ܐܝܟ ܕܠܐ ܕܠܠܐܢܬ ܬܫܒܐ ܢܦܫܗ ܡܢ ܦܓܪܗ
ܘܬܬܢܝܚ. ܘܬܡܢ ܒܪܡܫܬ ܕܗܘܐ ܓܠܝܐ ܒܒܘܪܐ ܕܢܘܪܐ ܙܩܝܦܬܐ
ܐܬܟܢܫ ܦܓܪܗ ܘܕܡܘܬܐ ܕܥܒܕܘܗܝ ܕܠܘܬ ܐܠܗܐ ܗܘ.
ܘܒܝܩܘܬܐ ܕܙܩ̈ܝܐ ܥܬܝܩܐ ܕܐܢܘܬܐ ܐܬܟܠܠ. ܘܡܛܠ ܕܐܢܫ
ܠܐܠܗܐ ܦܐܪܐ ܕܥܘܡ ܠܓܒܢܗ ܦܟܠ. ܦ̈ܝܘܗܝ ܫܘܗ ܡܬܠܡܕܢܐ
ܕܠܘܬ ܐܠܗܐ ܐܬܠܐ ܕܥܠ ܓܒܐ ܕܢܗܘܐ. ܘܒܟܠܗ ܙܒܢ ܕܗܢܐ
ܡܕܝܢܐ ܫܠܝܚܐ ܒܗ ܒܒܕܢܐ ܕܒܘܫܪܐ ܕܡܕܝܢܘܬܗ ܒܗ
ܒܡܕܝܢܬܐ ܐܦܠܘ ܗܘܕܐ ܘܬܠܡܐ ܬܡܝܢܘܬܐ ܗܕܐ ܕܝܢ
ܕܒܘܦ̈ܬܐ ܐܬܚܙܝܘ ܡܢ ܡܓܒܘܢܐ ܕܗܢܐ ܡܥܡ ܒܢܝܐ
ܢܡܠܘܢ ܕܡܢ ܫܘܬܐ ܠܐܬܟܠܘܢ .٠.

ܘܟܕ ܗܠܝܢ ܚܙܐ ܗܘܐ. ܙܥܘܪܐܝܬ ܡܢ ܟܠܗܘܢ ܩ̈ܢ ܐܢܫܐ ܟܠ
ܡܠܬܗ ܕܡܫܝܚܐ ܐܫܡܥ ܗܘܐ. ܘܟܕ ܚܙܐ ܚܝܠܗ ܕܗܘ ܕܐܘܕܝ.
ܒܗ. ܗܘ ܗܘܐ. ܘܟܕ ܕܢܚܐ ܫܡܫܐ ܗܠܝܢ ܫܪܝ ܬܘܒ ܒܣܘܕܐ
ܐܬܬܢܝܚ. ܘܒܫܘܡܠܝܐ ܕܡܕܒܪܢܐ ܘܕܝܢܐ ܡܫܝܚܘܬܐ ܒܢܬ
ܐܘܪܚܐ ܐܬܡܠܝ ܒܗ ܘܐܬܬܣܝܡ. ܘܟܫܝܪ ܗܘܝܐ ܒܝܢ ܩ̈ܘܠܐ ܗܘ̈ܕܐ
ܠܦ̈ܬܓܡܐ ܕܒܢܬ ܠܗ ܒܡܕܒܪܢܘܬܗ ܐܬܡܠܟ. ܘܗܢܐ ܐܦ ܠܒ
ܒܐܝܠܢܐ ܐܬܚܒܫ ܘܐܫܬܦܪ ܒܢܝܢ ܕܝܢ ܡܠܠ ܕܡܢ ܦܠܛܝܢܐ
ܒܢܘܡ ܐܬܬܣܝܡ ܗܘܐ. ܒܢ ܒܢܝܫܐ ܕܗܘ̈ܕܐ ܕܒܗܢܐ ܐܬܪ
ܒܦܠܚܘܬܐ ܐܬܬܟܝܠ. . . ●

ܡܕܝܢܬܐ ܕܦܠܣܛܝܢܘܣ ܒܢܝܐ ܡܕܝܢܬܐ ܒܢܝܬ ܗܕܪܝܢܘܣ
ܕܐܪܙܘܦܐ ܕܒܩ̈ܦܘܠܝܢ.

ܫܢܬܐ ܗܘܬ ܕܗܕܪܝܢܘܣ ܕܐܪܘܦܐ ܘܡܠܟܐ ܕܪܗܘܡܝܐ ܫܢܝ ܡܢ
ܡܕܝܢܬܐ ܒܝܬ ܗܘܐ ܘܟܢܫܐ ܕܦܠܣܛܝܢܐ ܐܘܪܫܠܡ ܡܕܝܢܬܐ
ܐܬܬܗܝܗ ܗܘܐ. ܗܘ ܕܒܗ ܒܢܝܢܐ ܠܦܠܣܛܝܢ ܡܕܝܢܬܐ ܡܢ
ܫܠܝܛܘ ܐܬܒܢܝ ܗܘܐ. ܐܬܬ ܗܘ ܕܝܢ ܬܘܒ ܡܕ̈ܝܢܬܐ ܕܫܠܡܐ
ܕܗܕܪܝܢ ܕܟܠܗ ܠܒܪ ܡܢ ܗܠܝܢ ܡܕ̈ܝܢܬܐ ܕܠܡܕܒܪ ܠܒܠܝܗܘܢ ܩ̈ܢ
ܐܢܫܐ ܡܬܠܒܝܢ ܗܘ. ܒܡܕ̈ܝܢܬܐ ܒܪ ܟܠ ܡܕܒܪ̈ܢܐ ܕܒܕܬܗ
ܕܐܠܗܐ ܟܠܝܘܕ ܦܩܕ ܗܘܐ ܕܢܒܢܘܢ. ܒܡܕ̈ܝܢܬܐ ܕܝܢ ܐܚܪ̈ܢܝܬܐ
ܦܩܘܕܢܐ ܗܘܐ ܡܢܝܐ ܕܠܟܘܠ ܐܢܫ ܫܘܝܐܝܬ ܐܠܝ ܗܘܐ
ܕܠܡܬܒܢܝܐ ܕܠܐ ܢܫܢܐ ܟܠܗܘܢ ܒܢ̈ܝܐ ܕܟܠ ܡܕܝܢ ܒܢ̈ܝܢܐ ܘܢܝܫܐ.
ܐܚܪܝܢܐ ܢܒܢܘܢ ܘܐܬܗܘܡ ܠܗܘܢ ܢܡܘܣܐ ܕܠܫܘܪܝܐ ܢܒܢܘܢ
ܐܝܟ ܗܢܘܢ ܗܘܘ ܒܪ ܦܘܩܕܢܗܘܢ ܕܦܠܘܚܐ ܕܒܢܝܢܘܬܗܘܢ
ܠܡܣܪܒܘ ܒܢ ܐܠܗܐ ܡܠܟܐ ܕܟܠ ܢܟܝܢ ܗܘܘ. ܘܟܕ ܗܠܝܢ ܕܡܢ
ܡܠܟܐ ܦܩܝܕܝܢ ܗܘ. ܒܒܢܝܐ ܡܬܡܛܠܝܢ ܗܘ. ܠܦܘܠܚܢܐ ܠܦܠܚܬܐܘܣ
ܟܕܪܐ ܡܕܝܢܬܐ ܕܦܠܣܛܝܢܐ ܠܐܘܪܫܠܡ ܒܪ ܬܘܒ ܐܬܬܗܝܗ ܗܘܐ
ܐܬܝܠܕ ܘܒܒܢܝܐ ܒܕܡܘܬ ܡܠܟܐ ܒܟܠܗܝܬ ܐܬܠܒܝ ܗܘܐ.

ܠܕܝܢܐ ܟܐܢܐ ܕܐܠܗܐ ܕܥܠ ܟܠ. ܘܟܕ ܗܠܝܢ ܒܡܠܐ ܪܡܐ ܠܗܘܢ
ܐܡܪ ܗܘܐ. ܘܕܠܐ ܕܚܠܬܐ ܘܕܠܐ ܐܪܗܒܘܬܐ ܬܡܢ ܦܐܫ
ܗܘܐ. ܒܦܘܪܥܢܐ ܕܕܝܢܐ ܗ̇ܘ ܕܬܡܢ ܦܐܫ ܝܬܒ ܗܘܐ. ܫܩܠܘܗܝ
ܡܦܠܚ̈ܢܐ ܘܓܢܒ ܟܠܗܘܢ ܕܟܝܘܬܐ ܢܬܚܟܠ. ܚܝܐ ܗܘܐ ܓܝܪ
ܕܐܢܫ ܢܫܟܚ ܕܡܢ ܡܠܐ ܕܩܛܠܘܗܝ. ܕܗܘܝܐ ܫܒ̈ܝܐ ܡܬܚܫܠܝܢ
ܗܘܘ ܘܫ̈ܒܝܐ ܟܠ ܛܘܒܝܢ ܡܟܪܙ ܗܘܐ. ܘܡܛܠ ܕܐܝܟܐ
ܕܐܬܚܙܝܘ ܗܘܘ ܩ̈ܠܝܐ ܗܠܝܢ ܒܟܪܟܐ ܕܢܦܩ ܒܒܪ ܗܘܐ.
ܟܪܣܬܗ ܗܘ ܛܒܝܐ ܡܨܥܬ ܡܕܝܢܬܐ ܐܬܛܒܝܐ ܡܛܦܝܣ ܗܘܘ
ܠܗ. ܘܟܕ ܘܥܬܗ ܗܝ ܕܟܗ ܡܣܟܢ ܟܪܝܐ ܡܟܠ ܗܘܐ ܩ̈ܛܠ.
ܘܡ̈ܬܥܝܬܐ ܐܝܟ ܕܠܘܬܐ ܢܫܝܢ ܐܬܦܬܝܒ ܗܘܘ. ܘܡܬܪܗܒܐܝܬ
ܕܦܘܪܥܢܐ ܢܫܟܚܘܢ ܡܬܚܫܒܝܢ ܗܘܘ. ܕܘܟܠܝܢܘ ܕܝܢ ܩ̈ܛܠܐ ܟܪ
ܒܠ ܕܗܠܝܢ ܗܘܢܐ ܐܬܗܦܟ ܦܘܪ. ܘܡܢ ܡܗܘܬܐ ܕܒܘܪܐ ܠܗܘܕܐ
ܐܦܦܘܗܝ ܡܛܠ ܕܐܣܒܪ ܕܠܐ ܥܘܠܐ ܡܪܫܘܬܗ ܘܡܟܠܬܗ ܡܗܘܡ
ܟܪܝܐ ܕܒܘܪܐ. ܘܐܗܘܒܟܐ ܫܒܬܐ ܕܡܗܘܡ ܟܪܝܐ ܐܝܟ ܩ̈ܠܟܐ
ܡܪ̈ܫܝܥܐ ܟܠ ܗܘܕܐ ܦܓܪ ܗܘܐ ܕܠܥܝܢ ܢܬܦܘܡ. ܟܪܡ ܕܝܢ ܟܕ
ܗ̇ܘ ܗܘܕܝܐ ܕܟܗ ܡܟܠܠ ܗܘܐ ܐܥܬܦܠ. ܐܠܐ ܫܘܒܗ ܥܙܝܙܐ
ܡܢ ܐܠܗܐ ܠܐ ܐܬܦܩܡ. ܐܦܠܐ ܠܥܝܢ ܡܠܠܐ ܡܢ ܟܪܘܙܘܬܐ
ܡܥܠܐ ܗܘܐ. ܘܟܝܠ ܡܢ ܠܘܬ ܐܠܗܐ ܩ̈ܠܟܐ ܕܥܠ ܚܠܦ
ܬܟܬܘܒܐ ܕܐܟܣܢܘܣ ܦܘܪܥܢܐ ܡܓܠ. ܘܚܠܐ ܡܥ̈ܢܝܐ ܠܒ
ܡܢ ܡܕܒܚܐ ܐܬܟܒܠ ܗܘܐ ܗܕܝܡ ܠܟܠ ܐܢܫ ܬܗܘܕܐ ܪܒܐ ܐܢܫ
ܗܘܐ. ܗ̇ܘ ܓܝܪ ܕܠܥܝܢ ܐܬܦܠܒ ܗܘܐ ܟܪ ܥܒܬܗ ܒܟܘܡܟܬܐ
ܕܐܠܗܐ ܚܠܬܢܝܬ ܡܟܠܠ ܗܘܐ. ܘܟܡܟܢܘܬܐ ܠܒܢܝܐܬ
ܡܥܬܒܪܗ ܗܘܐ ܘܐܡܝܢ ܗ̇ܘ ܕܥܠ ܟܪܗ ܕܗ̇ܘ ܕܐܘܕܝ ܟܗ
ܐܬܘܗܝ ܗܘܐ. ܘܒܦܪ̈ܘܦܐ ܢܡܪ̈ܐ ܘܦܝܫܐ ܟܠܒ̈ܐ ܕܬ̈ܡܟܗܘܢ
ܥܐܠ ܗܘܐ. ܘܡܛܠܬܐ ܕܐܠܗܐ ܒܐܪ̈ܢܐ ܕܒܠܗܘܢ ܒܬ̈ܪ ܐܢܫܐ
ܙܟܐ. ܘܕܚܝܠܝܢ ܠܐܠܗܐ ܒܠܫܢܗܘܢ ܠܟܠ ܐܢܫ ܡܓܙܪ ܗܘܐ.
ܘܚܠܦ ܬܘܕܝܬܐ ܠܐܠܗܐ ܥܒܕ ܬܫܒܘܚܬܐ ܩ̈ܕܡܐ ܗܘܐ.

ܒܒܥܐ ܕܗ̈ܘܕܝܐ ܕܟܠܐ ܐܬܚܒܫܘ ܘܐܝܟ ܐܬܐܠܨܐ ܥܩ̈ܝܒܐ ܘܫܘܪ̈ܝܐ
ܒܢ̈ܫܬܗܘܢ ܒܐܦܝܠܘܣ ܕܐܠܗܐ ܐܬܟܠܠܘ. ܗܘ ܐܝܢܐ ܕܡܬܠܠܬܗ
ܐܦ ܪ̈ܚܡܘܗܝ ܐܬܦܫܛܘ ܗܘܘ. ܘܡܢ ܟܠܗ ܒܥܡܪܐ ܕܚ̈ܫܘܗܝ
ܥܘܫܢܘܗܝ ܕܠܘܬ ܗܘ ܐܝܢܐ ܕܐܘܕܝܘ ܒܗ ܐܝܟܢܐ .ܘ.

ܢܗܡܐ ܕܝܢ ܕܐܘܕܝܘ ܒܗ ܐܝܬܘܗܝ ܗܘܐ ܥܒܕܬܐ ܒܬܪ
ܐܫܪ ܕܡܬܕܝܢܘܬܗܘܢ ܕܗܢܘܢ ܕܐܡܪܝܢ ܠܒܫܘܢ ܐܬܦܠܓܬ.
ܘܒܗ ܕܝܢ ܒܢܘܡܐ ܗܢܐ ܐܦ ܪ̈ܗܘܡܝܢܘܣ ܒܐܝܠܦܢܐ ܡܕܝܢܬܐ
ܐܬܗܕ ܡܢ ܦܘܠܦܠܢܐ ܕܝܢ ܐܝܬܘܗܝ ܗܘܐ. ܗܘ ܪ̈ܗܘܡܝܢܘܣ
ܘܡܥܡܥܢܐ ܐܝܬܘܗܝ ܗܘܐ. ܐܦ ܡܥܡܘܢܝ ܒܫܢܐ ܡܢ ܡܘܪ̈ܐ
ܕܡܗܪ̈ܐ. ܐܦ ܗܘ ܡܫܠ ܒܗܕܐ ܐܬܡܠܟ ܘܐܒܗܬܗܘܢ ܕܗܠܝܢ
ܕܒܪܗ ܐܠܗܘܬ ܗܘܕܐ ܒܗܘ̈ܪܐ ܡܕܝܢܐ ܐܦ ܪ̈ܗܘܡܝܢܘܣ
ܦܘܠܝܢܐ ܠܗܘܢ ܕܡܢ ܕܝܠܬܗܘܢ ܒܥ̈ܒܕܬܐ ܕܦܘܠܝܢ ܕܪ̈ܗܘܐ
ܢܩܠܝܢ ܗܘܘ. ܒܡ̈ܠܘܗܝ ܕܠܘܫܡܐ ܠܗܘܢ ܡܢ ܕܒܢܝ̈ ܟܠܐ ܗܘܐ.
ܘܠܟܠܗܘܢ ܕܢ̈ܠܬܐ ܕܡܢ ܐܠܗܐ ܡܬܡܗܪ ܗܘܐ ܘܒܡ ܒܢܝܐ ܗܘ
ܐܝܢܐ ܕܠܦܘܠܘܬܐ ܒܦܘܠܝܢܐ ܐܬܕܒܪ ܐܡܪܝܢ ܕܢܒܥܠ ܘܐܬܡ
ܒܐܝܠܦܢܐ ܢܚܡܗ ܠܕܝܢܐ ܡܪܒ. ܘܒܪ ܥܡܒܕ ܕܦܡܕ ܠܗܘܢ̈ ܕܢܝܢܐ
ܐܝܟ ܕܢܒܚܫܘܢ ܘܚܦܢܘܢ ܡܬܗܪܡܐܢܬ ܡܢ ܕܝܠܬܗܘܢ ܕܢܒܚܫܘܢ
ܡܢ ܘܒܚܬܗܘܢ ܐܬܥܒܕܘ. ܗܘ ܕܝܢ ܗܢܐ ܒܪܢܐ ܦܠܢܐ. ܕܗܡܒܪ
ܗܕܐ ܚܝܬܐ ܒܫܬܐ ܠܐ ܐܫܒܚ. ܘܐܝܟ ܕܟܠ ܚܢܘܢ ܕܒܫܘܒܚܐ
ܒܒܗܡܐ ܡܒܫܡ ܗܘܘ. ܕܡܢ ܫܘܦܐ ܢܦܠܘܢ ܪܘܡ ܗܘܐ. ܘܒܕܡܒܗܬ
ܥܡܥܢܐ ܢܘܠܦܢܐ ܕܡܓܕܬܐ ܕܐܠܗܐ ܡܕܡܒܫܘܢ ܐܕܝܫ ܗܘܐ ܒܕ
ܦܠܐ ܗܘܐ ܘܡܦܪ. ܕܠܐܢܫܐ ܡܬܕܒܪܝܢ ܐܢܫܘܢ ܐܘ ܩ̈ܢܝ ܐܢܫܐ
ܘܠܒܘܡܒܐ ܕܬܫܒܘܢ ܢܦܫܘܢ ܠܒܘܢ ܡܬܪܚܡܝܢ ܐܢܫܘܢ.
ܐܪ̈ܫܒܘ ܒܢ̈ܝܢܐ ܕܬܪ̈ܒܝܬܗܘܢ ܠܡܪܘܡܐ ܘܠܟܠ ܡܢ ܟܠܡܐ ܠܟܠܗܘܢ
ܠܐܠܗܐ ܘܠܦܪܘܩܐ ܕܒܠܗܘܢ ܗܦܘܟܗ ܕܟܠܡܐ ܬܕܒܘܢ.
ܘܠܐ ܬܬܠܘܢ ܠܦܘܠܝ. ܦܘܡܕܢܐ ܕܐܬܦܠܠ ܠܒܘܢ ܘܬܬܫܢܐ
ܠܒܘܢ ܦܘܠܝܬܐ ܕܠܐ ܐܠܗ. ܕܦܘܠܚܢܐ ܕܥܒ̈ܕܐ ܘܐܬܕܒܪܘ ܐܦ

ܕܐܠܗܐ ܐܝܬܘܗܝ ܗܘܐ. ܘܡܠܟܘܬܐ ܫܡܝܢܝܬܐ ܠܘܬ ܟܠ ܐܢܫ
ܐܝܬܘܗܝ ܗܘܐ. ܘܗܝ ܗܕܐ ܗܘܬ ܠܗ ܥܠܬܐ ܠܡܬܐ ܠܡܘܕܝܢܘܬܗ
ܕܥܒܪܐ ܘܡܛܠ ܕܫܪܝܐ ܗܘܐ ܕܢܒܝܢܐ ܗܘ ܥܠ ܟܠ ܐܢܫ ܪܕܘܦܝܐ
ܘܕܫܠܝܘܬܐ ܫܡܝܢܝܬܐ ܢܦܠܬ ܗܘܬ ܘܫܡܝܢܝܐ ܐܝܟ ܕܡܢ ܡܕܡ ܚܫܘܟܐ
ܕܟܠܗ ܫܡܝܢܝܐ ܡܬܚܪܦ ܗܘܘ. ܘܠܫܡܪܬܐ ܫܡܝܢܝܬܐ ܕܦܬܓܡܐ
ܡܬܕܒܪܝܢ ܗܘܘ. ܘܐܬܚܙܝ ܕܠܘܬ ܫܡܝܐ ܕܡܢܬܐ ܒܫܠܝܘܬܗ
ܢܩܘܡ ܩܠܝܠܐ ܕܫܠܐ ܒܩܠܗܘܢ، ܫܠܝܘܬܐ ܢܬܒܥܐ. ܘܠܗܝܢ ܒܬܘܗܝ
ܕܒܢܝܐ ܕܐܠܗܐ ܗܘ ܒܝܬ ܚܝܘܗ ܢܚܡܐ ܫܕܪ ܗܘܐ. ܘܟܬܒܐ
ܕܠܘܬܗܐ ܠܫܘܢ ܕܡܢ ܕܫܠܝܘܬܗ ܠܡܚܝ ܡܬܓܒܝܢ ܗܘܘ.
ܡܬܩܕܡ ܗܘܐ. ܘܠܗܘܢ ܡܢ ܫܡܪܬܐ ܕܟܬܒܐ ܚܠܝܐ ܗܘܐ. ܘܟܠܗ
ܕܐܡܪܝܢ ܠܡܫܝܚ ܥܠ ܡܕܒܪܢܘܬܐ ܠܗܘܢ ܡܫܡܫ ܗܘܐ. ܘܟܕ
ܗܠܝܢ ܐܠܦܘ ܫܠܝܚܐ ܘܡܪܟܒܢܐ ܒܪܘܚܐ ܦܫܪ ܗܘܐ. ܠܟܘܠܗܘܢ
ܩܠܝܠ ܘܒܪܥܬܗ ܡܕܡ ܕܢܐ ܡܪܟܒܗ. ܗܘ ܕܝܢ ܐܝܟ ܕܝ ܐܢܫܐ
ܕܪܘܚܐ ܕܐܠܗܐ ܡܠܝܐ ܗܘܐ. ܕܟܠܟܐ ܬܒܬ ܩܠܐ ܐܦܪܝ ܗܘܐ
ܒܐܪܥܬܐ ܕܡܠܘܗܝ. ܘܟܠܟܐ ܩܠܐ ܕܫܡܝܢܬܐ ܕܐܠܗܐ ܐܝܬ
ܗܘܐ ܒܗܝܢ ܦܪ. ܠܐ ܗܘܐ ܝܟܢܐ ܗܘ ܕܐܬܡܪ ܘܟܬܪ ܗܠܝܢ ܠܟܝܬ
ܐܘܪܚܐ ܐܬܬܕܪ ܗܘܐ. ܘܟܬܪ ܡܩܪܬܐ ܬܘܒ ܠܕܢܚܐ ܡܪܟܒܗ.
ܘܟܢܫܘܬܐ ܡܩܦܬܐ ܠܟܠܗ ܦܢܘܗ ܕܠܐ ܢܝܟܡ ܡܬܟܢܫܝܢ ܗܘܘ.
ܟܕ ܒܪܘܬܐ ܕܪܒܝܗ. ܠܘܩܒܠ ܕܢܐ ܝܩܦܐ ܗܘܬ. ܘܟܢܫܬܗ
ܠܘܩܒܠ ܟܠܗ ܦܠܚܘܬܐ ܦܐܡ ܗܘܐ. ܘܟܣܢܩܐ ܡܩܢܐ ܒܕܩܢܬܗ
ܡܫܬܢܝܢ ܗܘܘ. ܘܠܫܪܬܐ ܟܕ ܐܠܐ، ܠܕܢܚܐ ܐܦ ܠܗܘܢ ܕܝܒܝܗ
ܕܕܢܚܐ ܡܫܡܫܝܢ ܒܡ ܐܬܠܝܠܐ ܫܕ ܟܪ ܘܦܟܗ. ܠܫܟܘܫܐ
ܐܫܬܠܡ. ܘܬܡܢ ܒܗܕܐ ܕܡܫܟܐ ܐܡܟܢܐ ܟܠܗ ܒܡ ܠܠܝܐ ܡܬܝܒ
ܗܘܐ. ܘܟܬܪ ܡܩܪܬܐ ܬܠܬܐ ܡܕܡ ܕܢܐ ܬܪܝܢܘܗܝ ܫܡܐܝܬ
ܐܬܦܪܟܗ ܘܡܣܪ ܠܗܘܢ ܕܢܒܝܘܗܝ ܠܩܠܝܐ. ܘܦܢܘ ܟܕ ܡܟܕܝܢ
ܗܘܘ ܐܡܟܪܝܢ ܗܘܘ. ܠܝܫ ܗܘ ܒܠܫܕܘܗܝ ܐܠܗܐ ܩܠܝܐ ܕܥܠ
ܢܒܝܝܢ ܐܢܫܝܢ ܘܟܕ ܗܠܝܢ ܩܠܝܐ ܡܕܡ ܒܗܠܝܢ ܒܟܐ ܐܡܟܪܝܢ ܗܘܘ.

ܠܗ. ܢܘܡܐ ܕܝܢ ܐܢܬܬܗ، ܗܘܐ ܫܡܗܬܐ ܒܣܝܪ̈ܢ ܢܫ̈ܐ. ܒܫܢܬܐ ܡܕܡܟܬܐ ܕܐܪܕܘܦܝܐ ܕܟܪ̈ܣܛܝܢܐ. ܗܢܐ ܗܟܝܠ ܡܕܒܪܢܐ ܦܪܡܝܛ ܐܫܬܠܡ ܒܡܘܬܐ ܡܪܝܪܬܐ. . . .

ܡܕܒܪܢܘܬܐ ܕܐܠܦܝܘܣ ܘܕܪܐ ܘܕܪܡܛܝܘܣ.

ܒܫܢܬܐ ܡܕܡܟܬܐ ܕܐܪܕܘܦܝܐ ܕܟܪ̈ܣܛܝܢܐ.

ܒܗ ܕܝܢ ܒܙܒܢܐ ܗܘ. ܟܕ ܗܘܐ ܕܒܐܬܪܐ ܗܘ. ܕܩܒܠܬ ܒܗܘܢ ܩ̈ܢܘܢ ܠܩ̈ܠܝܠܐ ܡܬܟܬܒ ܗܘܐ. ܡܢܟ ܗܘܐ ܘܫܘܦܪܐ ܕܟ̈ܠܝܬܐ ܕܐܘܪܚܐ ܒܟܐܪܐ ܗܘ ܡܬܟܬܢ ܗܘܘ. ܡܕܡ ܕܝܢ ܠܒܐܪܐ ܗܘ ܡܦܩܢܐ ܗܘ ܕܒܐܬܪܐ ܘܠܐܘܪܚܐ ܕܡܫܡܫܢܐ ܒܝܕ ܗܘܐ ܘܡܢܗܘܢ ܒܡܪܚܡܢܘܬܐ ܕܩ̈ܠܝܠܐ ܐܫܬܪܝܘ ܗܘܘ. ܠܗ̈ܘܕܐ ܕܝܢ ܕܐܠܗܐ ܐܝܟ ܕܠܗܘܢ ܕܟܬܝܒ ܡܢ ܠܩ̈ܠܝܠܐ ܘܩܠܝܠܐ ܒܥܕ̈ܬܐ ܝܗܒ ܗܘܐ. ܐܦ ܗܟܝܠ ܐܢܫܐ ܕܐܢܬܬܗ، ܗܘܐ ܡܫܡܫܢܐ ܒܥܕܬܐ ܕܒܪ ܡܕܝܢܬܐ ܒܕܡܘܬ ܐܡܪܐ ܬܡܝܡܐ ܡܢ ܓܙܪܐ ܐܬܕܒܪ ܗܘܐ. ܡܛܠ ܕܐܦ ܗܢܝܐ ܐܢܬܬܗ، ܗܘܐ ܐܦ ܒܟܢܫ. ܐܦ ܕܝܢ ܫܡܫܗ، ܗܘܘ ܢܕ̈ܘܟܘܗܝ، ܟܕ ܡܫܡܫܝܢ ܠܗ. ܘܦܪ̈ܐܘܗܝ ܒܟܘܢܐ ܕܗܘ ܐܦ ܡܕܡܟܐ. ܫܕܐ ܡܛܠ ܐܟܘܪܬܐ ܕܡܘܡܬܗ. ܘܕܬܪܬܝܢ ܕܒܡܟܪܐ ܐܠܝܨܐ ܡܬܕܒܪ ܗܘܐ. ܘܕܢܚܝܘܗܝ ܠܡܒܪܟ ܝܬܝܪ ܡܢ ܐܦ ܡܫܘܚ ܗܘܐ. ܘܟܕ ܟܠ ܡܕܡ ܕܢܐ ܒܡܕܒܪܢܘܬܐ ܕܟܠ ܐܢܫ ܡܫܝܚܐ ܙܘܪ ܗܘܐ. ܘܟܕ ܩ̈ܠܝܠܐ ܕܐܠܗܐ ܡܕܡ ܕܢܐ ܐܡܪ ܗܘܐ. ܠܟܠ ܫܢ̈ܝܢ ܕܡܫܡܫ ܒܝܫܐ ܐܫܬܠܡ ܗܘܐ. ܘܗܪ̈ܟܐ ܡܩ̈ܢܐ ܡܢ ܒܬܪ ܝܗܒܐ ܡܕ̈ܢܚܐ ܗܒܝ ܗܘܐ. ܘܬܘܒ ܡܢ ܒܬܪ ܗܠܝܢ ܠܒܫܬ ܐܗܘܪܐ ܐܫܬܠܡ ܗܘܐ. ܘܬܡܢ ܒܠܗ ܐܡܡܟܐ ܘܒܠܗ ܠܠܝܐ ܒܐܪ̈ܥܐ ܫܘ̈ܢܝܢ ܕܗܘܐ ܬ̈ܟܠܬܗ، ܐܬܡܟܬܚ ܗܘ. ܐܬܟܬܒܘܗܝ ܕܝܢ ܕܗܠܝܢ ܐܩ̈ܠܝܢܐ ܐܦ ܐܠܦܘܣ ܒܕܢܐ ܕܝܬܗܐ ܫܡܪ ܗܘܐ. ܒܢܫܗ ܕܝܢ ܐܢܬܬܗ، ܗܘܐ ܡܢ ܩ̈ܪܒܢܐ ܕܐܠܬܪܦܝܘܣ ܡܕܝܢܬܐ. ܘܡܕܝܢܬܐ ܕܡܘܪܐ ܒܟܘܬܐ ܕܩ̈ܘܪܐ ܘܡܕܘܟ̈ܝܢܐ ܡܥܠܪ ܗܘܐ. ܗܘ ܕܝܢ ܗܢܐ ܡܕܡ ܕܢܗܘܐ ܗܘܐ ܡܕܒܪܢܐ ܒܪܘܪܐ ܘܡܠܦܢܐ ܕܡܠܬܐ

ܠܐ ܢܛܠ ܗܘܐ. ܟܕ ܕܝܢ ܠܬܪ̈ܝܢ ܣܩܡ ܠܗܘܢ ܗܘܐ. ܘܟܕܡ
ܠܬܠܬܐ. ܘܥܕ̈ܡܐ ܗܦܟܢܘܬܐ ܐܦ ܟܠܗ ܥܒܕܐ ܕܠܐ ܗܘܟܪܬܐ
ܡܟܪܙ ܗܘܐ. ܡܢ ܗܘܟܐ ܕܝܢ ܕܡ̈ܠܐ ܐܠܗܘܬܐ ܠܐ ܠܠܝܐ ܘܠܐ
ܐܣܟܝܡܐ ܬܟܠ ܗܘܐ. ܕܗ ܟܠ ܐܣܟܝ̈ܡܘܗܝ، ܘܟܠ ܟܘܡܪܘܗܝ ܢܟܦܐ
ܡܫܠܡܘܬܐ ܐܝܬ ܗܘܬ ܠܗ. ܡܟܝܟܐ ܕܡܟܝܟܘܬܐ ܘܟܢܝܫܘܬܐ
ܠܟܠܗܘܢ ܟܪ̈ܐ ܡܢܟܗ ܫܠܡܗ ܐܦ ܟܠ ܡ̈ܠܐ ܕܐܠܗܘܬܐ.
ܐܟܝܢܘܬܐ ܐܝܬ ܗܘܬ ܠܗ. ܐܦ ܡ̈ܠܐ ܟܪܝܗܬܐ ܕܟܝܢܐ ܠܐ ܗܘܐ
ܟܪܝܐܝܬ ܡܕܟ ܗܘܐ. ܟܠܗܘܢ ܕܝܢ ܡܢ ܟܢܫ ܐܝܬܘܗܝ ܗܘܐ.
ܘܟܠܗܘܢ ܕܟܕܘܬܐ ܟܬܠܬ ܝܘܡܢ ܥܡܟܝܢ ܗܘܐ. ܦܪܡܟܝܬ ܪܘܚܐ
ܗܘܐ ܗܘܐ. ܘܟܠܗܘܢ ܐܫܝܢܐ ܠܟܝܢܐ ܡܢܝܐ ܠܐܪܡܟܝܐ ܡܬܪܦܡ
ܗܘܐ ܘܐܫܝܢܘܬܐ ܕܡܟܝܢܬܐ ܐܦ ܡܢ ܡܕܡܟ̈ܝܬܐ ܠܗܘܟܠ ܫܠܡܘܬܗ
ܕܟܫܐ ܐܝܬܘܗܝ ܗܘܐ. ܘܪ̈ܘܚܐ ܡܢ ܡܕܡܟܘܗܝ، ܘܟܝܢ ܗܘܘ. ܟܕܥ
ܗܟܠ ܕܡܢ ܟܢܫ ܠܗܘܪܐ ܡܕܝܢܬ ܟܡ ܫܟܪ̈ܘܗܝ، ܡܟܘ̈ܪܝܐ ܐܥܬܕܪ
ܗܘܐ. ܘܟܕ ܟܥܒܕܬܐ ܡܢ ܬܪ̈ܟܢܗ ܕܡܕܝܢܬܐ ܠܗܬ ܗܓܡܘܢܐ
ܐܟܠܗܘܢ، ܘܟܪܥܒܕܗ ܟܡܟܠܡ ܡܕܡܟܐ ܐܡܓܪ ܠܗ ܕܢܟܐ ܗܘ. ܐܟܢܐ
ܕܟܠܗܝܘܗ ܡܬܡܘܪܐ ܗܘܐ. ܕܦܠܐ ܠܝ ܠܡ ܕܬܕܟܝ ܠܐܠܗܐ ܘܗܘ
ܟܡܠܐ ܙܡܟܐ ܐܡܟܪ ܗܘܐ. ܕܠܝܬ ܐܠܗܐ ܐܠܐ ܐܢ ܫܕ ܟܠܝܫܕܘܗܝ،
ܟܟܘܕܐ ܘܟܪܘܟܐ ܕܟܠ. ܗܕ ܕܝܢ ܗܘ ܕܢܟܐ ܡܢ ܡܣܘܬܐ ܕܡܟܠܬܗ
ܕܗܘܕܐ ܟܠܟ ܗܘܐ. ܟܝܢܐ ܐܫܝܢܐ ܠܗܘܟܠ ܡܠܦܢܐ ܕܥܪܪܐ
ܐܬܟܬܕ ܗܘܐ. ܘܥܡ ܡܟܠܬܗ ܡܕܡܟܬܐ ܘܥܠ ܠܐܫܝܪܬܐ ܘܐܡܟܪ
ܠܗ ܕܠܬ̈ܟܠܬܐ ܕܐܬܐܡܣܘ̈ܗܝ ܗܘܐ ܐܪ̈ܟܟܐ ܟܡܟܝܢܐ ܢܕܟܝ ܗܘܐ.
ܗܘ ܕܝܢ ܗܘܕܐ ܡܕܝܟܐ ܕܐܠܗܐ ܐܦ ܟܠ ܗܘܕܐ ܡܟܠܬܐ ܡܬܪܐܝܬ
ܟܫܝ ܘܡܟܠܬܗ ܕܢܗܘ ܙܟܐ ܕܗܩ̈ܐܝܡܘܗܝ ܕܡܩ̈ܢܐ ܬܟܐ. ܗܿ، ܕܐܡܓܪ
ܕܠܐ ܥܡܝܢܐ ܡܪܘܬܐ ܕܩ̈ܘܟܝܐ ܐܠܗܐ ܠܡ ܫܕ ܡܟܪܐ ܢܗܘܐ ܘܫܕ
ܦ̈ܠܟܐ ܘܡܟܠܠ ܗܘܝ ܦܬܓܡܗ ܕܠܬ̈ܟܠܬܐ ܝܓܪ ܗܘܐ. ܗܘ ܫ
ܟܕܘܟ̈ܪܘܗܝ، ܠܟܗܘܬܐ ܐܥܬܠܡ ܗܘܐ. ܘܪܥܗ ܕܦܘܟܝܐ ܟܪܥܒܕܗ
ܐܥܬܠ ܗܘܐ. ܘܡܟܪܕܬܐ ܕܠܠܬܐ ܟܐܘܪܝܐ ܕܥܟܟܐ ܐܬܦܓܫ

ܕܡܠܟܘܬܐ ܒܪܘܡܐ ܕܡܕܝܢܬܐ ܐܬܩܠܠ. ܡܛܠ ܕܐܝܟ ܕܒܐܓܘܢܐ ܡܬܬܪܐ ܬܘܒ ܐܬܦܬܚ ܗܘܐ. ܘܟܕ ܐܟܘܬܐ ܕܢܣܒ ܡܟܝܠܐ ܠܡܘܕܐ ܐܟܝܐ ܐܬܩܠܠ ܐܦ ܥܡܗܘܢ ܐܪܒܐ ܘܢܣܒܐ ܕܐܬܒܩܪܬܐ ܬܘܒ ܬܘܒ ܐܬܩܠܠ. ܘܒܪܡܫܬܐ ܕܢܩܘܡ ܕܩܝܡ ܚܕ. ܐܦ ܓ̈ܠܝܢܐ ܐܚܪܢܐ ܒܪ̈ܘܚܢܝܬܐ ܐܚܪܢܝܬܐ ܥܠܝܡܐ ܕܫܡܥܘܢ ܒܡܕܝܢܬܐ ܗܘܐ. ܘܠܐ ܗܘܐ ܒܠܚܘܕ ܠܡܪ̈ܢܐ ܒܥܒܕܐ ܗܘܬ ܗܕܐ ܠܒܪܘܬܐ ܐܠܐ ܐܦ ܠܕܪܐ ܗܢܐ ܕܝܠܢ ܕܠܐ ܫܩܠ ܐܬܒܥܬ ° ° ° °

ܐܓܘܢܐ ܗܢܐ ܕܒܐܬܪ ܐܬܪ ܐܬܓܠܝܘ ܕܐܝܟ ܢܦܫܐ ܕܒܬܪܗܘܢ ܐܝܟ ܕܒܫܡܗܘܢ ܒܐܬܪܘܬܗܘܢ ܒܫܡܝܢ ܗܘܘ ܐܢܫܐ ܕܡ ܡܬܝܠܐ ܐܢܫ ܕܐܘܟܡ ܕܐܡܪ ܒܠ ܦܘܡܗܘܢ ܕܒܫܡܬ ܕܒܫܡܗܘܢ ܗܘܬ. ܘܐܦ ܒܫܡܗܘܢ ܢܨܝܚܘܬ. ܦܘܡܗܘܢ ܕܒܫܡܗܘܢ ܒܫܡܐ ܒܠܗ ܕܬܠܡܝܕܐ ܡܫܬܒܚܝܢ. ܡܛܠ ܕܐܦ ܟܡܐ. ܕܐܡܪ ܐܝܟ ܡܫܘܚܬܐ ܡܦܟܝܢܐ ܕܢܨܘܚܬܐ. ܗܘ ܦܘܩܐ ܕܒܠܘܢ ܓ̈ܒܐܢܐ ܕܚܝ. ܐܓܘܢܣܘܢ ܗܕܝܢ ܕܦܘܡܗܘܢ ܐܬܦܠܓܘ ܢܨܚܢܐ ܠܗܠܝܢܐ ܘܠܒܪܝܬܐ ܕܟܠܗ ܐܪܬܐ.

ܡܕܝܢܬܐ ܕܪܘܡܐ. ܒܫܢܬܐ

ܡܕܝܢܬܐ ܕܐܘܪܗܝ ܕܒܡܘܬܗܘܢ.

ܡܕܝܢܬܐ ܕܒܠܘܢ ܗܘܐ ܗܘܢ ܕܒܠܘܡܢܐ ܐܬܚܙܝܘ. ܦܪܘܣ ܡܬܦܪܐ ܗܘܐ. ܒܚܪܐ ܒܝ ܐܢܫܐ ܐܠܗܐ ܐܬܚܘܝ ܗܘܐ ܡܛܠ ܕܐܦ ܡܢ ܡܕܝܢܬܗ ܠܡܫܒܚܘܬܗ ܦܠܚܬܐ ܚܝܗ ܐܝܠܝܢ ܗܘܐ. ܘܡܢ ܒܝ ܩܠܐ ܗܘܐ ܘܒܘܪܐ ܒܡܕܝܢܬܐ ܕܒܗ ܘܒܡܕܝܢܬܐ ܐܝܠܝܢ ܐܬܚܘܝ ܗܘܐ. ܘܒܡܫܘܬܐ ܕܢܚܡܘܢ ܠܦܪܘܣ ܡܫܝܚ ܗܘܐ. ܐܡܝܢܐ ܕܐܦ ܡܢ ܡܕܝܢ ܡܕܝܢܬܗ ܢܬܬܪ ܕܦܪܘܣܐ ܡܬܬܐ ܢܒܝܗ ܪܒܐ ܗܘܬ. ܠܢܝܫܗ ܕܡܢ ܒܥܠܝܐ ܐܠܗܘܬܐ ܡܫܒܠ ܗܘܐ ܐܡܝܢܐ ܕܐܦ ܦܪܘܣ ܒܫܠܐ ܕܐܠܗܐ ܦܐܡ ܗܘܐ. ܡܬܐܡܠܬܗ ܕܡ ܠܥܒܕܐ ܗܘܬ ܒܠܚܘܕ. ܘܡܬܬܗܘ ܗ̈ܢܐ. ܘܡܢ ܗܠܝܢ ܬܪ̈ܝܢ ܡܕܝܢ

ܢܬܒܥܐ ܗܒܠ ܕܡ̈ܘܬܐ ܓ̈ܠܝܬܐ ܘܬܫܥ̈ܝܬܐ ܥܒܝ̈ܕܬܐ ܕܝܘܠܦܢܐ
ܐܠܗܐ ܘܟܘܢܢܐ ܗܘ ܕܠܐ ܡܬܦܠܓܐ ܒܟܬܒܐ ܢܒܝ̈ܘܗܝ،
ܘܠܡܬܪ̈ܬܘܗܝ ܬܡܗܬܐ ܐܝܟ ܚܕܬܐ ܐܡܝܢܬܐ ܦܪܩ ܒܢ̈ܝܢ
ܢܒܝ̈ܘܗܝ. ܡܬܕܡܪ ܐܝܟܐ ܕܝܢ ܒܠ ܚܠܝܘܬܗܘܢ ܘܡܬܒܣܡ ܒܠ.
ܐܦ ܡܘܕܝܢܘܬܗܘܢ ܦܬܝܟܐܬ ܐܡ̈ܝܢܬܐ ܘܦܠܚܐ ܚܠܝܬܐ
ܕܢܦܫܗܘܢ. ܘܥܒܕ̈ܗܝܢ ܕܪ̈ܚܡܝܗܘܢ ܘܦܪܗܣܝܐ ܕܡܫܬܡܠܝܬܗܘܢ
ܘܒܪܘܪܬܐ ܕܡܫܒܚܗܘܢ ܘܡܬܒܪܝܢܬܐ ܕܢܘܟܪ̈ܝܗܘܢ ܘܥܘܪܪ̈ܬܐ
ܕܦܓܪܗܘܢ ܘܕܠܐ ܐܬܚܙܝܘ ܒܪ̈ܚܡܝܗܘܢ. ܘܕܟܠ ܚܝ̈ܘ
ܗܘ، ܒܝܬܗܘܢ ܘܕܠܐ ܘܚܘܬܐ ܡܐܪܒܥܬܐ ܐܬܚܙܝܘܢ ܗܘܘ.
ܘܐܦ ܚܘܒܐ ܕܐܠܗܐ ܘܕܡܫܝܚܐ ܚܝܠܐ ܕܡܬܥܪ ܡܢ ܟܠ
ܕܠܬܠܬܝܗܘܢ ܢܦܫ̈ܗܘܢ ܫܪܝ ܗܘܐ ܠܗܘܢ. ܠܐܠܗܐ ܓܝܪ
ܬܠܬܐ ܕܒܠ ܐܝܟܘ. ܘܠܗ ܡܢ ܟܠܗ ܚܝܠܗܘܢ ܪ̈ܚܡܘ. ܘܐܓܪܘ
ܕܢܦܫܗܘܢ ܕܠܐܬܗ ܒܡܕܪܝܢ ܕܠܗܘܬܗܘܢ ܥܒܕ ܠܗܘܢ. ܘܐܬܪܚܡܘ
ܡܢ ܠܘܬܗ ܘܐܬܦܢܝܘ ܒܠ ܡܫܐܠ̈ܬܗܘܢ ܘܒܬܒܥܬܗ ܩ̈ܠܐ ܕܗܘ
ܡܕܝܢܐ ܕܡܢ ܡܪܡܘܗܝ ܐܬܩܪܝ ܗܘܐ ܡܬܦܫܝܢ ܗܘܘ. ܒܪ
ܐܡܝܢ ܗܘܘ ܕܟܠܗ ܢܦܫܗ ܡܢ ܡܫܝܢܐ ܒܝܬܐ ܐܘ ܐܘܠܝܢܐ
ܐܘ ܐܪܕ̈ܘܦܝܐ ܐܘ ܒܦܢܐ ܐܘ ܡܘܬܐ ܐܘ ܫܦܟܐ ܐܝܟ ܕܟܬܝܒ
ܕܡܦܠܛܝܢ ܠܗܘܢ ܡܢܬܗ ܐܝܢܝ. ܐܬܚܙܝܢ ܐܝܟ ܐܡܪ̈ܐ ܠܢܟܣܬܐ
ܘܒܪ ܡܘܪܒ ܬܘܒ ܗܘ ܗܢܐ ܫܘܪܐ ܕܐܠܗܐ ܠܡܘܒܕܢܘܬܐ
ܕܡܢ ܒܢ̈ܝܐ ܠܐ ܡܬܕܒܪܐ ܐܝܟ ܕܟܠܗ ܟܠܗܘܢ ܐܢܫ ܐܢܫ ܚܠܦ
ܗܘ ܕܐܒܝܕ. ܘܡܬܕܒܪܝܢ ܒܟܠܗܘܢ ܒܢܝ̈ܬܐ ܒܫܘܒܚܗ ܕܐܠܗܐ ܦܪܩ
ܒܪܗ. ܘܡܬܟܣܦܝܢ ܒܠ ܟܠܗܘܢ ܕܟܠܬܐ ܘܐܩܠܝܢܐ ܐܒܪ ܘܡܟܪ
ܕܡܟܣܐ ܐܢܐ ܕܠܐ ܡܘܬܐ ܘܠܐ ܚܝ̈ܐ. ܘܠܐ ܡܠܟ ܘܠܐ
ܕܟܬܒ. ܘܠܐ ܚܝܠܐ ܘܠܐ ܪܘܡܐ ܘܠܐ ܥܘܡܩܐ ܘܠܐ ܒܪܝܬܐ
ܐܚܪܬܐ ܢܟܫܘܢ ܕܢܦܪܫܢ ܡܢ ܚܘܒܗ ܕܐܠܗܐ ܕܒܡܫܝܚܐ ܝܫܘܥ
ܡܪܢܐ. ܒܗ ܗܒܠ ܒܗܘ ܗܘ ܦܘܠܘܣ ܗܘ ܕܒܚܝܠܐ ܕܡܪܗ
ܡܬܚܝܠ ܗܘܐ. ܗܘ ܕܡܘܢܥܗ ܒܡܫܬܐ ܕܪܘܚܐ ܡܕܝܢܬܐ

ܕܥܠ ܡܘ̈ܬܢܐ ܕܒܠܘܓܝܢܐ ܕܐܡܝܪ ܠܐܘܣܒܝܘܣ ܩܣܪܝܐ.

ܡܘ̈ܬܢܐ ܩ̈ܫܝܐ ܕܐܠܗܐ ܫܕܪ ܕܠܡܫܝܚ ܘܡܪܢ ܢܩܘܒ
ܡܫܝܚܐ ܘܠܐܠܗܐ ܕܥܠ ܟܠ ܘܫܠܝܛܐ ܕܟܠ. ܡܛܠ ܡܢ ܢܩܦܘܢ
ܘܫܬܩܘܢ ܐܣܓܘ. ܘܠܐܦܘܣܐ ܕܫܠܘܬ ܐܠܗܐ ܐܬܡܪܓܘ.
ܘܟܣܝܘܬܐ ܕܡܘܫܚܬܐ ܐܬܓܠܝܘ. ܘܠܡܘܬܐ ܘܣܓܝܐܐ ܗܘܐ ܠܗܪ
ܡܢ ܫܢܐ ܕܒܪܝܐ ܒܪܘ. ܘܟܠܗܘܢ ܐܝܬܝܗ ܕܡܫܬܘܕܝܬܐ ܐܬܚܒܠܘ.
ܘܬܫܒܘܚܬܐ ܕܐܝܬܝܗܘܢ ܠܫܘܒܚܬܐ ܠܐܠܗܐ ܡܩܪܒܝܐ ܕܟܠ
ܡܢ ܟܠ ܐܢܫܘ. ܡܛܠ ܕܟܫܝܢܐ ܥܡܝܢܐ ܐܬܚܙܝܘ ܗܘܘ.
ܘܒܓܘ ܕܗܘ ܕܢܗܒ ܐܝܟ ܕܠܡܫܬܘܕܝܢ ܡܕܝܢܝܢ ܗܘܘ.
ܘܬܫܒܘܚܬܐ ܘܐܡܝܪܐ ܘܪܒܘܬܐ ܠܐܠܗܐ ܘܠܒܪܗ ܘܠܪܘܚܐ
ܕܩܘܕܫܐ ܡܩܘܡܝܢ. ܘܢܫ̈ܬܐܘܢ ܕܡܘ̈ܬܢܐ ܕܗܘ̇ ܠܦܠܓܘܬܐ
ܕܡܫܟܚܐ ܒܡ ܒܢܝܐ ܕܢܦܫܐ ܘܕ̈ܚܠܝܐ ܡܫܡܥܝܢ ܘܐܝܠܝܢ ܕܝܢ
ܕܩܕܡܝܢ ܐܢܫܝܢ ܥܠ ܒܡܘ̈ܪܕܢܐ ܕܝܠܗܘܢ. ܘܐܬܦܩܕܘ ܐܦ
ܡܢ ܒܬܟܐ ܕ̈ܓܠܝܢܐ. ܕܢܬܬܘܦ ܒܡܘܕܪܝܢܐ ܕܩ̈ܪܝܐ. ܢܬܬܦ
ܒܡܦܘܢ ܐܦ ܐܢܫܝܢ. ܘܢܦܩܐ ܕܒܬܬܒ ܬܫܒ̈ܘܚܬܘܢ ܕܠܘܡܠ
ܫܠܝܛܐ. ܫܪܘܢ ܕܟܠܝܢ ܡܬܓܕܪܝܢ ܡܢ ܦܘܡܟܐ ܕܟܠܗܘܢ
ܕܘܟ̈ܝܢܘܢ ܡܘܡ̈ܝܢܐ. ܘܠܐ ܗܘܐ ܒܡܢ̈ܝܬܐ ܕܒܥܐ̈ܐ ܕܥܒܕܝܢ
ܦܘܫܝܢ ܬܫܒ̈ܚܬܗܘܢ ܐܝܠܐ ܒܝܘܪ̈ܬܐ ܕܡܦܬܚ ܒܡܡ̈ܬܝܢܐ ܐܦ
ܠܐ ܒܩ̈ܝܢܐ ܘܒ̈ܡܫܚܬܐ ܐܪܥܝܬܐ ܕܠܐ ܢܩܐ. ܐܠܐ ܒܡܠܬܐ
ܪܘܚܢܝܬܐ ܗܝ ܕܡܬܡܠܠܐ ܡܢ ܐܠܗܐ. ܘܗܘܝ ܒܒܝܬܗ ܘܕܒܢ̈ܝܐ
ܡܬܥܢܐ.

° ° ° ° ° °

www.ingramcontent.com/pod-product-compliance
Lightning Source LLC
Chambersburg PA
CBHW030319170426
43202CB00009B/1061

* 9 7 8 3 7 4 2 8 6 0 1 9 4 *